The Brightest Arm of the Savannah

The Augusta Canal 1845-2000

For Jim
My canal boat-mate
Ed Cashin
June 30, 2005

By Edward J. Cashin

Library of Congress Control Number: 2002110808

ISBN Number: 0-9716309-0-9 Hardcover
                0-9716309-1-7 Softcover

Published by the Augusta Canal Authority
Augusta, GA

Printed by The Stinehour Press
Lunenburg, VT

Design by Clemons & Company, Inc.
Aiken, SC

When in 1844 "the cold damps of commercial death seemed to be settling around" Augusta, "you... threw the Augusta Canal, the brightest arm of the Savannah, around us."

Georgia "will soon be known not only as the State of rivers and of railroads, but as the great manufacturing State of the South, and Augusta will be the 'Lowell.'"

Mayor Thomas Miller to Henry H. Cumming, *The Augusta Chronicle*, November 1, 1850.

The Augusta Canal Authority gratefully acknowledges a generous grant from Monsanto/Searle Corporation to underwrite the research and preparation of the manuscript for this book.

Contents

List of Illustrations

INTRODUCTION

—————

When Jeanie Allen approached me on behalf of the Canal Authority with a commission to write the history of the Augusta Canal, I had mixed feelings about doing it. Having grown up in Augusta and lived here most of my life, I thought that I knew about its history. I had touched on the highlights of the canal history in *The Story of Augusta* and wondered if there was anything else to tell. On the other hand, like many Augustans, I had never really looked closely at the canal. I came to the conclusion that we can live near something and not pay attention to it through a series of un-scientific experiments. On several occasions when giving talks on the history of the canal, I would start by having my listeners imagine that they were crossing the Butt Bridge and turning right up Greene Street toward Sacred Heart Cultural Center. In doing so, they crossed over the canal at 14th Street. I would ask which way did the canal flow at that point? (Perhaps the reader will hazard an answer.) Invariably, the audience would be thrown into confusion, half answering one way and half the other. (Count yourself correct if you said it flowed to your left, toward the river at Hawk's Gully.) So, for me the past year has been one of discovery, of research along paper trails and walks along towpath trails. A rich and interesting history emerged, the essentials of which I hope have been captured in these pages.

In preparation for the actual writing, my wife Mary Ann and I went on a tour of canals in New England, New York and one in Canada. We visited William Shank, Director of the American Canal and Transportation Center in York, Pennsylvania, and looked through his library of canal literature.

ix

We were impressed with the long history of the canals and the chronological progress of canal building from ancient Rome, through the great Canal of the Midi in France, to the English canals and then to the New England canals. New England and New York engineers, having learned their trade in England, brought their expertise to Augusta. Therefore, the Augusta Canal had an impressive historical provenance. We came to realize that there is a burgeoning international interest in historic canals, and that tourists flock to them as though they were discovering some ancient treasure.

Lowell, Massachusetts, has turned its canal system and the old mill buildings from a liability into an asset. The National Park Service has a fine industrial museum along the canal; visitors watch a film on the development of the industrial revolution in America as reflected in the history of Lowell. We took a boat tour on the canal and had the intricate mechanism of the gates and locks explained to us. A dormitory formerly used to house the famous "Lowell girls" who worked the factories is now a museum, with details of daily life posted in the various rooms. The restoration of the canal system seems a success. Adapting the many huge former factories to modern uses is Lowell's most formidable challenge.

We visited the Erie Canal Museum in Syracuse and followed the Erie Canal to Lockport's dramatically high locks at Lake Erie. The little towns along the way capitalize on the tourism the canal attracts. Like the Lowell Canals the Erie is not used commercially, only for the tourist trade. Our favorite was the Rideau Canal at Ottawa, Canada. The quaint Bytown Museum tells the story of Colonel John By of the Royal Engineers who built the canal in 1826 to connect the Great Lakes with Montreal. The War of 1812 convinced the British that the St. Lawrence was too vulnerable to the pesky

Americans who might want another war. I am indebted to Jean McNiven of the Museum for a copy of Robert Legget's *Rideau Waterway*. Today the log rafts, barges and steamers of old have given way to pleasure craft. A recent *AARP Bulletin* ran a story on the popularity of restored canals: "Now from Rhode Island to Illinois, from Pennsylvania to Georgia, they are being restored and transformed into community assets." The mention of Georgia in the story is a reference to the attempts to rewater the Savannah and Ogeechee Canal. A few brave volunteers are trying to clear the canal of debris at the Ogeechee end. However, it will be enormously expensive to rewater the canal all the way to the Savannah, and the Chatham County Commission has shown little enthusiasm for the project.

Another realization we came to during our tour was that whereas all these people are going to a great expense to restore long-empty canals, none of which are being used for their original purposes, the Augusta Canal has been here all along, quietly doing the job it was intended for, furnishing water to a thirsty city and power to industry. Only the Petersburg boats are missing from the modern canal and at the time of this writing, two replicas of the Canal boats are being constructed. No one that I have spoken to knows of any other power canal still operating in the country for its original purpose; Augusta's is unique.

In preparing for this history, I read through the canal records and the city council minutes from 1844 to 1901 in the vaults of the Augusta Municipal Building. I am grateful to the gracious ladies in the office of the clerk of commission for their friendly assistance, and for allowing me to use the commission chambers, with all the venerable-looking mayors staring down from their portraits around the walls. For the material from 1901 I used the city yearbooks, and from 1845 to 1985, I scanned the pages of *The Augusta Chronicle*. A great help was the book of minutes of the Flood Commission, 1908-1919; I thank Herbert Elliott, Jr. for the loan of his copy. For the recent past I relied on the files of the Augusta Canal Authority. The dozens of notebooks compiled during the research have been deposited in the archives of the Augusta Canal Authority in the hopes that they will be helpful to other students of the canal. In addition, I perused the holdings at the Center for Lowell History at the University of Lowell, the Southern Historical Collection at the University of North Carolina at Chapel Hill, and the rich resources of the Special Collections at Augusta State University's Reese Library.

I thank Tom Robertson, Turner Simkins, Hugh Connolly and Bill Baab for reading the draft of this narrative and for their corrections and suggestions. I appreciate Jeanie Allen's thorough proofreading and polishing of the draft. I gratefully acknowledge the assistance of Michael White, who knows the canal better than anyone else, who has helped me from the beginning and who has done the map work for this book. Dayton Sherrouse deserves credit for gathering the illustrations in this volume. Finally, Karen Wesson has labored long and patiently to format the volume, and I owe her a heartfelt thanks.

Edward J. Cashin
September 1, 2000

CHAPTER ONE

The Setting

When Henry Cumming and his friends plotted the route of the future Augusta Canal on a brisk November day in 1844 they knew that hard rock lay above the shoals of the Savannah River, and softer rock below, but they had no idea of the ancient forces that caused the rock to form in the first place. In the hundred years since then geologists have learned to read the history embedded in stone. The development of North America alone has been the result of many mountain building episodes and periods in which entire mountain ranges were eroded to mere hills and plains. It is almost mind-boggling for the layman to imagine such tremendous events, but the evidence can be seen in the landscape today.

Only since the 1960's have scientists understood plate tectonics, and since then they have been struggling to describe the process to the rest of us. The earth's inner core is intensely hot, molten rock, as anyone who has witnessed a volcanic eruption can testify. Visitors to Yellowstone National Park can observe smoking fumaroles and bubbling hot springs and realize that they are standing on a thin portion of the crust of the earth's surface. It is a relatively recent discovery that the earth's crust is not solid, rather it is cracked into huge plates upon which our continents and oceans are riding. Furthermore, these plates are in motion. It is this motion of the earth's crustal plates that has formed, reshaped, and then transformed continents and oceans many times over, leaving only the process as the true permanent player in the history of this planet.

For tens of millions of years now, the Pacific plate has been crowding into and sliding beneath the North American plate. One of the most curious sites in Mount Baker National Park in the state of Washington is a "green" mountain with a different composition of rock than its neighbors. The Park Service explains the astonishing fact that this mountain's rock strata was scraped off the Pacific plate as it crunched its way under the North American landmass and pushed over to where it is now.

While the western United States has towering, young mountain ranges with a geologic history easy to read and learn from, the eastern United States has a much older history of mountain range development and decline, and an older geologic history in general. When the roots of the Rockies of western North America began their rise, the Appalachians of eastern North America had already been formed and were mostly eroded down to the stumps they are at the present time.

The story of earth properly starts at the Big Bang, but this narrative will begin more modestly at about a billion years ago when all the continents were one land mass. This supercontinent broke up as tectonic plates separated and pieces floated apart. After a few hundred million years a reverse process brought the various segments together again to form another super-continent that geologists call "Pangaea." None of this information will surprise school children, because they learn about Pangaea as early in their education as the previous generation learned about "continent." Pertinent to our story is the fact that a collision some 300 million years ago created enormous pressure where the edges of the land masses crushed into one another. Some of this fused rock can be seen at Heggie's Rock in Columbia County, in the quarry on the Richmond-Columbia County line, or in the deep quarry at Camak. Climbers on Stone Mountain near Atlanta can see the results also. Rock strata that was not fused might have been cracked in the collision, or in a subsequent upheaval. Two of these cracks, or "faults" run near Augusta, one through Belair in Columbia County, and one through the Savannah River Site across the Savannah River from Augusta in South Carolina.

Pangaea itself broke up as its predecessor had done. Today's continents, formed about 70 million years ago, resulted. A chunk of Georgia floated off to become a permanent part of Africa and another piece traveled off as part of Wales. Even as the continents separated, the erosion of the once mighty Appalachians had begun. The Appalachian chain, created at the formation of Pangaea, originally towered higher than today's Alps or Himalayas. Erosion over millions of years has reduced them by two-thirds of their height, or to put it more graphically, the Appalachians were once two miles higher than they are now. The sediment from the dissolution of the mountains formed the Atlantic Coastal Plain. The hard rock of the Appalachian Plateau ends at Augusta and the sedimentary rock of the coastal plain begins. The erosion process created not only the coastal plain, but the gentler, more friendly mountains of Georgia, North Carolina and upwards. Unlike the much younger Rockies and Sierras of the West, the Appalachians have acquired a skin of soil and a coat of foliage.

The age of dinosaurs ended 66 million years ago, as is now theorized, with a possible combination of the widespread death by diseases of most of the earth's dinosaur population, and the crash into earth of a giant meteor, creating a cloud of dust that blocked out the life-sustaining ultra-violet light of the sun. Small mammals survived to begin their reign on earth. Oceans retreated permanently from Augusta's area 36 million years ago, leaving the sand dunes of the ancient shoreline. The sea flooded and retreated from the lower Coastal Plain of Georgia many times before the arrival of pre-historic humans 15,000 to 20,000 years ago. Marine fossils from 36-38 million years ago can be found throughout the "Sandhills" of the Augusta area. Subsequent erosion by precursors of modern streams and the Savannah River at Augusta carved valleys through the soft layers of sedimentary rock. The remaining intact strata of marine and deltaic sediments, which themselves are like pages in the book of the Atlantic Coastal Plain's history, became ridgelines between the valleys we would come to know as "Sandhills." By about 500,000 years ago the major work of sculpting Augusta, Georgia's physical geography had been done. However, changes in the Atlantic's sea level would often affect the inner Savannah River Valley at today's Augusta, even as recently as 6,000 to 4,000 years ago when the flood plain deposits on which the city now sits were then beginning to be stabilized.

The reason for this discussion of geologic prehistory is that all the continental clashing, rifting, erosion, marine advances and retreats have fashioned the geographic milieu inhabited by people of the Savannah River Valley. The resulting physical geography has determined the possibilities of life in the

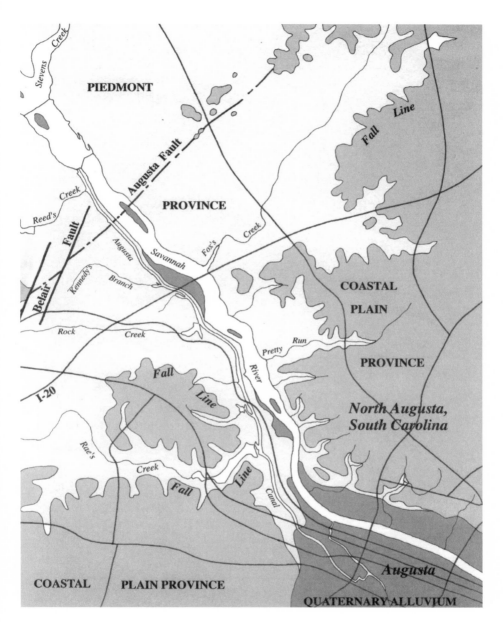

Figure 1. Geology determined the location of the Augusta Canal.
(Drawing by Michael White)

region. The place where the metamorphic rock of the southern Appalachians meets the sedimentary rock of the Coastal Plain, known as "the fall line," is a vicinity that would develop a predictable history. The Savannah River's flow through the 100 miles of Appalachian Piedmont ends abruptly at the fall line, with the flow changing to a more sluggish pace, and the fall line marks the inland head of navigation. As European colonial settlement began, boats could follow the Savannah River inland from its mouth at the sea up as far as present-day Augusta. Also, because the rocky shoals at Augusta are the farthest downstream on the entire river, they had been a place of natural crossing by animals for thousands of years. The shoals became, quite naturally, the crossing point on the Savannah River for prehistoric trails from coastal and mountain regions. Subsequently, in historic times it would become the natural market for the country around it, a place for trade and commerce. The produce of the Piedmont would be brought by mule, wagon, boat and train to be transported downriver to other markets. Equally important to this story is that the fall of the river has the potential of generating enormous power. When commerce began to fail in Augusta, Augustans turned to the river as a source of power. The result changed the history of the city.

CHAPTER TWO

The First People

———⟨❋⟩———

A college graduate of the 1950's would not have known about plate tectonics and the theories of continents colliding and dividing, but would have been familiar with theories about the earliest human occupation of the new world. The standard professional opinion then was that the first Americans crossed over the Bering Straits some time between twenty thousand and fifty thousand years ago. In 1997, James Axtell, a respected ethno-historian wrote, "The human history of America – we should not have to argue any longer – began when Asian hunters first crossed the Bering land bridge 15,000, perhaps 25,000, possibly 50,000 years ago, to make the Americas their permanent, if peripatetic home."[1] In other words we know no more now about the first arrival than we did fifty and more years ago.

The archaeological and historical professions have been reluctant to push human presence in the new world to an earlier date. The reason is partly our collective conservatism. For centuries no one seemed much concerned about antiquity. Christians then, and some still, regarded the Bible as a scientific as well as religious document. In 1606 an Irish bishop named Ussher examined the Bible carefully, added up the generations of the Old Testament, and came to the conclusion that creation occurred in B.C. 4004. Amazing as that detection might have seemed, the good bishop somehow discovered the precise time and day of the historic event, 9:00 A.M. on October 22nd. Not many people in 1606 quarreled with the bishop's conclusions, as far as we know, and some scientific creationists today think he was right, though they allow a narrow margin of error. The wide acceptance throughout the Christian world of a recent creation placed the burden of proof upon those arguing for an older beginning. Nevertheless, scientists have borne the burden and rolled back the ages of human origins. It is now commonly accepted by anthropologists that human precursors walked the earth millions of years ago, and that humans in their present form go back over a hundred thousand years. But so far, no one has suggested that human ancestors visited the new world. Humans came between 15,000 and 50,000 years ago and moved into Central and South America where they built up the great civilizations, the Olmec, Toltec, Inca, Aztec and others. It was assumed that the first people to visit the Savannah River region came only a few thousand years ago. Therefore, the 1998 discovery of stone implements dating from 15,000 to 20,000 years ago near the Savannah River in Allendale County caused a minor sensation among anthropologists and archeologists. Dr. Albert Goodyear of the South Carolina Institute of Archeology led the team of excavators at the Topper Site. He told reporters, "This pushes the prehistory of the Americas and certainly of the South farther back in time than any of us once thought possible." An expert from the Smithsonian Institution echoed the thought, "Until recently no one would have accepted the idea of artifacts this old. But in the last few years there has been a total change of thinking about finds like this. These may turn out to be the oldest tools in North America."[2] The find should be of more than casual interest to the inhabitants of the Central Savannah River Area because it extends their human prehistory and adds another element to their cultural heritage.

If the professionals do not know when the first Americans came to the new world, it has not been for want of trying. Language historian Johanna Nichols of the University of California attacked the problem from a different direction. Theorizing that it takes 6,000 years for a language to break down into two or three variations of the language, and figuring that there are now about fifteen language groups in the Americas, she puts the initial crossing at 30,000 to 40,000 years ago. She believes that the first comers penetrated deep into South America prior to 14,000 years ago, and that as the last glacier retreated from North America and the climate warmed they returned northward, and that new waves of immigration crossed over the Bering connection 12,000 years ago and again as recently as 5,000 years ago.

A team of Emory University scientists headed by Dr. David Wallace analyzed the mitochondrial DNA of living Native Americans, and reported in 1992 that they believe there were three separate migrations and that the first occurred before 30,000 years ago.[3] It will be interesting to see how Dr. Goodyear's discovery in Allendale County will affect the calculations of the linguists and DNA detectives.

Charles Hudson, a leading authority on Indian history, suggests that the Arctic passage into America destroyed most of the old world parasites and that therefore the American Indians lost their immunities to many diseases. That theory explains their known vulnerability to European illnesses.⁴ However, the first people would have been susceptible to germs carried by prehistoric American animals, so early humans in America, like their brethren on all continents, continued to die from disease, some in epidemic proportions. The first Europeans who introduced old world germs into new world people, also died by the thousands from new world diseases.

From the uncertain time of the first immigration until 9,900 years ago, the people and their culture are known as "paleoindian," a term meaning early Indian. As the last of at least four glaciers released its hold upon North America from 20,000 to 10,000 years ago, the climate improved and grasses flourished. Humans looked the same as now, but the animals they hunted 10,000 years ago and earlier were quite different. The extinction of the great woolly mammoths might have been hastened by the arrival of the first hunters, and the mastodons with their enormous curving tusks still roamed about. Giant sloths were fair game. An early spear point was found embedded in the remains of a giant sloth in a cave in Clovis, New Mexico. Points of similar manufacture, called Clovis points, are considered evidence of the presence of early Americans wherever they are found. Other prey included beavers weighing as much as 500 pounds, tapirs, llamas, bears, bison, and deer. And there was the curious glyptodent, an armor-plated reptile, four feet tall and eight feet long.⁵ Alligators probably crowded the glyptodent out of their marshy habitats and into extinction. For thousands of years humans wandered about following game over natural trails, several of which converged at the fall line of the Savannah River. One or more of these bands of hunters and their families left the stone cutting tools that were found by Dr. Goodyear.

Although nothing remarkable happened to change the

life style of the early people between 9,900 and 8,000 years ago, archeologists call that period "early archaic." Moderns might wonder at the lack of progress of those people who lived nomadic lives and did the same thing generation after generation, but their way of life could be considered the most successful in American history or prehistory since it lasted so long. The wanderers seem to have been healthier than their descendants who stayed in one place. The revolutionary change in American prehistory occurred during the "Middle Archaic" period, 8,000 to 5,000 years ago. Some clever or unusually hungry nomad decided to break open a clam and eat it. Soon his or her entire band preferred staying and eating shellfish to roaming about after game. Technological improvements followed. These early people learned to dig pits and cook shellfish by heating stones and dropping or dipping them into the liquid. Shellfish mounds or middens are landmarks of the Middle Archaic era. Soapstone, found in the Piedmont, became the preferred heating tool, and perforated pieces of soapstone are other clues to the existence of shellfish eaters. One of these bands wandered into the Savannah River Valley, found the shellfish abundant and settled upon an island known today as Stallings Island and located just above the headgates of the Augusta Canal. Kenneth Sassaman has studied the Stallings Island people more assiduously than anyone since William Claflin wrote his report in 1931. He believes that the first residents of Stallings Island arrived as early as 4,000 years ago, but should not be classified as part of the classic Stallings Island culture because they did not use pottery. He refers to them as the Mill Branch Culture. Pottery-makers from below the fall line of the Savannah River moved into the Stallings Island neighborhood and intermingled with the early occupants to create the Stallings Island Culture of 3,700 to 3,500 years ago. Beautifully

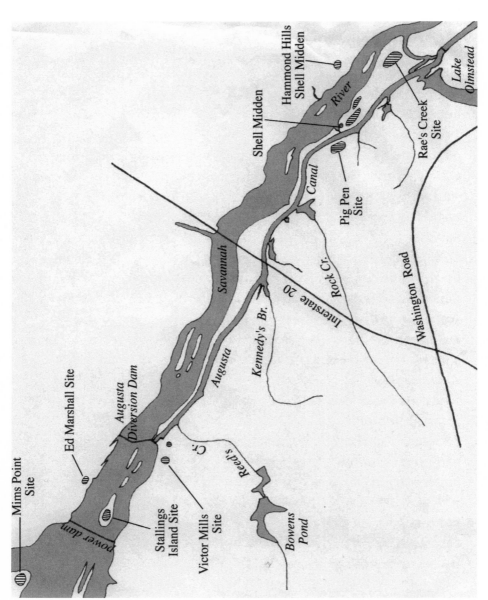

Figure 2. Excavation sites along the canal provided information about pre-historic human occupation of the area. *(Drawing by Michael White)*

decorated bone pins and uniquely decorated pots characterize the era.[6]

Charles C. Jones, Jr. first excavated Stallings Island and other prehistoric sites near Augusta. His published accounts attracted the interest of William H. Claflin, Jr., who made the study of Stallings a life-long pursuit. He visited the island with his father in 1906, and returned to do exploratory digs in 1908, 1921 and 1925. His findings prompted the Peabody Museum of Harvard University to undertake a thorough study of the site. C.B. Cosgrove and his wife, both members of the Peabody staff, arrived in Augusta on December 28, 1928 and remained until March 1, 1929. Their extensive notes and his own observations provided material for Claflin's report titled *The Stallings Island Mound Columbia County, Georgia*, published by the Museum in 1931.[7] The report made Stallings Island famous among archeologists, both professional and amateur. An unfortunate by-product of the attention to Stallings was an onslaught of amateur collectors, called looters by the professionals, who removed artifacts from their original sites. (For scientists, such activity is like tearing the pages out of a book, rendering the history unreadable.)

The principal mound on Stallings measured 512 feet by 300 feet, and had an average elevation of 23 feet. The Peabody team located 24 fireplaces, 110 cooking or storage pits, 3,500 pottery shards, 500 bone artifacts, as well as hundreds of stone and shell artifacts. The abundance of net sinkers, over 2,500, indicated that the islanders fished in the shoals of the Savannah River. They also made their own fishhooks. The many arrowheads of various sizes meant that they hunted small game such as squirrel and larger animals such as deer. The grinders and mortars revealed that they grew maize and ground it into meal. The large number of piercing tools, awls, pins and needles, indicated sophisticated leatherworking, very likely by the women. Men would have used the grooved axe heads, the gouging and chiseling tools for woodwork. The striking feature of Stallings Island Culture is the attention to personal adornment, as evidenced by the decorated pins, gorgets, and bead necklaces.[8]

Surprisingly, no pipes of any kind were found at Stallings, so the familiar pipe-smoking ritual belonged to a later time. Nor did the islanders bury their dead with personal effects, as was the practice later. The Peabody team found clay floors of dwellings, but did not come to conclusions about the kind of housing of the Stallings people. The housing question presented a challenge to modern archeologists. Dan Elliot, digging at a Stallings era site at Lovers Lane in East Augusta, found evidence of structures in several sets of postholes. Ken Sassaman discovered similar signs of structures in another Stallings site at Mims Point, South Carolina, in digs in 1992, 1993, and 1995. His team found signs of three possible structures, each with a pair of hearths, one or more storage pits, and a series of shallow basins. The dwellings were round or oval, four to five meters in size, and arranged around a central common ground. Sassaman suggested why the pottery of the Stallings culture is so circumscribed around the Savannah River fall-line zone. Women made the pottery and in a matrilineal society, women stayed home generation after generation. However, as Sassaman observed, the social rules that bound women to home and hearth may have led to the abandonment of the Stallings villages and the end of the unique culture. Parasites accumulate in the trash pits of sedentary places and after two hundred years the villages must have become unsanitary, even pestilential. In any case, the Stallings people returned to the wandering and more healthy ways of their ancestors and left the Savannah Valley. Nevertheless, by their prolonged stay they awake the curiosity and challenge the imagination of modern residents of the same region.[9] Their artifacts, those exhibited at the Augusta Museum of History, and those secreted away in the possession of private collectors, remind us that we, like those ancients, are custodians of a precious environment.

For a thousand years people came and went along and across the Savannah Valley near the site of Augusta. They camped but did not stay. However, about two thousand years ago they began to settle down again. The period from about 1000 B.C. until 1600 A.D. is known as the Mississippian because the first excavations of the period were located on sites bordering the Mississippi River. This was the era of the mound-builders and chiefdoms. Several chiefdoms with their characteristic mounds were located on the Savannah River above and below the fall line. David Anderson, in *Savannah River Chiefdoms*, described the period as one in which "the way of life was characterized by sedentary communities, intensive maize agriculture, platform mounds, and a ranked hierarchical society."[10] A chiefdom might extend over several villages, depending upon the authority of the chief. That dignitary lived in an exalted style, was carried about on a litter, attended by dozens of servants, and was entitled to a privileged burial upon the mound, with his most precious belongings, sometimes including his favorite wives. The successful chieftain afforded security for his people, a requisite for the labor-intensive work of building mounds. Success depended upon his ability to command a fighting force to fend off intruders and keep client villages in subjection, for the period was one of chronic warfare.

The naturalist William Bartram came upon the mounds of the Savannah River's largest chiefdom in his 1775 visit to George Galphin of Silver Bluff, twelve miles below Augusta on the Carolina side of the Savannah River. He described, "various monuments and vestiges of the residences of the ancients."[11] The site is known today as Mason's Plantation, and remains to be thoroughly investigated. The always inquisitive Bartram found another mound village above the fall line when he visited Fort James at the confluence of the Broad River and the Savannah. The largest of several mounds was conical in shape, forty to fifty feet high, with a flat top and a circumference of two to three hundred feet at the bottom. Chiefdoms vied with one another to erect the most impressive mounds, much as the European medieval villages competed to erect impressive cathedrals during the same time period. The Broad River site is known by the name of a property owner, Rembert's Plantation site. David Anderson dates the rise of the Mason's and Rembert's chiefdoms to the early part of the Thirteenth Century. Closely associated with the Mason's mounds were those at the nearby Hollywood site near the Savannah River in Richmond County below Augusta.[12]

The Ocmulgee National Monument Park near Macon affords the visitor an insight into the lifestyle of the villagers of a Mississippian era mound center. Two of the huge mounds at Ocmulgee are in a good state of preservation, the council house has been restored, and the fine museum houses artifacts from the site. By contrast, the Rembert mound has entirely disappeared, and the Mason's nearly so. David Anderson believes that years of dry weather, combined with raids from larger chiefdoms to the east and west, caused the demise of the Savannah River chiefdoms. By 1450 they were abandoned. He suggests that the Savannah River people moved to the Oconee, noting that the natural trail followed by DeSoto was clearly marked from the Oconee to the Savannah, indicating traffic between those rivers.[13]

The fact that the Savannah Valley had been abandoned a

hundred years before DeSoto's expedition passed through is a new idea for modern residents of the area to ponder. Tradition is tenacious, and it is a local tradition that the village of Cofitachiqui, with its legendary queen, lay on the banks of the Savannah River, at Silver Bluff, or possibly even Beech Island. William Bartram thought the ruins he saw near Silver Bluff had been constructed by Spaniards.[14] Since at least 1690, traders at Savannah Town wondered at the whereabouts of Spanish silver mines. The name Silver Bluff and the "Spanish cut" in the Savannah River may have been souvenirs of the old rumors.[15] Albert James Pickett in his 1851 history of Alabama located Cofitachiqui at Silver Bluff, saying he had learned of it from an Indian. In 1901, James Mooney of the Smithsonian Institute added his authority to the Silver Bluff site. The matter seemed to be settled once and for all in 1935 when the special commission created by Congress and headed by the distinguished John Swanton of the Smithsonian concluded that Cofitachiqui was at Silver Bluff, and that DeSoto had gone up the east side of the Savannah River, and that his route went through Highlands and Franklin, North Carolina. Those two towns still display signs that say DeSoto passed through and seem disinclined to take them down in the face of new evidence.[16]

Unfortunately for local boosters, all these authorities had it wrong. In 1980 Charles Hudson, Marvin Smith and Chester DePratter of the University of Georgia analyzed a document that had escaped the notice of the previous scholars. Written by a member of the Juan Pardo expedition of 1566-68, it gave specific information about the location of Cofitachiqui and other towns visited by DeSoto. Thanks to recent archeological discoveries, Hudson was able to piece together a new interpretation of DeSoto's route that is now generally accepted by scholars, though some grumblers remain. Hudson tells his -

and DeSoto's - story in his excellent 1997 book *Knights of Spain, Warriors of the Sun*. He relates how the chiefdom of Ocute on the Oconee River considered itself at war with the chiefdom of Cofitachiqui on the Wateree River, and how DeSoto had to cross the empty wilderness in between. DeSoto's 500 men and their Indian escort crossed on the shoals of the Savannah River; the chronicles of his expedition mark the beginning of the written history of the Augusta area.[17]

Written records supplement archeological findings and provide a more complete account of human occupation of the Savannah River Valley and the fall-line zone through which the canal runs. Native Americans continued to move about, and the Savannah River occupants never stayed very long. A century after DeSoto's passing, the Westos Indians occupied both sides of the river near the fall line. The first settlers of Charlestown in 1670 heard unsavory stories about them from local Indians. They were an allegedly cruel people who had a reputation for eating their captives. They settled on the Savannah after having been driven out of Virginia, but they continued to be supplied with guns by Virginia traders. A party of Westos visited Charlestown in 1674 to open trade, and Henry Woodward, one of the founders of Charlestown, accompanied them to their villages on the river they called the Westobu. Within sight of the village, Woodward fired his gun in salute and must have been surprised at the "volley of fifty or sixty small arms" the Westos fired in answer. The Spanish never supplied guns to their Indian allies, so these weapons must have come from Virginia. Woodward opened a trade in deerskins and Indian slaves with the Westos that lasted about five years. The Charlestown merchants resented the middleman profits the Westos demanded for deerskins, and connived with another transient tribe known as the Savannahs or Shawnees to make war on the Westos, promising them guns as a reward for the favored situation on the river. After starting it in 1680 by killing several Westos who had come to Charlestown for a talk, the Carolinians let the Savannahs do the fighting. In 1682, a Charlestown merchant wrote, "We are at peace with all but those common enemies of mankind, those man eaters...by name of Westos..."[18] The remnant of the Westos sought refuge among the Creek towns with whom they had traded, and the victorious Savannahs occupied the fall zone. Their principal village, located at today's Beech Island, was known thereafter as Savannah Town, and the river became the Savannah instead of the awkward-sounding Westobu.

The late Harold Maness of Beech Island, South Carolina, searched in the British Library and found a map by William Gascoyne dated 1685 that depicts an "old fort" on the west bank of the Savannah River. The reference is interesting and intriguing. Such a structure would be the earliest colonial fort in the Augusta area. Henry Woodward visited the Creek towns on the Chattahoochee in 1685 and opened direct trade between the Creek Nation and Charlestown. Around that time Charlestown merchants established warehouses and began outfitting trading caravans at Savannah Town. However, that does not explain why the structure on the west bank should be called an "old" fort. It is possible that earlier Woodward or another Carolinian had built a fortified trading house among the Westos who lived on the west bank.[19]

The Savannahs were still there in 1708 when the Governor of South Carolina reported, "About one hundred and fifty miles south west from Charles Town is seated on the aforesaid river (the Savannah) a Nation of Indians called the Savannahs. They are settled in three towns and consist of about one hundred and fifty men."[20] The French called the Savannahs

"Chouanons" and a French map of the period shows them situated on the east bank of the river.[21] They were pestered by raiding Cherokee and Catawbas and soon resumed their wanderings into Pennsylvania and Ohio.

Another transient band who lived for a while on the Savannah were the Apalachees from the lower Chattahoochee. Former South Carolina Governor James Moore led a brutal raid upon the Spanish Apalachees, who were mostly Christian, in 1704. He burned several Spanish missionaries at the stake and brought back hundreds of captives to be sold into slavery in Barbados. A number of intimidated Apalachees followed along to the Savannah River and settled near the Savannahs. The Apalachees sought a measure of revenge against the Carolinians by joining the Yamassee in an uprising against the traders among them in 1715; ninety Carolinians were killed. The Louisiana French took advantage of the war to forge closer ties with the Creek Nation. They built Fort Toulouse at the forks of the Alabama River, and claimed everything their Creek allies claimed. A map made by the French royal cartographer in 1718 shows "La Louisiane" extending to the Savannah River.[22] The Carolinians ignored the French claim, but recognized that of the Creeks by signing a treaty with the Creek "Emperor" Brims in 1717 after the Yamasees had been driven into Florida. The Apalachees returned to their homeland.

Thoroughly alarmed by the Yamassee attacks, the Carolina authorities built Fort Moore at Savannah Town to guard their Savannah River frontier, and in 1721 they constructed Fort King George on the Altamaha to protect the Spanish border. In addition, Carolina attempted to attract friendly tribes to the Savannah to act as a buffer against future raids by French allied Indians. This policy explains why James Edward Oglethorpe's Georgians who would act as a buffer against potential enemies received such a warm welcome in Charlestown. But before the Georgians, the Yuchis and the Chickasaws settled upon the Savannah River as a screen for Carolina. The Yuchis, whose name has been spelled Uchees, and Euchees, were an interesting and enigmatic people. Their name comes from their own tradition. We are the "Tsoyala yuchi," they said, "the children of the sun from far away."[23] They have also been called the Hologe and Hogoheegee.[24] Their language and customs were unlike any of the other southeastern people. Scholars have linked their culture to that of the Mediterranean region, and speculate that the ancestors of the Yuchi came across the Atlantic. Thor Heyerdahl proved that a crossing could be done by sailing with seven companions in a papyrus reed boat from Morocco to Barbados in 1970. The Yuchis built their houses and buried their dead differently from neighboring people, making it easier for archeologists to iden-tify their settlements. They were widely settled in the southeast before the invasion of the various tribes known as Muscogulgees or Creeks. DeSoto's expedition passed near the Yuchi town of Chisca, in the mountains of eastern Tennessee. Scouts reported that there was no gold in Chisca and that it was almost inaccessible, so the Spaniards marched on.

A century and a half later the Yuchi experienced a severe defeat by Cherokees led by two renegade Carolina traders. The Yuchis left Tennessee and some settled among the Creeks upon the Chattahoochee and some joined the Savannahs and Apalachees on the Savannah River just before the Yamasee War of 1715. Like their neighbors they joined the Yamasee and like the others they left at the conclusion of that affair. However, the Carolina traders persuaded some of the Yuchis to leave the Chattahoochee and come back to the Savannah, where they set-tled upon the west side of the river. Their principal village was known as Mount Pleasant, near the present town of Newington. They were there in 1735 when German Salzburgers founded Ebenezer. Baron Von Reck visited Ebenezer and drew portraits of the Yuchi as they went about their daily business. The drawings are now housed at the Royal Library in Copenhagen, Denmark. One shows a Yuchi hunting party: a man carries a gun and on his back a bag containing "all sorts of utensils and kitchenware like a kettle, spoons, etc."[25] The man and woman wear woolen blankets called "strouds" for the town of Stroud in England where the thick cloth was manufactured. Clearly the Yuchis had become dependent upon the trade goods furnished by Carolina traders. Georgia's founder Oglethorpe took the side of the Yuchis when Carolinians tried to put their cattle on Yuchi land. As a result, the Yuchis volunteered to fight alongside the Georgians in their invasion of Spanish Florida in 1740. After that war, the Yuchis began to move upriver, settling for a time near George Galphin's trading post at Silver Bluff. William Stephens, the Trustees' secretary in Savannah, noted in his journal in 1746 that the Yuchis had deserted their town at Mount Pleasant, "chusing to settle farther up." Some of them lived for a time above Augusta upon the creek that bears their name "Euchee Creek." There they were exposed to Cherokee raids, and they retired to the Chattahoochee to join the rest of their people. They achieved an uncommon degree of prosperity by the time the naturalist William Bartram visited their town in 1775. He said it was a "beautiful town" with many young people. Their houses were neatly plastered inside and out, and roofed with cypress shingles. He noted that their language was different from that of the neighboring Creeks. "They are in a Confederacy with the Creeks, but do not mix with them," Bartram observed.[26] Most of the Yuchis were forced to move to Oklahoma with the Creeks during the 1830's, but they continued to preserve a distinctive language and tribal identity.[27]

The Indians most closely associated with colonial Augusta were the Savannah River Chickasaws. In 1722, as part of their policy of buffering their frontier with friendly tribes, the Carolina government invited any Chickasaws who wished to do so to settle upon the Savannah River, promising to supply them until they could support themselves. A chief named Squirrel King and his followers accepted the invitation. The pioneer naturalist and artist Mark Catesby found them near Savannah Town in 1723. "To the Hospitality and Assistance of those friendly Indians, I am much indebted," he wrote.[28] The Carolina authorities would have preferred Squirrel King to occupy a site on the lower Savannah River, but the chief declined, saying that he liked it where he was. Subsequently the governor of South Carolina assigned a grant of 21,774 acres to the Chickasaws, directly opposite today's downtown Augusta. The Chickasaws, proving themselves good neighbors, crossed the river to help Roger Lacy and Richard Kent construct Fort Augusta in 1736 and 1737. As a reward, Lacy informed William Stephens that he "had lately run out a little Town near him, for the settlement of some of the Chickasaw Indians."[29] The place Lacy referred to was thereafter called New Savannah, to distinguish it from Savannah Town across the river.[30]

Lacy's overture to the Chickasaws represented a phase of the on-going contest between South Carolina and Georgia for control of the Indian trade. At Oglethorpe's request and over the objection of the Carolina agents, Parliament passed a bill in 1735 giving Oglethorpe control of the trade west of the Savannah River. Oglethorpe established the fort and town of Augusta to enable him to regulate the Indian trade. The act had the unexpected consequence of causing the Carolina traders at Fort Moore to cross the river and become Georgians. For that reason, Augusta was quickly populated with traders and merchants who did business with Indians. Squirrel King volunteered to join General Oglethorpe's invasion of Florida and his warriors gave a good account of themselves in their encounters with Spanish-allied Indians. Squirrel King proudly presented the head of a slain enemy to Oglethorpe, and was disappointed when the general declined to accept the trophy.[31]

In 1742, when the South Carolinians and most of the Indians deserted Oglethorpe in the face of a Spanish counter-invasion, Squirrel King's men stood by the Georgians in the Battle of Bloody Marsh on St. Simon's Island. Captain Daniel Pepper, commandant of the Fort Moore garrison, reported the triumphal return of the warriors on August 21, 1742, "The Squirrel King and Mingo Stoby and the rest of the Cheekesaws with their wives came in with the War hoop from Frederica, and broght several Sculps to this garrison which they saluted by the discharge of their Guns and three hurraas which I returned with my Cannon."[32]

In 1758 the officious Indian Superintendent Edmond Atkin interrogated the Chickasaws at their camp at New Savannah. By then Squirrel King had died and Tuccatoby (or Succatebee) King acted as spokesman for his people. Atkin's tone was severe. The King had given the Chickasaws a fine tract on the other side of the river. Why had they abandoned it? The chief replied that it might have been because of their enemies who made life unsafe over there. Atkin scoffed at that. The Chickasaws had the reputation of being fierce warriors. He had never heard that they were afraid of their enemies. He had heard that when Augusta was first settled the Chickasaws swam across the river and drank too much and some of them drowned when trying to return to the Carolina side. Tuccatoby King considered the idea for a moment, then replied, "Tis true, had it not been on that Account partly, we might still be living on the same land." Atkin pressed on. How long had the Indians been on the Georgia side? None of the Chickasaws could remember exactly. Atkin chastised them for moving, "Our king don't allow his children to sell or take his lands to their own use," he said. What would the Chickasaws do when white people settled all around them? Tuccatoby King saw no problem in that eventuality. Moving held no terrors for them; they would simply go somewhere else.[33]

Fortunately for the inhabitants of Augusta, the Chickasaws remained at New Savannah a little longer. When painted Cherokee warriors joined the French and threatened Augusta in the winter of 1760, the Chickasaws camped outside Fort Augusta. They said that the English fight was their fight, and that they were prepared to live and die with the English. They went off with a Carolina army under Governor William Henry Lyttelton to fight the Cherokees and then returned to defend Augusta against Cherokee reprisals. When the Cherokees attacked Fort Moore across the river, Lachlan McGillivray led a party of Chickasaws out to drive the invaders away.[34]

The Chickasaws were highly praised by Superintendent John Stuart and the four governors who attended the great Indian Congress at Augusta in November 1763. The French had been expelled from the continent; now the Indians were all the children of the great white father across the ocean. The assembled Chickasaws, Choctaws, Catawbas, Creeks, and Cherokees signed a treaty giving the land between the Savannah and the Ogeechee Rivers to the Georgians. The treaty was epochal in the history of the Savannah River Valley in that it signaled the end of the nearly 20,000 years of Indian occupation. Indians came and went along the traditional trails in large numbers before the American Revolution. John Stuart held several congresses in Augusta, including another treaty conference in 1773, but after 1763 the Indians came as visitors, not as inhabitants. The Savannah River Chickasaws did as they had promised Edmond Atkin they would: when the neighborhood became too crowded they moved to their western homeland.[35]

In 1986 Augusta celebrated its 250th anniversary. An honored guest on the occasion was Overton James, head of the Chickasaw Nation in Oklahoma. He said that he and his people remembered Squirrel King, and that he would gladly participate in the proceedings. In a ceremony at St. Paul's Church, Chief James presented a pipe to Mayor Charles DeVaney. He said that his people had taken care of the neighborhood while they were here, but could not be responsible for what had happened since they left.[36]

CHAPTER THREE

Eighteenth Century Connections

———◦———

A lthough the Augusta Canal was the product of the Nineteenth Century, it had colonial and early federal connections. The land it traversed was already historic, and the persons and events along the right of way are part of the story of the canal itself. Rae's Creek is one of the more obvious physical connections with the canal because the two flow together. Rae's Creek was originally known as Kenyon's Creek. We know very little about the man Kenyon, because the Carolina Indian records for that period are lost. However, he must have been one of the Carolina merchant-traders based at Savannah Town. Very likely he kept his cattle on the Georgia side because the riverbank below Kenyon's Creek was called Kenyon's Bluff. He would have needed a sizable acreage for pasture, but he could not have actually owned the land. Until Oglethorpe's 1739 treaty with the Creeks, the site of Augusta was Indian land and officially off-limits to whites.[1] Samuel

Eveleigh, a prosperous and opportunistic Charlestown merchant with warehouses at Savannah Town, suggested to Oglethorpe that Kenyon's Bluff would be the ideal location for a fort and a town. As early as November 20, 1734, he offered to build the fort at his own expense in return for a three-to-five year monopoly of the Indian trade.[2]

James Edward Oglethorpe had no intention of allowing Eveleigh or any other Carolinian to monopolize the trade west of the Savannah. He listened to Tomochichi and other tribal leaders who accused the traders of once again cheating the Indians as they had before the Yamasee War. Oglethorpe knew about the French aspirations to control all the territory west of the Savannah River, and he worried that the trade, improperly conducted, could drive the Creeks into an alliance with the Louisiana French. Therefore he returned to England, and in 1735 obtained from Parliament legislation that gave control of the western trade to Georgia and that, incidentally, made him the Indian commissioner. He returned in 1736, and on June 14, 1736 ordered the surveyor Noble Jones to go up to Kenyon's Bluff and lay out a town of forty lots to be called Augusta, in honor of the recent marriage of Princess Augusta of Saxe-Gotha to Frederick, Prince of Wales.[3]

William Stephens, soon to be appointed Secretary to the Georgia Trustees, traveled upriver in July 1736 and reported that the traders of Savannah Town were agitated about the new law requiring Georgia licenses for trade west of the Savannah River. Many of them were in the process of moving across the river to Augusta. Stephens admired the view from the future site of Augusta; he expressed the opinion that the Savannah would soon be famous for the volume of its commerce. He liked the way in which the river "glides smoothly on as the River Thames at Putney."[4]

One of the Carolina "boomers" who moved across the river was a wealthy trader named Kennedy O'Brien. He asked for and received 500 acres along Kenyon's Creek for his plantation. O'Brien had no way of knowing it, but the site he selected had been frequently occupied by others before him. Archeologists tested the site before the 1989 construction of the Riverwatch Parkway linking Augusta and Interstate 20 and discovered artifacts dating back 8,000 years, in addition to some pieces from the Seventeenth and Eighteenth Centuries. O'Brien did not remain in Augusta long; in company with many other Georgians, he criticized the Trustees' regulations and moved to Charlestown, where he died in 1741.[5]   John Rae acquired O'Brien's property on Kenyon's Creek. He called it Stony Creek, but soon it became generally known as Rae's Creek and remains so today.

John Rae was born at Balycreen, County Down, Ireland, around 1708. He and his wife Catherine came to Georgia on May 8, 1734 and secured a lot in Savannah. Oglethorpe and the Trustees were glad to see people who paid their own way. Oglethorpe employed Rae as master of the Trustees' scout boat that made frequent runs along the coast. After 1739 Rae acquired his own riverboat, or periagua, and engaged in transporting commodities from Savannah Town and Augusta to Savannah. Rae must have become acquainted with Kennedy O'Brien because both men signed a petition protesting the Trustees' policies. Rae entered into partnership with Isaac Barksdale, a veteran Indian trader. Barksdale secured deerskins and Rae transported them to Charlestown.

A better business opportunity soon presented itself. In 1744 Archibald McGillivray, head of Charlestown's largest trading company, retired from the firm and returned to his native Scotland, leaving his license to his relative Lachlan

McGillivray. Patrick Brown took over the company, moved to Augusta, and invited Rae and Barksdale into partnership. The new company soon monopolized the Georgia Indian trade under the name Brown, Rae and Company. When Brown followed the successful trader's pattern of retiring to a plantation to live like a gentleman, Rae promoted two talented younger men, Lachlan McGillivray and George Galphin, to partnership. The three referred to themselves as "the surviving members of Brown, Rae and Company." Rae tended the store in Augusta, supervised shipments of deerskins and furs downriver and became one of the leaders in building Augusta into a proper town. In 1749 he and three other resident merchants offered to build a church if the Trustees would send altar supplies and arrange for a minister. The Trustees were glad to acknowledge such an act of civic virtue and did their part. The baptismal font they sent over may still be seen in the vestibule of St. Paul's Episcopal Church in downtown Augusta. The present church is the fourth or more likely the fifth to stand on the same site along the banks of the Savannah.[6]

For ten years Lachlan McGillivray lived deep in Upper Creek territory in the town of Little Tallassee on the Coosa River. The proximity of his residence to the French Fort Toulouse at the junction of the Coosa and Tallapoosa allowed him to collect intelligence on French activity, and made him a valuable agent of the Governors of South Carolina and Georgia. McGillivray married a mixed blood woman named Sehoy Marchand, and fathered a family of one boy and two girls. His Charlestown-educated son, Alexander McGillivray, grew up to be the recognized leader of the Creek Nation. Because of his honesty and genuine friendliness, McGillivray gained enormous influence among the chiefs of the Upper Creek towns along the Coosa and Tallapoosa Rivers.[7]

George Galphin established his post at the important Lower Creek town of Coweta, the home of Emperor Brims earlier in the century, and of his successors Chigilly and Malachi. Galphin, like John Rae, was a native of Ireland. Unlike Rae, he left his wife behind when he came to this country in 1737. He took at least two wives and had several children by them, all of whom he acknowledged. (He would also "marry" two black women and one white when he retired from the Indian country.) Like McGillivray, his personality was well suited to Indian diplomacy. The Lower Creeks trusted him even more than the agents appointed by the crown to supervise them.

Both men retired from the Indian country at the outset of the French and Indian War. Lachlan McGillivray became a hero when he led a group of Chickasaw and Creek Indians and drove away a raiding band of Cherokee Indians during the Cherokee War of 1760. McGillivray and Galphin were primarily responsible for persuading the Creek Indians to come to Augusta in 1763 and give up their land between the Savannah and Ogeechee Rivers. The Creeks had fought on the same side as the Georgians against the Cherokees, but they obliged McGillivray and Galphin and gave the land over to the Georgians.[8]

Lachlan McGillivray acquired the tract just east of John Rae's house, near where the Creek and Cherokee trails diverged from the main road later named Broad Street.[9] He fortified the house with a stockade during the Cherokee War, as did Rae. After that war, Rae and McGillivray followed the example of Patrick Brown and moved to plantations outside Savannah. Rae called his residence Rae's Hall, and McGillivray's was Vale Royal. George Galphin owned property below McGillivray's in Augusta, but preferred to live at his plantation at Silver Bluff, twelve miles below Augusta, near where a Mississippian Chiefdom was once centered. The three partners continued to be firm friends. They engaged in an ambitious project that involved bringing settlers from Ireland to settle a place they called Queensborough on the Ogeechee River. Several thousand Irish became Georgians as a result, though most of them preferred to live on their own farms rather than cluster together in Queensborough.[10] John Rae died in 1772; Lachlan McGillivray and his half-Indian son Alexander remained loyal to the King.

During the American Revolution the McGillivray tract was the scene of an important battle. After McGillivray moved to Savannah, his house in Augusta was managed by William Trevin. John and William Bartram stayed overnight with Trevin when they visited the town in 1765. Indian Commissioner John Stuart held several Indian Congresses in Augusta, including an important one in 1773 when the Cherokees and Creeks ceded their lands above the Little River to the King. By that time, Robert Mackay had acquired McGillivray's 500-acre property including the stone house eighty yards from the river known as the White House. Mackay preferred calling his estate "Garden Hill." During the British occupation of Augusta from June 1780 to June 1781, Lt. Col. Thomas Brown used the Mackay House to store Indian supplies. The Mackay House became the target for an attack in September by 600 refugee Georgians under Elijah Clark. A bitter, four-day battle ensued, with Brown and his Rangers barricaded in the White House. On the fifth day British reinforcements from Ninety-Six, South Carolina, rescued Brown. Lieutenant Colonel John Harris Cruger, of the New York Loyalists, assumed command in Augusta and hanged thirteen patriots according to Lord Cornwallis' standing order that any man who had taken an oath not to fight and who again took up arms would suffer that fate. The event became of more than local significance when Cornwallis dispatched a force under Major Patrick Ferguson to intercept the retreating Clark. Instead,

Clark's friends from the North Carolina mountains caught Ferguson atop Kings Mountain. The patriot victory has been called the turning point in the war in the South, but it would not have occurred if not for Clark's raid upon the Mackay House.[11]

The Mackay House was severely damaged during the battle, and demolished after the war. When President George Washington visited Augusta in 1791 he was taken to see the battlefield. A tobacco merchant named Ezekiel Harris bought the White House tract and in 1797 built the imposing house still standing on upper Broad Street near Chafee Park. Harris divided the estate into lots and ever since the neighborhood has been known as Harrisburg. During the 1920's the Augusta Chamber of Commerce began to make extravagant claims about local history; one was that the Harris House was actually the Mackay House. The house was "restored" to what it might have looked like during Lachlan McGillivray's residency, and troops of school children listened with bated breath for the groans of the patriots who were supposedly hanged from the back stairway. In preparation for the national bicentennial Martha Norwood, a historian for the Historic Preservation Office in Atlanta, thoroughly researched the property and demonstrated that the house was Harris', not McGillivray's. What fooled so many Augustans was that the property retained the name White House Tract even after the house itself was destroyed.[12]

President Washington authorized a federal arsenal for Augusta after his 1791 visit to the city. The work was neglected until after the War of 1812 when President James Monroe visited Augusta and urged the War Department to get busy on the project. The federal government bought that part of the White House Tract nearest the river for the new arsenal. A cornerstone later found at the site revealed that the construction was carried out under the supervision of Lieutenant Walter J.

Phillips. Unfortunately the location proved to be unhealthy and deaths caused by fevers decimated the garrison. Captain Matthew Payne recuperated at Senator Freeman Walker's plantation on the Hill and persuaded the army to buy the Walker plantation and move the arsenal buildings to the Hill. The new buildings were disassembled, carefully marked, transported to the new location and reassembled.[13] The army retained title to the river property when the canal cut through in 1845. As will be seen later in this chronicle, the great Confederate Powder Works and the huge post-war mills added to the historical importance of the old McGillivray tract. The property encompasses Augusta's history, from Indian trading house to Harrisburg mill village.

Rae's Creek has other interesting colonial connections. The present house at the sharp curve of Skinner Mill Road in west Augusta was the site of the colonial residence of Dr. Humphrey Wells, revolutionary war leader and a personal friend of the naturalist William Bartram. Wells purchased the 300-acre tract in 1773 from James Brewer, who had received the land as a royal grant in 1769. Bartram stayed with Wells as he traveled through the Augusta area on at least two occasions. Dr. Wells served on Georgia's Executive Council in 1779, and on the first Augusta commission in 1780. He died in 1781.

His widow Abigail sold the tract to John Hall in 1788 and it went through several hands after that until Seaborn Jones bought it in 1805. In 1806, Jones exchanged the property for land in Screven County belonging to William Skinner. Known as Major for his Revolutionary War services, Skinner was somewhat of a celebrity by virtue of the fact that President George Washington breakfasted at Skinner's Screven County residence while the President and his escort were on their way to Augusta. Skinner built a new mill downstream from the mill that Wells had operated, and the road passing his house has been called Skinner Mill Road ever since. An air of mystery attaches to the history of the house. In 1820 Major Skinner invited his family to dinner. While they waited, he took a shotgun, entered a closet under the stairway and shot himself. No one knew why. He had been seen the night before burying something in the back woods, something valuable according to family tradition.[14] There is the tantalizing possibility that the present house, still in the Skinner family, was the residence of Dr. Wells and therefore the oldest house in the Augusta area. However, an experienced historical preservationist crawled about under the house and informed this writer that in his opinion the house dated from about 1820.

The first map made of Augusta shows a shallow lagoon later used to channel the third level of the Augusta Canal. Lt. Col. Archibald Campbell, the commander who led the British army from Savannah to Augusta in January 1779, needed a map and the one drawn for him depicts colonial and revolutionary Augusta. During his short occupation of the town, Campbell made his headquarters at John Rae's house, then the home of John Rae, Jr. The house is clearly marked on the map. Campbell's description of Augusta is worth repeating:

"Augusta consisted of a Number of straggling Houses, arranged in a long Street lying parallel to the River, at the Distance of 100 yards. The great Road leading from the lower Country entered the South end of the Town at Right Angles to this Street, and after passing it, extended to the Ferry, which goes across to South Carolina. The Plain to the Southward of the Ferry Road extended four Miles in Length, and terminated in a Swamp at the Bend of the River, a little below Moore's Bluff. To the Northward of the Ferry Road, this Plain was about two Miles in Length and terminated in a Ravine, from whence the Country began to rise gradually from the Savannah River this Plain was about 3 Miles in Breadth' one thousand yards of which from the Banks of the River had been cleared of Wood and tolerably well cultivated. From the Ferry Road, Alligator Pond of about 80 feet in breadth and ten feet depth, extended one Mile and a half in a parallel Direction with the River, at the Distance of One thousand Yards."[15]

For several decades to come this long pond or lagoon

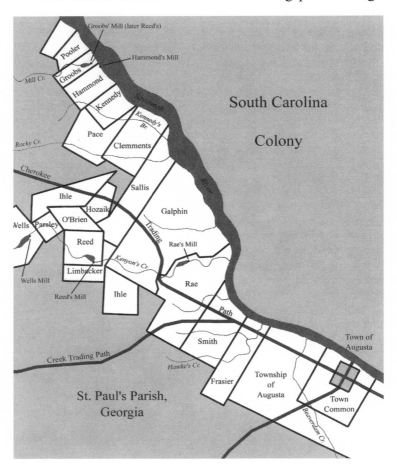

Figure 3. Colonial landowners, mill sites and road patterns.
(Drawing by Michael White)

divided the town into "lower" and "upper" sections. Because Martin Campbell owned land adjoining the lagoon the depression through which it flowed was known as Campbell's Gully. "Lagoon" is too generous a term for the long narrow drainage ditch. Lt. Col. Campbell must have seen it after a rainfall; most of the time it was a muddy nuisance. During the 1820's or 30's a progressive city administration filled in the ditch, but a depression in the ground remained. This depression was chosen by the canal engineers for the third level of the canal by which the canal water would be returned to the river.

The neighborhood immediately west of Campbell's Gully was known as Springfield even before the Revolution. The village that grew up here in the decade after the Revolution became the home of the first African-American congregation in the United States, Springfield Baptist Church. Its pastor, Jesse Peters Galphin, was one of the founders of the church when it began around 1773 at George Galphin's Silver Bluff plantation. Galphin gave permission for the slaves of his plantation to organize the church. Galphin died during the war, and after the war Jesse Peters moved with many of his congregants to Augusta.[16] The minutes of the Canal Commissioners reveal that when excavation of the third level of the canal was undertaken, workers uncovered the fountainhead of an old spring. Perhaps that is the reason, other than the low-lying nature of the land, that the area came to be known as Springfield.

Before Springfield was annexed to Augusta in 1798 it had its own tobacco warehouse and other stores. It could also claim "the governors plantation" for that term was used by the Augusta newspaper to describe George Walton's Meadow Garden residence. Walton thought on a grand scale, worthy of a man who had risked his life to sign the Declaration of Independence. He served on Augusta's first commission government in 1780 and again in 1783 when the commission took control of the town and established Richmond Academy. He served on the governing board of the prospective state university and hoped to locate it on his property on the Hill. He divided his 250 acres on the brow of the Hill and called it "College Hill." As Superior Court Judge, he fretted over the welfare of Augusta like an anxious parent. As governor in 1788 he lived at Meadow Garden. He led the delegation that welcomed President George Washington to Augusta in 1791.[17] Both men were ardent advocates for river improvement and canal building as a means of facilitating commerce and fostering union. Washington hoped to connect the Potomac and Ohio Rivers by a canal, and to construct a canal on the James River around the falls at Richmond, Virginia. According to his biographer, Washington foresaw a centrally planned system of canals and rivers that would go everywhere, bringing navigation almost to every man's door.[18] Washington's interest in waterways had caused him to host the Mount Vernon Conference in 1785, the meeting that led to the constitutional convention two years later. Walton escorted the President to the shoals of the Savannah River and, given their mutual interest, the two must have discussed the possibilities of improved river transportation.

Walton toured north Georgia and eastern Tennessee in 1798, two years after the admission of Tennessee to the Union. The mountain country was occupied by the Cherokee Nation, but Walton looked to the future. He believed that the Tennesseans as well as the Cherokees would want to export their produce through Augusta in preference to the Spanish ports of Mobile and New Orleans. "In fact," he told the Richmond County Grand Jury on May 23, 1799, "there is no stream in our country equal to the Savannah River, and the full magnitude of the sea-port town of Savannah, and of this city, are already so advanced... that there is no doubt of their remaining the principal magazines of the trade of this country for a great length of time, and the lessons of experience teach us, that commerce accustomed to flow through certain chanels [sic] are diverted to new ones with difficulty. I do believe, therefore, with confidence from the impressions I have received that the western trade will pass through this place, and produce a prosperity in it surpassing all present expectation, and we will have the happiness of knowing and experiencing that as much health is enjoyed in it as in any town of the United States of its numbers."[19]

The connection of the Savannah and Tennessee river systems, only about ten miles apart between the present towns of Clayton and Mountain City in Rabun County, has been a tantalizing fantasy for Augusta promoters ever since George Walton. Earlier in the year 1799 the state legislature, meeting in the new capital of Louisville, enacted a bill "to incorporate a company for the improvement of the navigation of that part of the Savannah River between the town of Petersburg and the City of Augusta."[20]

William Longstreet acted as foreman of the Grand Jury who congratulated Judge Walton for his encouragement of commerce. Longstreet had invented a steam engine and was engaged in rigging it to a riverboat. He finally accomplished his purpose in 1808; his engine powered a pole-driven craft on the river. Unfortunately for his fame and for the future of his invention, Robert Fulton had demonstrated a more practical paddlewheel steamboat on the Hudson River the year before.

Interestingly, the Augusta Canal would cut across Meadow Garden. The canal basin adjoining Walton's former residence would be the termination point for Petersburg boats from upriver. Walton certainly would have approved. Remarkably the house and the canal basin – though smaller –

survive to this day, side by side, at the end of the first level at 13th Street, both house and canal honored by their listing as National Historic Landmarks.

Rae's Creek continued to figure in Augusta's history. Early in the Twentieth Century Augusta entrepreneurs planned a residential complex and a golf course bordering Rae's Creek. Lake Aumond is all that remains of their dream. The glory days of the creek awaited the advent of another golfing enterprise. Rae's Creek fed the "Lake Course" of the Augusta Country Club during the early years of the century. When Bobby Jones laid out the Augusta National Golf Course, he used the creek imaginatively on holes eleven through thirteen. Amen Corner at the twelfth hole is famous throughout the golfing world for its water hazard.[21]

Despite its often placid appearance, Rae's Creek is subject to flooding after heavy rains. How to properly manage Rae's Creek and harness its power has been a continuing problem for canal engineers from George Walton's day to the present.

Figure 4. Rae's Creek Spillway, circa 1894.
(Courtesy of the Augusta Museum of History)

Figure 5. This portrait of Henry Cumming is in the possession of David Hugh Connolly, Jr., great-great-great grandson of Henry Cumming.

CHAPTER FOUR

Planning the Canal

Henry Harford Cumming (1799-1866) was the fifth child of Thomas and Ann Clay Cumming. Thomas Cumming, a prosperous merchant and Augusta's first mayor (then called "intendant") under the city charter of 1798, set a standard of civic service for his sons to follow. William, eleven years older than Henry, lived up to those standards in a way that might have intimidated his younger siblings. William was a natural leader, tall of stature and with a "leonine appearance" as his nephew described him. He distinguished himself in the War of 1812 in service on the Canadian border, and emerged from the war with the rank of colonel. Thereafter, he comported himself as one of Augusta's leading citizens and the city's designated orator on all celebratory occasions.[1]

Henry's younger brother Alfred, much like William physically and intellectually, strove to emulate the older son, and as a result quarreled bitterly with him. William and Alfred refused to speak to one another for over twelve years. Alfred served as mayor of Augusta in 1839 and went on to the governorship of the Utah Territory, where he became a good friend of Brigham Young. Unlike William and Alfred, Henry was somewhat frail as a young man, as introspective and retiring as they were outgoing. For those studious qualities his Summerville neighbor John Forsyth, United States Minister to Spain, appointed Henry his attaché in 1819. At the time Forsyth was engaged in the delicate diplomacy that led to the acquisition of Florida from Spain.[2] Fortunately, the appointment was meant to be something of a lark and Henry never actually got to Spain. Instead, he traveled extensively for three years through England, France, Switzerland and Italy, and returned to his home with a liberal education, including a fluency in French and an acquaintance with the canals of those countries.

Cumming began the practice of law in partnership with George Crawford, later Governor of Georgia and Secretary of War in the administration of Zachary Taylor. In 1824 Henry married Julia Bryan, daughter of Joseph Bryan of Hancock County, a woman whose intellect matched his and whose letters to her sister Maria have been published by Carol Blesser under the title *Tokens of Affection: Letters from a Planter's Daughter in the Old South*. The couple had seven children and the need to support his increasing family caused Henry Cumming to become a workaholic. It is all the more surprising that he gave so much time to the canal project.[3]

Henry embraced the best of the Old South traditions, not as ostentatiously as his brother William, who fought three well publicized duels with George McDuffie, the future governor of South Carolina, over an imagined insult. Henry was brave enough: on one occasion he risked his life to save a man from a mob, depending only on his moral authority and his standing in the community. In another instance he interceded on behalf of a black man who was being mistreated by a policeman. It was typical of him to feel a sense of obligation to his city, and especially the poor of Augusta, when the depression of the 1840's set in. As Cumming observed, "In 1845 the prospects of the city were so gloomy that many of its citizens had abandoned or were preparing to abandon it."[4] Charles C. Jones, Jr., Augusta's distinguished historian who knew the Cumming family well, wrote of Henry Cumming, "He seems to have studied the subject of how to utilize the vast waterpower of the Savannah River for years, and never rested until triumphing over all obstacles, he saw the water finally turned in."[5]

The golden age of canals coincided with Henry Cumming's life span. He was only five years old when the great Middlesex Canal opened in 1804. Chartered in 1793, the Middlesex linked the Merrimack River with Boston. The man who became famous for engineering the project had no training as an engineer; in fact the profession was unknown in America and was in its infancy in England. Loammi Baldwin's previous claim to fame was that he had developed the Baldwin apple. Nevertheless, a group of wealthy Boston businessmen selected him to build their canal. He had to borrow instruments from an English engineer, fortunately then in America, to do the surveying. He had the assistance of his sons, Loammi, Jr., James F. and George R. Baldwin. The sons later played important roles in Georgia's canal building. Despite obstacles, the Middlesex Canal was completed in 1804, twenty-seven and a half miles in length, with twenty locks and eight aqueducts. Never mind that the wooden locks needed constant repair, and the wooden aqueducts leaked; everyone considered the Middlesex Canal a great success because it diverted the traffic of the Merrimack River to Boston instead of Newburyport. Loammi Baldwin lived only three years after the opening. His last instructions to his sons were, "Do all the good you can and cherish the Middlesex Canal."[6] Ironically the Baldwin sons built the Boston to Lowell Railroad that put the Middlesex out of business.

Canal historian Ronald E. Shaw commented on the experimental nature of early canal building: "Only with an awareness of repeated failures and problems overcome can we understand the slow introduction of the Canal Era in America and reach a valid assessment of the place of internal improvements in the politics and economic development of the early American republic."[7] Henry Cumming would become painfully aware of the experimental nature of canal work when George Baldwin gave him the wrong calculations regarding water flow, and Charles Estes would experience the same kind of experimental guesswork when Charles Olmstead made a monumental underestimate of the cost of canal enlargement.

Another pioneer canal project connected the South Carolina Santee River with the Cooper River and Charleston. Its construction engineer was John Christian Senf, a Swede by birth, and a Hessian officer by profession, one of the Hessians who fought under British General John Burgoyne and were made prisoners at Saratoga. Henry Laurens realized Senf's potential value to South Carolina and arranged to have him paroled to that state. Senf gained his citizenship by switching to the American side. After the war he became the state's chief engineer. A "vain and jealous man" as one historian called him, and difficult to work with, Senf nevertheless managed to complete the twenty-two mile canal in seven years with slave labor. He constructed two double locks and eight single locks and eight aqueducts. The canal rose thirty-four feet from the Santee River over a ridge, and descended sixty-nine feet into the Cooper River.[8] The state built a series of short canals, one of which connected the Catawba River to the Santee. The system proved a major boon to upland cotton planters, though the canal would periodically go dry. The railroad from Charleston to Columbia, completed in 1842, marked the end of the canal era in Carolina.

The completion of the Middlesex and the Santee-Cooper canals prompted President Thomas Jefferson to regard canals as a means of linking the Mississippi Valley with the eastern seaboard. His Secretary of the Treasury Albert Gallatin outlined a bold plan for four trans-Appalachian water routes: the Mohawk-Hudson, the Allegheny-Susquehanna, the Monongahela-Potomac, and the Tennessee-Savannah systems. Thus George Walton's dream of connecting the Tennessee and Savannah lived on in Gallatin's plan. In fact a General Millar of Rabun County actually attempted to dig a canal connecting the Little Tennessee and Tallulah Rivers. In 1873 water drawn from Black Creek in Mountain City operated Izell's Mills and emptied into the Stekoa Creek at Clayton in Rabun County.[9]

The dream of a water route to the west continued to intrigue Georgia legislators. In 1815 the legislature enacted a bill providing funds for removing obstructions in the Savannah River from Augusta to Petersburg at the mouth of the Broad River, stressing the economic advantages of river improvement. The legislature increased the initial appropriation of $10,000 to $15,000 in 1817 to show earnestness of intention. Commissioners charged with the project included William Cumming, the gregarious brother. We can assume that Henry shared an interest in improved river navigation even at that early stage of his life. Georgia spent approximately $40,000 by 1826 clearing the river as far as Panther Creek, a tributary of the Tugaloo. For years Georgia and South Carolina discussed cooperative arrangements for supervising river traffic, but could never come to an agreement. After 1830 Carolina lost interest in rivers and invested in railroads.[10]

Enough obstructions were removed from the river to allow "Petersburg boats" sixty to eighty feet long, seven feet wide, and shallow-drafted, to navigate from Broad River to Augusta. The pilot, or patroon, and his six-man crew risked, and sometimes lost their lives shooting the rapids they called the "Ring Jaw" just below Petersburg. They would have smooth water for two or three miles, then more shoals with names like Garden Shoals, Little River Shoals, Scott's Shoals, Blue Jacket, and Whirligig. At the smooth stretches between the shoals the boats would stop at plantation docks along the way to pick up cotton, the patroon blowing a trumpet-sounding horn to signal his coming. They could carry as much as sixty bales of cotton, three tiers high, together with corn, oats, barrel staves, and anything else the people along the way wanted to send to Augusta. The current carried the boats downriver, the pilot manned his trailing oar and the hands fended off boulders on each side.

Figure 6. Petersburg boat at the headgates loaded with cargo.
(Augusta Canal Authority Archives)

The pilot would call out "Georgia" for the crew to watch out for trouble on the Georgia side and "Carolina" if on the other. The long pull upriver was a nightmare, three men on each side had to push on poles to propel the craft, their shoulders would become bruised and bloody from pressing on the butt-end of the pole. Even so, the boats could carry as much as 18,000 pounds of cargo, mostly farm and household commodities. It took three days to reach Petersburg from Augusta. During most of the Nineteenth Century the colorful boats plied the river; twenty-five were active in 1877. When Petersburg was abandoned by its inhabitants, the boats left from McCord's dock in Lisbon on the Carolina side; almost half the river trade came from Carolina. Petersburg boats made up most of the traffic on the Augusta Canal.[11]

PETERSBURG BOATS
ON THE
AUGUSTA CANAL

Figure 7. A Petersburg boat in the canal basin at 13th Street.
(Drawing by Bill Blackard)

The completion of the Erie Canal in 1825 induced canal fever throughout the eastern United States. Every hamlet aspired to become a "port city" even if they had to drag a barge through mud to make a connection with a waterway. In 1825 Georgia's Governor George Troup allowed his ambitious imagination to overcome his common sense when he proposed that the state might sponsor a canal system that would link the Tennessee River, not only with the Savannah, but also the Oconee, Ocmulgee and Chattahoochee Rivers.[12] A direct result of his enthusiasm was the creation of a state Board of Public Works charged with the supervision of canal construction. The Board decided to start in the low country rather than undertake the more difficult work in the mountains.

The state's first project linked the Savannah and Ogeechee Rivers, a few miles above the city of Savannah. The Board employed a young Irish engineer named Edward Hall Gill to oversee the construction. Only twenty years old at the time, this was Gill's first big job. Gill built six locks and completed fifteen miles of the waterway before leaving to become chief engineer of the Chesapeake and Delaware Canal, and to go on to a distinguished career as canal builder in Pennsylvania, Ohio, and Virginia. The canal reached the Ogeechee in 1830, but the revenue did not amount to the cost of chronic repairs. Banks leaked and wooden locks rotted quickly. The original company declared bankruptcy in 1836 and was sold under the sheriff's hammer for a fraction of the $190,000 it cost. Under new management, the canal was repaired, brick locks replaced wooden ones, and the canal paid for itself carrying lumber and other cargoes from Central Georgia down the Ogeechee to Savannah. In the waning years of the Civil War the canal happened to lie directly in the path of General William T. Sherman's "bummers" and they broke down the banks in several places. The canal refused to die; after 1865 it was fixed up, and its profitable commerce continued until the mid-1870's. Trade slowed and recurring outbreaks of fever in Savannah were blamed on the sluggish waterway. Before the turn of the 20th century the canal ceased to operate.

One of the most exciting aspects of the Ogeechee and Savannah Canal's history might well lie in the Twenty-first Century. Volunteers have begun to reclaim the canal as an historic site, a nature preserve, and, of course, a tourist attraction. The excavations and most of the brick locks remain, and the towpath has been converted into a hiking trail. A master plan calls for the restoration of the entire length of the canal from just above the intersection of highways Interstate 95 and 204 to the outlet near the Talmadge Bridge.[13]

Georgia's other canal project, the Brunswick and Altamaha, had even less success. The idea was good when first chartered in 1826. The Altamaha, which drains the Oconee and the Ocmulgee, had no adequate port. Brunswick had a fine port but no hinterland. The connection of the two via the Turtle River seemed a perfect solution. However, the work was mismanaged and delayed until 1834 when Thomas Butler King, a prominent planter on St. Simons Island, took charge. He hired Loammi Baldwin, Jr., famous for his work on the Middlesex Canal and as civil engineer of Boston. Baldwin Junior designed the Boston dry docks (a memorial plaque there acknowledges him as architect) as well as the Bunker Hill Monument. King could not have employed a more famous engineer.

Baldwin came South in 1836 and completed a survey of the route. However, his health declined and he died a year later. King secured the services of another New Englander, Edward Hammond, to supervise the work, and he transported five hundred mostly Irish workers from Boston to do the labor. The Irish quarreled with one another, objected to working with slaves, and most of them left or were fired and replaced by slave labor. In two years the canal had progressed just five miles when ancient fossils were discovered, including mastodon and mammoth bones as well as whale-bone fragments. The fossils proved to be the most successful aspect of the project. By the time the thirteen-mile water way was finished in 1842, the Central of Georgia Railroad offered a more convenient route to the interior. The canal carried timber to Brunswick until the early Twentieth Century when it was abandoned and became a dumping ground for hazardous wastes.[14]

There can be no doubt that Henry Cumming and Augusta's other businessmen knew about the Santee-Cooper, the Erie, and the two Georgia canals. They also knew that Augusta did not need such a canal. The Savannah River gave the city birth and the river continued to be the commercial lifeline. Since 1816 steamboats carried the bulk of the trade on the river. Augusta native Gazaway Bugg Lamar had an iron-clad steamboat made in England and assembled in Savannah for the Augusta-Savannah run. Its advantage was that it could navigate in only two feet of water, not unusual in dry seasons. The South Carolina Railroad, from Charleston to Hamburg opposite Augusta, provided an alternative means of transportation in 1833. With water and rail outlets to the sea, Augusta simply did not require a canal for transportation.

However, after the national depression of 1837, business declined in Georgia as all over the country. Smaller Georgia towns became deserted as people moved west to seek their fortunes in Alabama, Mississippi or the newly independent nation of Texas. If the depression continued, there was real danger that Augusta would become as deserted as Petersburg upriver and nearby Wrightsborough. Augusta found a solution to its economic malaise in the example of Lowell, Massachusetts. Lowell was the first successfully to use waterpower for heavy industry. Lowell today rightly boasts that it was the home of the industrial revolution in the United States.

The Lowell story begins with an ethically questionable instance of industrial espionage. Boston Brahmin Francis Cabot Lowell, owner of a cotton mill in Waltham, Massachusetts, visited friends in England. They showed him the top secret Cartwright loom but forbade any drawing or note-taking. The clever Lowell memorized the design, much as Samuel Slater had done for the first American mill in Pawtucket, Rhode Island. Back home, Lowell "reinvented" the loom for the Waltham plant. Although Lowell died in 1817, his associates formed a company and determined to build a larger mill at the Pawtucket Falls of the Merrimack River. The Boston Associates bought out the defunct canal company's charter and under the old name "Proprietors of Locks and Canals" enlarged the canal in 1822 with a crew of Irish workers. In front of the visitors center in Lowell today is a statue to the foreman of the work gang, Hugh Comisky. Comisky's men shored up the eroding earthen banks with huge granite blocks, still in place today and a testimonial to their skill.

The first factory began operation in 1824, with the Pawtucket canal furnishing water for the 3,584 spindles. As at the Waltham Mill all of the operations were under one roof; raw cotton went in and finished cloth came out of the mill. The company constructed side canals off the Pawtucket, the Merrimack in 1823, the Hamilton in 1828, the Eastern in 1836, and the Northern in 1848. By 1836 there were twenty-six mills operating along the various interconnected canals. The nine biggest mills employed over eight thousand workers. The Proprietors of Locks and Canals supervised the waterways and made its money by selling water to the mills. The same men sat on the boards of the canal company and the various mills.[15]

Just as it was innovative in the manufacture of cotton, the Lowell company also introduced a new form of social engineering. The company followed the old New England rule of "doing good while doing well," attracted young women from the countryside by offers of good wages ($1.85 to $3.00 a week), and supervised company lodging, compulsory church attendance, Sunday school, circulating libraries, and a lyceum series. One Harvard lecturer expressed appreciation for his attentive audience, "The hall was always crowded and four-fifths of the audience were factory girls. When the lecturer entered, almost every girl had a book in her hand and was intent upon it. When he rose, the book was put aside and paper and pencil taken instead...I have never seen such assiduous note-taking, no not even in a college class, as in that assembly of young women, laboring for their subsistence."[16] Foreign visitors like Charles Dickens and Anthony Trollope, who found much to criticize about America, were favorably impressed by the Lowell system. For businessmen in Augusta, already disposed to conduct themselves in a paternalistic fashion, the Lowell model seemed a way of transferring plantation values to the city environment.

If Augustans continued to observe the Lowell situation, they would have noticed that the mill owners lost much of their early paternalism. Operatives' hours were gradually lengthened to eleven, twelve, and even thirteen hours a day. Conditions in the factory worsened. Poor ventilation, flying lint, fumes from whale-oil lamps, and the excessive humidity needed to keep cotton thread from breaking, all conspired to break the health of the operatives. Young women who rushed from farms to a better life in the 1830's found work elsewhere by the sixties. In 1836 fewer than four percent of the women were foreign-born; by 1860 sixty-two percent of the work force were immigrants.[17]

Henry Cumming and his friends realized that Augusta's best hope of recovering from its business depression lay in industrialization. However, they knew nothing about how to get it done. The most pressing need of Augusta canal promoters was engineering expertise. How to locate the best place for a canal, how to build locks, how to calculate water flow, how much to charge for water use, they needed answers to these and other practical problems. Lowell had the experts with the answers. The recognized genius at Lowell was James Bechno Francis (1815-1892). Welsh by birth, he worked on canals in Wales before coming to the United States in 1833 to work for the Proprietors of Locks and Canals. In 1844 he was promoted to agent or supervisor of canals. He studied the flow and measurement of water and worked out a formula that is still taught in hydraulic engineering. Today, visitors who take the guided tour of the Lowell canals are shown the complex system of ten sluice gates at the head of the canal on the Merrimack River that Francis devised. Water from the Merrimack is diverted by a slanting (or "wing") dam into the head gates. Atop the dam is a flimsy-looking wall of plywood sheets (called wasteboards or flashboards) supported by thin carbon-steel rods. The wasteboards are deliberately designed to give way in a flood, so that the excess water would go downriver instead of down the canal. Augusta would use the same device at Rae's Creek aqueduct. Anticipating the worst, Francis built a guardhouse on the main canal. A massive portcullis of Georgia pine, twenty-five feet by twenty-seven, and seventeen inches thick, was suspended in the guardhouse through which the canal flowed. Francis was criticized for wasting money when he built the contraption, but in 1852 it saved the city from a devastating flood. Thereafter,

Francis could do no wrong. Dartmouth and Harvard conferred honorary degrees, and he was elected to the presidency of the Boston Society of Civil Engineers as well as the American Society of Civil Engineers.[18]

Thanks to the political influence of the late Senator Paul Tsongas and the infusion of federal funding in the 1970's, Lowell's industrial center, concentrated on the canal system, has undergone a renaissance. A modern visitors center and museum, the Boott Mill with its looms still operating noisily for tourists, the restored quarters of the women operatives, all afford the visitor a notion of what Lowell must have been like at the time when it was a model for cities like Augusta. A major difference between Lowell and Augusta is that the canal there is no longer used to power factories, and since 1901 it has not been used for transportation. It is a relic of the past, albeit a noble relic. As Lowell once served as an example of industrialization; now it can be a model of historic preservation and adaptive use of historic buildings. The remarkable fact about the Augusta Canal, of course, is that it is still being used for its original purpose, the furnishing of water for industrial power and for public consumption.

Unfortunately for Henry H. Cumming and his friends, James B. Francis had not completed his calculations about how much water was needed to operate a given number of spindles when Cumming needed the information. Cumming would have to rely on the advice of a member of the well-known Baldwin family. George R. Baldwin's calculations proved disastrously wrong, and finally James B. Francis had to provide Augusta with his more accurate formula.

Before Cumming turned to Baldwin for information, he sought out an expert nearer home in the person of the chief engineer of the Georgia Railroad, John Edgar Thomson.

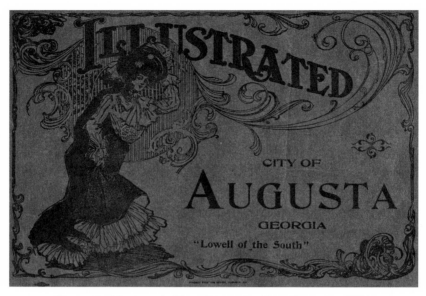

Figure 8. Illustrated, City of Augusta Georgia cover, 1907.
(Courtesy of Augusta Museum of History)

Thomson was born of Quaker parents on a farm outside Philadelphia in 1808. He learned the rudiments of surveying from his father and at age nineteen began work on the combination rail and canal system between Philadelphia and Columbia, Pennsylvania. Blessed with native common sense, he worked hard and won the respect of his fellows. By age twenty-one he was Principal Assistant Engineer charged with grading and bridging twenty miles of the right-of-way. After completing that job Thomson went to work for the Camden and Amboy Railroad. In 1832 Thomson toured England and Scotland, investigating techniques in the still new science of railroad engineering.[19]

On December 21, 1833, the Georgia legislature chartered the Georgia Railroad. James Camak, chairman of the Board of Directors, sought the advice of Major John Wilson in the selection of chief engineer. Wilson had hired Thomson for the Pennsylvania railroads and recommended him for the Georgia position. Camak's associate, William Williams, went to Philadelphia and signed a contract with Thomson on October 11, 1834. On January 5, 1835 Thomson arrived in Augusta and took lodgings at Mrs. Hall's on Broad Street. In spite of a miserable winter, he completed a survey as far as Greensboro by April. A labor force described as "European" (and probably Irish) was at work by September 1834. In order to finance the project, the company secured banking privileges from the state legislature on December 18, 1835, creating the Georgia Railroad and Banking Company. Construction proved expensive, over $10,000 for each mile of five-gauge track. By the end of the year 1836 the line reached Crawfordville. Railroad towns named after the engineer and directors blossomed along the line: Dearing, Camak, Thomson. William Cumming, a director, had a town named for him.

Figure 9. J. Edgar Thomson as president of the Pennsylvania Railroad. (From James A. Ward, *J. Edgar Thomson, Master of the Pennsylvania*.)

The European workers could not, or would not, endure the heat of a Georgia summer, so the company bought seventy-two slaves and hired two hundred others to do the work. The grand opening of the first ten miles took place with all appropriate fanfare on May 2, 1837. By the end of that year Thomson opened fifty miles of track for service. Progress slowed because of the national depression that followed, but by the end of 1839 trains ran on seventy-four miles of track.[20] Thomson welcomed the competition of the Savannah-based Central of Georgia, and he expressed impatience with Athens stockholders who were reluctant to extend the rails during the economic slowdown. "We have but few bold spirits among us, and even these seem cowed by the hard times," he wrote a friend in 1842. "If all the stockholders resided at Augusta and the terminus (the future city of Atlanta) we should be now at work above Madison, but Athens and Madison have both adverse interest in the progress of the work."[21]

The challenge that the Central might reach the terminus first and there connect with the state-owned Western and Atlantic alarmed the stockholders. "Where ever I now go," Thomson wrote three months later, "I hear nothing but the cry of go on with your work."[22] By July 1845 the line reached Decatur. Thomson suggested the name "Atlanta" for the terminus instead of earlier trial names, Junction City and Marthasville. He intended the name to symbolize the linking of the Atlantic to the West by rail. In addition to naming the town, he laid out the first streets. Thomson knew the importance of what he had done, "No object ...can enlist one's feelings like the execution of some great enterprise."[23] The construction of the Georgia Railroad made available to Henry Cumming an unprecedented wealth of engineering talent. Other than

Thomson himself, there were, E.D. Sanford, Fred Arms, and Frank Hight, all of whom would work on the canal.

Thomson's long residence in Augusta, twelve years in all, allowed him to become acquainted with most of the prominent businessmen of the city. He worked closely with John P. King, president of the Georgia Railroad Bank. King and Henry Cumming were early advocates of the canal project. The catalyst that prompted Cumming and his friends, most of whom were Whigs, to initiate the canal project might have been the visit of Henry Clay to Augusta in March 1844 as part of his presidential campaign. Evidence that they had met was Clay's letter to Cumming thanking him for his hospitality.[24] At the request of either King or Cumming, Thomson left off rail building, "I am called to Augusta," he wrote a friend on November 2, 1844.[25] Henry Cumming lost no time in explaining to Thomson what he wanted, namely an expert opinion on

Figure 10. John P. King
(Courtesy of the Augusta Museum of History)

whether a canal was feasible, and if so, where it should be located. On November 10, 1844, Cumming wrote his wife Julia, then at Mount Zion in Hancock County, that he, his brother Alfred, James Harper, and Robert Campbell had accompanied John Edgar Thomson and an Augusta engineer named William Phillips on an excursion six miles upriver "to the point at which it is proposed to commence the canal."[26]

Cumming paid Thomson to do a survey of his recommended route. That business kept Thomson in Augusta until May 1845, even as his rail line neared completion. Thomson's sketch of the proposed canal was prominently exhibited in John P. King's Georgia Railroad Bank to generate interest in the project. Thomson attended a public meeting on March 8, 1845 and answered questions about the practicality of the proposed construction. Later, he prepared a detailed drawing of the most difficult feature of the work, the aqueduct over Rae's Creek.[27] Thomson's contribution to the public acceptance of the canal was inestimable. He lent his prestige as the successful railroad builder to the project; without him, Henry Cumming might not have convinced the townspeople that the job could be done. In 1846 Cumming told the city council that Thomson had "from the beginning aided by his advice the proprietors of the works and your commissioners."[28] Thomson left Georgia in 1847 to take a position as chief engineer of the Pennsylvania Railroad, but retained a $2,000 salary and the title of chief engineer of the Georgia Railroad until 1852.[29] Thomson went on to become the head of the Pennsylvania Railroad and one of the most successful railroad executives in the country.

Cumming welcomed the support of *Augusta Chronicle* editors and publishers, J.W. and W.S. Jones. During the early 1840's the newspaper deplored the worsening depression and praised the efforts of the local Home Industry Society to provide work for the needy. Under the leadership of Daniel Hook, Augustans contributed money to buy cloth that was distributed to women who made clothing in their homes. In 1842 over a hundred women were thus employed. However, by the end of that year, the newspaper noted that there were no longer enough contributions to continue to purchase the raw cloth.[30] During 1843 the local papers urged "capitalists" to establish stores in Augusta, without result. The editors greeted the prospect of a canal for manufacturing with enthusiasm. On January 2, 1845 the editors presented a challenge:

> If Charleston may successfully introduce the manufacture of cotton by the aid of steam for propelling the machinery, with how much more success may Augusta embark in the enterprise when the river which forms one of her corporate boundaries affords a waterpower which would by the application of art, science, and capital render her the Lowell of the South.[31]

On January 3, 1845 the newspaper printed a letter from Joel Crawford urging southern manufactures. Beginning on January 31, *The Chronicle* ran essays by William Gregg of South Carolina who purchased the Vaucluse Mill in 1843 and manufactured coarse fabrics. He blamed a "want of energy" on the part of southern businessmen and "ignorance and laziness" on the part of those who ought to labor. Instead of blaming the tariff (the favorite target of John C. Calhoun and other politicians) we ought to blame ourselves, said Gregg. Gregg proposed employing black operatives as well as white. He cited the example of the Lowell partners building a canal on the Merrimack costing over a million dollars, while Augustans argued about spending $100,000.[32] Gregg provoked the

Augusta community into action, but paid a price for it. When he later bid to build a factory on the canal, he was refused. He had to be satisfied with erecting a mill on South Carolina's Horse Creek; he called it the Graniteville Mill.

Henry Cumming knew that in addition to persuading his fellow townspeople to agree to spend money on a debatable venture, something Augustans have always disliked doing, there was a stronger obstacle. The plantation model of success had become an obsession with Georgians. Cotton was king. Cotton production and cotton investment were identified with southernism. City folk tried to act like planters, in dress, politics and manners. On the other hand, factories were yankee inventions; places where cruel capitalists exploited workers and cast them out when they became old or ill. Cumming explained his problem this way, "We had been almost exclusively a commercial community. To many the thought of competing with the North industry was foolish, to others the very name manufacturer had become odious."[33] He had to appeal to a growing sense of southern nationalism, and argue that local industries would make the South independent of the North and of England. So patriotism was enlisted in the cause, as well as the profit motive and the real urgency of a worsening depression, as Augustans gathered to debate whether or not to undertake the city's first bold enterprise.

Building the Canal

CHAPTER FIVE

"It is the duty and ought to be the pleasure of every citizen to do something for the public good," so said Henry Cumming.[1] One of the advantages of studying history is that we can find role models, exemplars for our own lives. We could do worse than follow Henry Cumming's example. Augusta needed help badly in 1845. The lure of the West drew thousands of Georgians away to Alabama, Mississippi and to the independent State of Texas. Once promising east Georgia towns such as Jacksonborough, Wrightsborough and Petersburg became ghost towns. The Georgia Railroad proved to be only a mixed blessing because the railroad deprived Augusta drivers and merchants of the once-thriving wagon trade. Stores in upper Broad Street were particularly hard hit. James Harper, one of Cumming's closest colleagues, spearheaded a drive to build a bridge to South Carolina at 13th Street, but in the flood of 1840 the bridge was washed away. Mayor Thomas W. Miller

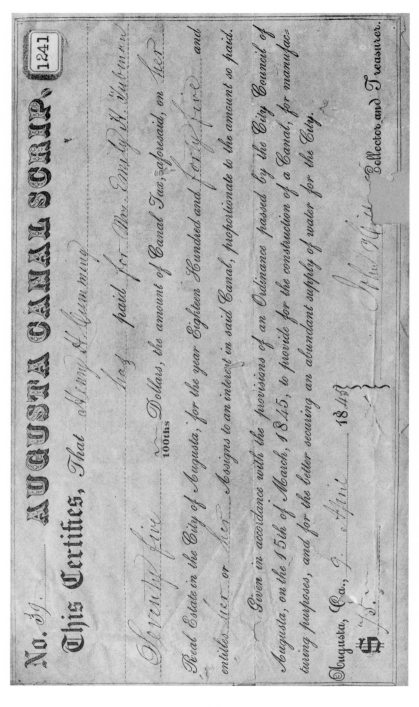

Figure 11. Taxpayers received stock in the Augusta Canal Company in proportion to the amount of taxes paid. Pictured is a certificate or scrip issued to Henry Cumming. *(Courtesy of Augusta Museum of History)*

looked back from the vantage point of 1850 to say that in 1844 Augusta was caught in the grip of "the cold damp of commercial death."[2]

Henry Cumming pondered what should be done for the public good and concluded that Augusta needed nothing less than an industrial revolution. The idea had been bruited about in the newspapers and the time had come for action. "Augusta must do something for the artisan," he said in one of his rare public statements, it "must provide a home for him where he will be duly respected...good schools must be provided, both public and private."[3] John Edgar Thomson had shown that waterpower could be brought into the city, but the magnitude of the undertaking was staggering and the cost prohibitive. With considerable misgiving, Cumming took the initiative, "Without taste or fitness for such offices, I sought to discharge a part of this admitted duty by promoting a public improvement which I thought would advance the prosperity of Augusta, the place of my birth, and the home of many honored friends."[4] Desperate for expert advice, Cumming wrote to a dozen engineers in the northern states, but in the end had to find the way by trial and error.

Other than his inexperience and that of his colleagues in the undertaking, the other major obstacle to launching the project was how to finance it. It was useless to expect help from the federal government. James Madison had vetoed John C. Calhoun's bill that would have funded internal improvements, and more recently Andrew Jackson had killed Henry Clay's bill for road-building in Kentucky. If Clay had been elected President in 1844, as Cumming and most of the canal backers had hoped, the government might have helped, but James Knox Polk had been elected and he had other things on his mind, such as the acquisition of Texas, California and Oregon. Nor would Georgia help. The state had spent money to improve rivers, and was in the process of building its own railroad, but it would not put up money for a canal in Augusta. Cumming credited a local banker, William D'Antignac, with the creative financial arrangement that made the canal possible.

Four local institutions agreed to put up seed money of one thousand dollars each: the Bank of Augusta, the Georgia Railroad Bank, the Augusta Insurance and Banking Company, and the Bank of Brunswick. The City Council of Augusta would issue bonds worth $100,000 and pay off the bonds by a special "canal tax." The estimate that the canal would cost that amount proved woefully short of the mark. Taxpayers would receive stock in the Augusta Canal Company in proportion to the amount of taxes paid. Possession of the stock certificates, or canal scrip, entitled the holder to vote for a Board of Managers for the Canal Company. Not everyone was pleased at being forced to become a stockholder, and some would join a lawsuit challenging the city's right to impose the tax. As it turned out, the city became the largest stockholder, and the sitting mayor became the head of the Board of Managers. As long as Henry Cumming and his friends were willing to serve on a Board of Commissioners appointed by the City Council, the Board of Managers left the operation of the canal to the Commissioners. Cumming called D'Antignac's plan "entirely original."[5]

D'Antignac explained how the canal might be financed to interested citizens on March 10, 1845. The tax would be minimal; the benefit to the city enormous. J. Edgar Thomson's plans on exhibition showed that the great work could be done. The canal, as proposed, meandered through all four city wards, exiting through a drainage ditch that emptied into the Savannah River below Augusta's East Boundary Street. The meeting attracted the attention of *The Charleston Courier* that called the undertaking, "One of the boldest steps ever yet taken in the

Southern States." The reporter noted that only one voice was raised in opposition to the proposal at that meeting.[6]

Following the meeting the City Council acted promptly on March 17 by enacting an ordinance creating a "Canal Board of Commissioners."[7] The ordinance charged the Commissioners with the task of "constructing a canal from Bull Sluice to the city for manufacturing purposes and for the better securing of an abundant supply of water to the city."[8] The Council appointed the following commissioners: Henry Cumming, James Harper, John Phinizy, John P. King, Charles J. Jenkins, Andrew J. Miller, and William D'Antignac. The Board held its first meeting on March 18 and elected Henry Cumming to its presidency, and William D'Antignac secretary. Local engineer William Phillips, born in Beaufort, South Carolina in 1804, who had consulted with Cumming from the beginning, was the only employed staff member. Phillips was hired as secretary and bookkeeper, and thus began twenty-three years of devoted service to an enterprise he came to regard as his own. Cumming parceled out the assignments; everything had been thought out ahead of time. One committee had to find a competent engineer, another committee set about securing the right-of-way from property owners along the proposed route, and another drew up the by-laws for the governance of the Commission.

The Board met again two days later to listen to J. Edgar Thomson explain the details of his plan of construction. By-laws were adopted. (In its first fervor, the Board fined its own members for lateness.) An application was drawn up to be submitted to President James K. Polk for permission to cut through the old Augusta Arsenal tract below the Ezekiel Harris house. Thomson probably recommended the hiring of the first engineer, because after only two weeks the Commissioners hired C.O. Sanford as chief engineer at a annual salary of $2,500. There must have been an unwritten understanding that Sanford would not remain long in Augusta. The engineer required the assistance of his nephew, E.D. Sanford, and the Board obligingly hired the nephew for $800 a year. The younger Sanford had worked for Thomson on the Georgia Railroad.

Thomson's survey had twelve sections to be separately contracted, so that work could begin on all simultaneously. The length of the sections was based on the presumed difficulty. The headgates and lock would comprise section one. Sections two to ten would be the main channel, or the first level, section eleven would be the short second level, and section twelve, the third level draining out through the first ward, was assumed to be the easiest. It turned out quite otherwise. An indication that Cumming had put the word out to prospective contractors is the fact that within a month, bids had been received on all sections. Within a strikingly short time, on April 25, 1845, the contracts were assigned for all sections except the headgates.[9]

The smooth interaction between Thomson's Georgia Railroad and the canal was once again evident in the selection of contractors. The firm of Timberlake and Timanus would soon finish their work on the railroad (the rails had reached the destination at the future city of Atlanta); they secured the contract for sections two and three, the longest and presumably the easiest sections along the first level. Another railroad company, Graves and O'Brien, won the right to construct three short sections, eight, nine and ten, that led into the city and terminated at McKinnie (13th) Street. In between, two local planters who happened to be brothers-in-law, were awarded contracts, probably because they had two of the larger plantations along the right-of-way. James Coleman would construct sections four and five across his own property with a work force of his own slaves. Benjamin Warren, a prominent businessman and judge, and the recent host of Henry Clay in his 1844 visit to Augusta, would build what everyone expected to be the most difficult section, number six, across the flood plain of Rae's Creek, as well as section seven. He would not have to construct the aqueduct that would carry the canal over Rae's Creek. The ambitious Timberlake and Timanus would attempt to do that work.

A persistent local legend that appears now and again in print is that Chinese workers were employed on the original canal. They were not. The Chinese first came to this country to work on the Union Pacific Railroad during the Civil War and some of them came to Augusta to help with the enlargement of the canal in 1875. Tradition also has it that many of the original workers were Irish and that may be so. In fact, there was an increase in the Irish population of the city in the 1840's. So many Irish families lived south of Most Holy Trinity Catholic Church that the neighborhood became known as Dublin, and the church was popularly known after its patron saint, St. Patrick. Irishmen worked on the Georgia Railroad, and it is logical to suppose that Irish were among the sixty men Timberlake and Timanus brought to Augusta; Graves and O'Brien had twenty hands on the job by April 30th, with more on the way.

Henry Cumming indicated the nature of the work force in September 1845 when he said that many of the men were white laborers "from our own neighborhoods and the Cherokee counties on the lines of the Georgia and Western and Atlantic Railroads." The railroads, he said, "Would furnish the labor of the (State's) hardy and industrious sons, many were already employed on the canal."[10] The heat of Augusta's summer discouraged many of the white workers, and after the second summer most of the workers on the project were black. Quite likely there are descendants of the black men who built the canal living in Augusta today.

The early rate of progress was astonishing. By April 30, 1845, Sanford had met with all the contractors working on the first level. Sanford did test borings along the right-of-way and found hard rock along the second section and part of the third. He changed Thomson's route as much as he dared in an attempt to circle the hill of mylonite rock. Sanford prepared detailed plans for the headgates, locks and dam, and decided to supervise this demanding section himself. However, Sanford's most controversial decision surprised the commissioners on May 17, 1845. He disagreed with the esteemed J. Edgar Thomson, arguing that the third level must not exit via East Boundary. A better route would be the old Beaver Dam Ditch and Hawk's Gully. John Phinizy, a commissioner and resident of the first ward, took heated exception to the suggestion, and threatened to resign if the original route was changed. However, Phinizy was undermined by a citizen of his own ward who wrote to the newspaper on May 30 noting that the East Boundary outlet would have the effect of lowering the river level at the Fifth Street docks. Furthermore, it would introduce flooding and "disfigure the beautiful commons."[11] A newspaper debate followed with "Justice" contending that any change of route would be a breach of contract with the citizenry who had voted for the original plan. "Fair Play" said that the property owners of the first ward caused the change by demanding too much money for yielding the right-of-way through their land.[12]

The argument divided the city and ended the harmony among the commissioners. Finally, on July 2, 1845 William D'Antignac made the motion to discharge the canal at some point above Campbell (9th) Street. Furious, John Phinizy threatened a lawsuit if the commissioners voted for the motion. The vote was taken. Henry Cumming, John Bones, James Harper, William D'Antignac, Charles J. Jenkins, and Andrew J.

Miller voted for the motion. Only Phinizy and Luke Mann opposed it and they promptly resigned.[13] The compliant City Council passed a new ordinance on July 7 amending the original and in effect leaving the choice of an outlet to the Commissioners. Feelings ran high in the first ward, the "Pinch Gut" neighborhood. On July 17, a public meeting in that ward expressed outrage at the change of route. It would "draw the shades of midnight on our prospects," said a speaker. Resolutions were adopted to refuse to pay the canal tax, and to initiate a court challenge to the city's right to extend its authority so far upriver and outside the city limits.[14]

The threat of legal action could delay and possibly end the entire operation. The canal opponents intended to do just that by securing an injunction to halt the work and then getting a legal opinion on the right of the city to impose taxes, to extend its city jurisdiction by fiat, to change the original route, and generally to act in the high-handed and arbitrary manner in which it was acting in this whole canal business. The complainants who filed the bill in Richmond County Superior Court were prominent citizens who could not be easily disregarded; most of them lived in the first ward: Martin Frederick, John W. Houghton (who would leave his fortune to the city for a school in the first ward), Thomas J. Walton, Benjamin F. Chew, David L. Curtis, and John Phinizy.

Commissioner Andrew J. Miller proved his worth as a member of the Canal Board. When the complainants secured an injunction against the collection of the canal tax, Miller represented the city in getting the injunction overturned. Even better, he introduced a bill in the Georgia Legislature when that body met in December 1845. The act contained twelve sections, but in essence it incorporated the canal taxpayers as stockholders in the Augusta Canal Company, and it affirmed the city ordinances of March 15th and July 7th. Interestingly one of the sections conferred the right to enlarge and extend the canal, should the need arise. The men who built the canal were confident enough of their ability to complete this huge initial project, and were already looking forward to improving it.[15]

Miller faced stiff opposition to his bill in the Senate by some who argued that wealthy Augustans were trying to take advantage of poor people. He had the votes to turn back amendments and to defeat a motion to table. But it was a near thing, the final vote was 19 for and 19 against; the president of the Senate broke the tie by voting aye. Even so, before the bill became law, Miller had to face two more days of debate by determined opponents who tried to kill the bill by making individual stockholders liable for lawsuits. Miller's legislation meant that when the lawsuit against the canal reached the Georgia Supreme Court that distinguished body could rule as it did, first that Augusta's charter of 1798 gave the Council broad enough powers to levy the tax and build the canal, and secondly it was a moot point because the Georgia legislature had added its legal authority to the city's, and no one disputed the state's right to tax for internal improvements.[16]

The litigation failed to slow progress in the least. The Commission secured the right-of-way with very little trouble from property owners Brayton, Hall, Byrd, Primrose, Poe, Carrie, Silcox, Robertson, Rich, and Nelson. Matthew Nelson owned the old Meadow Garden tract, including the home of George Walton, the signer of the Declaration of Independence. Thomson's plan called for the first level to terminate in a basin on Nelson's property. Fortunately for future generations of Augustans, Matthew Nelson did not sell his home, and therefore Augusta's oldest house was spared. Consent of the two largest property owners Warren and Coleman was secured by contracting with those gentlemen to build the canal across their farms, and to make a profit in so doing. The commissioners agreed to purchase John Skinner's entire plantation in order to gain the right-of-way through that estate. The commission also bought other property outside the proposed route as an investment. When the first level began to function, the property values near the canal would escalate.

In July 1845 Sanford recruited General H. Howard to construct the dam and headgates. The dam extended upriver to a small island, not across the river, and had the effect of diverting water into the headgates, simple drop-gates that could be raised or lowered. Henry Cumming placed an order for 150 barrels of Rosendale cement for underwater work, the first of many such orders.[17] Rosendale, a hamlet near Kingston, New York, furnished the finest hydraulic cement in the country. The Rosendale quarry supplied the cement for the foundation stonework and towers of the Brooklyn Bridge. The canal would suffer during the Civil War because of the inability to secure Rosendale cement to make necessary repairs. Howard had to blast through a ledge of rock east of the dam to allow passage of boats to the Carolina side. Carolinians insisted on creating that channel but in fact most of the Petersburg boats would prefer the safer waters of the canal rather that risk the rapids.

Timberlake and Timanus had perhaps the most scenic portion of the canal, if they or their workers had paused to admire the scenery. J. Edgar Thomson's survey line followed the topography of the land and the canal cut hugged the hills near their crest, while the river level dropped sharply as it descended the rapids. John Skinner owned most of the land along section two; he had inherited it from his father William Skinner, whose house still stands on the bend of Skinner Mill Road. Reed's Creek flowed into the river through the Skinner plantation, and engineer Sanford followed Thomson's plan to carry the canal over the creek in a ninety-foot aqueduct. Neither the Reed's Aqueduct nor the larger Rae's Creek Aqueduct functioned well. Henry Cumming asked George Baldwin of Boston to take a look at the completed Reed's Aqueduct. Baldwin predicted correctly that it was on the verge of collapse. He recommended letting it collapse and using the fallen aqueduct as a dam, with the overflow going into the canal. Hikers along the towpath bank of the canal today are impressed with the heavy cascade of water out of Reed's Creek into the canal. They might not realize that the junction of creek and canal is now a hundred yards or so above the original aqueduct.

Today, the Martin-Marietta Company Quarry occupies the original creek bed. The Skinner plantation contained valuable mylonite rock that furnished stone for Augusta construction projects during the Nineteenth and Twentieth Centuries, but for Timberlake and Timanus, the impervious rock proved an expensive nuisance. They had to blast their way through, driving up their costs.[18] Opposite the old mouth of Reed's Creek is an escape gate put there during the 1875 enlargement of the canal. In case of excessive flow in the creek, the gates could (and can) be opened and the water drained into the river far below. In fact, during the heavy rainfall that soaked Augusta in 1990, Reed's Creek flowed back into its former course and flooded the vast pit of the quarry. When considering the three hundred foot depth of the quarry, and the thin wall of rock that separates it from the canal, one hopes that Augusta will not soon experience an earthquake.

The hypothetical hiker along the scenic towpath should be reminded that the present, post-1875 canal is three times wider than the Thomson-Sanford original. (In fact, the cut of the old canal from the quarry to near the I-20 bridge is now hidden by a low ridge on the land side of the canal, and what one sees along this portion is entirely the 1875 Olmstead canal.) After cutting through the quarry, Timberlake and Timanus had a relatively easy task digging the third section. The river falls away from the canal along section three and part of section four. The lowlands between the towpath bank and river conjure up images of pre-historic Indian camping grounds, and invite the hiker to investigate nature trails. Near the present Interstate 20 bridge the piedmont rock merges with the sand hills at the beginning of the coastal plain. The bridge crosses at the first low point in the land-side hills since the hike began at the headgates.

James Coleman won the bid to construct the relatively short sections four and five across his Bedford Plantation. He had a workforce of ninety slaves on his plantation and put seventy of them to work on the canal. Nature cooperated in maintaining a natural low embankment on the land side so that only a levee on the riverside needed to be constructed. Rock Creek flowed through Coleman's plantation, and today forms a pond known as Warren's Lake emptying into the canal. Coleman and the Canal Commissioners argued about whether or not Coleman could use the canal water to run a mill on his property. The engineers worried that any outlet might affect the amount of water available at the terminus of the first level; the Commission offered to sell Coleman two acres of the Nelson property near the terminus for a flour mill. Coleman did not particularly like the offer, but when the Commission warned that they would not put a culvert under the canal as an outlet for the creek and instead simply flood his plantation, he agreed.[19]

Coleman wanted to be cooperative, but controversy seemed to follow him about. When he bought a huge Hotchkiss Wheel to power his mill the Commissioners ordered him to replace it with a smaller one.[20] Coleman finished his saw and

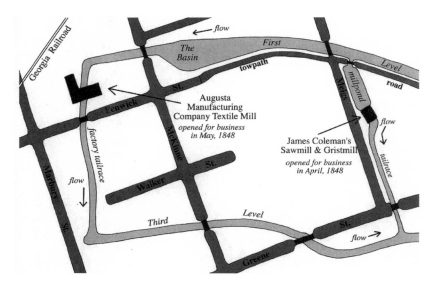

Figure 12. Map showing the location of Coleman's Mill, the first to operate on the canal, and followed shortly by the Augusta Manufacturing
Company. *(Drawing by Michael White)*

grist mill by April 24, 1848 and earned the distinction of operating the first mill on the canal. On that day, *The Augusta
Chronicle* noted, "Mr. Coleman's Mill is now cutting lumber
and grinding corn using canal water."[21]

At Rock Creek, or Warren's Lake, the river comes into
the hiker's view and the remainder of section four and the entire
stretch of section five to the 1899 Pumping Station seems dan-
gerously close to the river. At one point the towpath is shored
up by a concrete embankment. Near the pumping station the
hills on the land side disappear and two nineteenth century
structures take advantage of the fact. The old Augusta and
Knoxville Railroad crosses here, as do the huge pipes that carry
canal water four miles inland to the reservoir on Highland
Avenue. The absence of high ground from this point on and the
fact that the towpath was actually higher than the opposite bank
of the canal meant that the property north of the canal would be

subject to recurring floods. Most of the land here belonged to Judge Benjamin Warren, Henry Clay's host in 1844. Warren secured the contract to build across his own plantation. Section six from just below the pumping station to today's Lake Olmstead was more difficult than the previous sections because the landside bank had to be built up as well as the towpath. Engineer Sanford thought that "the heaviest work" would be along the short section seven, the flood plain of Rae's Creek. In retrospect, it would have been much easier to have adopted a plan similar to that of Charles Olmstead in 1875 and dam up Rae's Creek. The creek flowed twenty-five feet below the bottom of the canal, and Thomson's plan was similar to many in the North and Europe in that he intended to convey the canal over the creek in a wooden aqueduct 188 feet long, founded upon stone piers. This kind of work was beyond the capacity of Benjamin Warren or any other amateur; the contract was awarded to the busy Timberlake and Timanus Company.[22] Warren hired out twenty of his slaves to work on the aqueduct. The solid rock of the Appalachian Plateau at this point had been buried under tons of sediment, and the contractors found it nearly impossible to set the piers securely upon bedrock.

The Georgia Railroad construction partnership of Graves and O'Brien won the contract to build sections eight, nine and ten, carrying the canal down to McKinnie (13th) Street. All sections were low-lying and the banks had to be built up on both sides. The most historically significant segment was number eight, roughly from Rae's Creek to Broad Street. It was on this land that Elijah Clarke fought a four-day battle with British Lieutenant Colonel Thomas Brown and his Ranger and Indian allies. It was this tract that tobacco merchant Ezekiel Harris divided into lots and called the area "Harrisburg," a name that is used today for the wider neighborhood. In 1819 the federal government purchased part of the old 500-acre tract nearest the river for the Augusta Arsenal, and, although the Arsenal had been removed to the Hill, the Army still owned the land through which the survey ran. As mentioned earlier, Henry Cumming had to write to President James Polk to get clearance for the canal. Cumming also had to deal with a difficult officer in the person of Colonel George H. Talcott, commanding officer of the Augusta Arsenal. After the Commissioners put a bridge over the canal at Talcott's request, he decided that he did not like the location. The commissioners obliged by moving it.[23]

The ninth section extended from Broad Street to Hawk's Gully (15th St.); the tenth from there to McKinnie (13th) where the first level terminated in a wide boat basin, and where the Augusta Manufacturing Company, chartered in the December 1845 session of the Georgia legislature, would locate its mill.

Henry Cumming pushed work on the first level, to the neglect of the second and third levels, because he needed to show results to the citizenry, many of whom remained skeptical of the practicality and the value of the canal. Two hundred men were already at work on the construction, and in September 1845 the Commission authorized contractors to hire additional workers, setting May 1846 as the target date for completion. As in most great projects, that deadline could not be met. Because of the shortage of white laborers in Augusta, Cumming sent William Phillips, the board secretary, to Savannah and Charleston to recruit laborers at the handsome salary of $12 a month. Meanwhile the Board hired fifty black workers for $85 each for a year.[24]

Each time a problem occurred the costs escalated and Cumming had the unpleasant job of going before the City Council and asking for more money. The original estimate was in the neighborhood of $100,000. C.O. Sanford asked for

$25,000 more in December 1845, and another $25,000 in August 1846, raising the total cost at that point to $156,000. Cumming heard angry mutterings from taxpayers. Nobody in Augusta had any idea what to charge for the waterpower once the canal was in operation. Cumming sent Sanford to the North to interview all the experts he could find to ascertain a fair rate. C.O. Sanford's nephew and assistant, E.D. Sanford, took over the chief engineer's job of supervision during his uncle's two month absence.

Even after the older Sanford reported back to the Commissioners in January 1846, Henry Cumming was not satisfied that the Commissioners really understood the mathematics of water flow. He invited George Baldwin, the son of the famous Loammi Baldwin, to Augusta to look over the situation and give his opinion on the amount of horsepower the canal could furnish and how much would be required to operate a given number of spindles in a mill. Baldwin spent the first two weeks of April in Augusta, examining the canal and writing his report. He admitted that his figures were not based on actual experiments. Costs even in Lowell differed from mill to mill. With that caveat he calculated that a five-foot deep canal could supply 380 horsepower and should be able to drive a mill with 3,584 spindles.[25] (Inexplicably, William Phillips later interpreted Baldwin as stating that 380 horsepower would work 10,000 spindles.)[26]

The most interesting part of Baldwin's report, as far as the canal history is concerned, is that it provided the first description of the waterway as it neared completion. A dam of 1,200 feet stretched directly upriver to a small island, creating an entrance into the headgates. The lock chamber measured eleven by seventy-five feet. Headgates consisted of six sluices each six feet wide and seven feet high; each could be shut by means of a wooden dropgate. Stone "rip-rapping" protected the canal bank on the riverside from flooding. The canal itself measured twenty feet across at the bottom; the towpath bank rose eight feet from the base of the canal.

Reed's Creek ran nearly level with the bottom of the canal, and a ninety-foot wooden aqueduct carried the canal over the creek with little room to spare. As mentioned earlier, Baldwin thought that it was a mistake to put an aqueduct there, and he correctly predicted that it would soon collapse. However, that would be no problem, because the fallen aqueduct would serve nicely as a dam, allowing the creek to flow directly into the canal. Rae's Creek flowed twenty-five feet under its aqueduct, a 187-foot wooden trunk upon stone piers. Five culverts carried smaller creeks under the canal; eleven wooden bridges crossed farmlands and thirteen bridges crossed roads, all high enough to allow the passage of Petersburg boats.

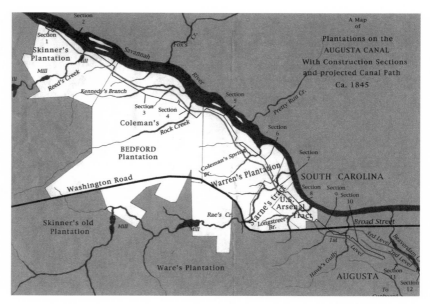

Figure 13. Map showing the twelve construction sections of the original canal and the property owners. *(Drawing by Michael White)*

Guard gates that could be lowered were located at the upper end of the first level and the exit of the third level. The first level measured 36,000 feet in length, the second as projected would extend 3,000 feet and the third 7,000, for a total length of nearly eight and three-quarter miles. Because the first level when completed would require an outlet, an abbreviated second and third level had to be part of the first construction; water would flow through the proposed factory at Thirteenth Street and run between Twelfth and Thirteenth streets into the third level and out Hawk's Gully.[27] The extension to the full length of the second and third levels would wait upon the completion of the first level. Baldwin's report indicates how impressed he was with the magnitude and complexity of the Augusta effort. Many skeptics in Augusta and across the engineering community doubted that the project would ever work, and if it did, whether it could pay for itself.

In his pep talks to the worried City Council members, Henry Cumming emphasized the importance of completing the first level before extending the second and third levels. He assured the Council that real estate along the canal, including the properties now owned by the Commission, would increase in value when the water began to flow and boats brought their cargoes to the basin at Thirteenth Street. He predicted that upriver farmers on both sides of the river would bring their produce down the canal. Of most interest to Augusta promoters, he announced the "early formation of a local company for the establishment of a cotton mill.[28]

In late October Graves and O'Brien finished work on the tenth section. C.O. Sanford checked over the entire length of the canal for last minute improvements, then with great expectations on the part of many and trepidation on the part of the Commissioners, the headgates were opened for a test on

November 23, 1846. Friends cheered and opponents were silenced when the canal filled and flowed, obedient to the engineer's calculations. *The Augusta Chronicle*, the leading supporter of the project from the beginning, expressed the universal sentiment, "A brighter day is dawning for our city."[29]

Between the time the first shovel was dug and the water was let in, the United States had declared war on Mexico and the local "Richmond Blues" took ship for Texas. On December 31, 1846 a soldier on the Texas frontier wrote to the editor of *The Chronicle*, "How does the canal come on? How many factories?"[30] The editor could reply that the canal had come along nicely, and the first factory would soon be built.

CHAPTER SIX

Threats to the "Brighter Day":
The Third Level and the Aqueduct

T he beneficial effects of the opening of the first level were immediately evident. Henry Cumming told Mayor Lewis D. Ford that after water had been let in "the whole enterprize began to attract considerable attention, not only among our own citizens but among intelligent and experienced men from abroad."[1]

On January 28, 1847 the Canal Commission invited Jabez Smith of Petersburg, Virginia, an expert on the building of factories, to advise on the best location for a new factory. Smith remained in Augusta to supervise the construction by contractor William Goodrich. It should not be surprising that the same men who sat on the Canal Commission were also prime movers in the promotion of the factory. The December 1846 session of the legislature chartered the Augusta Manufacturing Company; on January 19 stock was offered to the public, on February 11 Martin Dye, John P. King, Amory

Figure 14. Print showing newly constructed Augusta Factory. The functional building retained classical touches such as the cupola and a portico. *(Courtesy of the Augusta Museum of History)*

Sibley, John Bones and William D'Antignac called a stockholders meeting, and on March 3, 1847 the Board of Directors met and organized. William D'Antignac, an officer of the Canal Commission, was named president of the company. Coleman's saw and grist mill and the great factory were the first tangible fruits of the canal.[2]

Figure 15. Augusta Factory Stock Certificate, 1906. *(Courtesy of the Augusta Museum of History)*

However, there were other positive effects. The initial success of the canal encouraged Augustans to plan other bold steps. James Harper, one of the most faithful attendees at the Canal Commission meetings, spearheaded a new effort to rebuild the upper bridge over the river at McKinnie (13th) Street to replace the one washed away by the flood of 1840. John Bones, another commissioner, secured subscriptions to bring the first telegraph lines to Augusta. William G. Goodrich built a new factory on Reynolds Street that could, according to advertisements, "mass produce" doors, shingles and sashes. Goodrich became Augusta's first great builder. Other than the Augusta Factory, he constructed Artemas Gould's Italianate mansion on the Hill at the corner of Walton Way and Milledge, as well as Carolina Governor James Hammond's "Redcliffe" in Beech Island. Historic preservationists suggest that he built the Woodrow Wilson boyhood home on the corner of Seventh and Telfair. His later works include the Augusta Cotton Exchange and the synagogue on Telfair Street behind the courthouse, built in the style of a Roman Temple. James Hope and Thomas Metcalf reorganized the Augusta Steamboat Company. Across the river William Gregg made a bold move of his own. He began his mill village at Graniteville, South Carolina, in the Horse Creek Valley.[3]

The return of the Richmond Blues from the Mexican War added to the celebratory mood in the city. So did the arrival in town of the great orator Daniel Webster, on May 18, 1847. Webster himself was indisposed, so his welcoming banquet went on without him. On June 20, Herbert Stallings offered pleasure boat rides along the canal for fifty cents a passenger, marking the first recorded recreational use of the canal. Clearly, the canal had dispelled "the cold damp of commercial death" from the Augusta atmosphere.

Figure 16. Pleasure boat on the Canal.
(Photo courtesy of the Augusta Museum of History)

In celebration of the rebirth of their city, Augustans decided to build a monument honoring the Signers of the Declaration of Independence, two of whom lay buried nearby, George Walton near New Savannah, and Lyman Hall at his estate known as Montevallo, located at Shell Bluff. The legislature authorized the removal of the remains of the Signers in its 1847 session, and the handsome obelisk was erected in front of the County Courthouse in the following year for the reinterment ceremony. No one knew where Button Gwinnett was buried. It is not claiming too much to say that the new mood dampened the incipient secessionist movement in Augusta, and Augusta leaders managed to moderate Georgia's position in the crisis of 1850. John C. Calhoun called a meeting of southern states in Nashville for the purpose of seceding if slavery were banned in the Mexican Cession territory. The delegates there opted to follow the "Georgia Platform" written by Augusta resident and Canal Commissioner Charles J. Jenkins favoring Henry Clay's compromise bill.[4] Georgia preferred to go with Henry Clay's compromise and to stay with the Union. Canal optimism had something to do with it.

Chief Engineer C.O. Sanford decided to rest on his laurels and on May 5, 1847 proposed a new arrangement. He would leave town but retain the title of Chief Engineer, with his nephew doing the work in Augusta as Assistant Engineer. The two would be paid a total of $1,500 as well as travel costs for the Chief Engineer. Perhaps because they saw a savings in salary (C.O. had received $2,500 and E.D. $800) the Commissioners agreed to the proposition. However, no one seemed satisfied, neither the Sanfords nor the Commissioners. E.D. resigned within the year, and so did the Chief Engineer. That left the faithful local man, William Phillips, with the responsibility of correcting early mistakes. He worked uncomplainingly at his salary of $800 during the year 1848 and was rewarded with the title of Chief Engineer and a pay raise to $1,500 in January 1849.[5]

While maintaining a public air of optimism, Cumming and the commissioners wrestled with huge and almost unsolvable problems. The third level caused trouble and the aqueduct proved a nightmare. The first contractors for section twelve, Williamson and Timberlake, succeeded in digging the short outlet from McKinnie (13th) Street to Hawk's Gully, and made it possible to run water through the first level by November 1846. Cumming hoped that they would extend the cut along Beaver Dam Ditch back to Jackson (8th) Street, but by August 1847 he admitted that the contractors had "failed utterly" to fulfill their contractual obligations. David Collins and Daniel Crawley were hired to finish the job, but they failed also.[6]

It seemed so simple at first. The third level was supposed to be the easiest part because it followed the old drainage ditch called "Alligator Pond" on a British map made during the Revolution, and "Beaver Dam" Ditch by the locals. Since then, the ditch had been filled in, but a depression remained. Cumming told the City Council, "The city will have the full benefit of the surplus earth in removing forever all traces of those unseemly depressions marking the site of former lagoons." In March 1849 Cumming, Phillips and a group of the commissioners walked along the intended route of the third level with another contractor, William Eve, and pointed out what needed to be done. Cumming afterward admitted that they had no idea of the quality or condition of the subsoil.[7]

Eve went to work with a will, and immediately ran into trouble of various kinds. Quicksand and hidden stumps of ancient trees were problems. So was a buried spring that may account for the origin of the pre-revolutionary name of "Springfield." Far worse was the stench of exposed organic matter deposited in the bed of the old lagoon thousands of years before. People in the neighborhood began complaining of the evil-smelling matter thrown up by the workmen's shovels. Physicians warned about the danger of pestilence when the hot weather came. William Phillips recommended changing the route between Campbell (9th) and Jackson (8th) to higher ground. Cumming put the best face on it in his report to the City Council, the altered route would "furnish an ample quantity of earth to cover all the injurious matter that may be thrown out in the progress of the works."[8] To his credit, Eve succeeded where others had failed, and then put his crew to work on the second level, opening a channel from McKinnie to Jackson streets. That part went smoothly. At last, on July 23, 1850 water ran through the entire length of the first, second and third levels.[9] The commission would have celebrated except for the troublesome Rae's Creek Aqueduct. Henry Cumming had intended to resign when the three levels were finished, but he felt that he could not do so as long as serious doubts remained about the stability of the aqueduct.

By constructing the second and third levels, the Canal Commission created a problem that lasted through the remainder of the Nineteenth and for most of the Twentieth Century. Previously when the river flooded, water flowed up through Hawk's Gully, down Beaver Dam Ditch and out into the wetlands once referred to as "the Cupboard" and today as Phinizy Swamp. A necessary by-product of the canal would be a new sewer system rerouting the drainage into the third level and out Hawk's Gully.[10] The new system never worked very well.

C.O. Sanford, in his last report to the Commissioners on December 11, 1847, assured those gentlemen that the Rae's Creek Aqueduct had settled as far as it would and that there would be no more trouble with it. Henry Cumming wondered about that advice and once again turned to J. Edgar Thomson

Figure 17. Hawk's Gully during a flood.
(Courtesy of the Augusta Museum of History)

for his opinion. Thomson replied on February 17, 1848 that his plan was sound, but that the contractors (and presumably the Sanfords) had allowed a poor quality of stone to be used. Further, they had cut corners by not using hydraulic cement on the piers. Even while the structure continued to sink, E.D. Sanford flatly stated on December 29, 1847 that "the canal may now be said to be in excellent order." He handed in his resignation three months later. William Phillips inherited the problem of a slowly settling aqueduct.[11]

The Commissioners authorized Cumming to take whatever steps were necessary to shore up the aqueduct. He consulted with Georgia Railroad engineers William Hight and Fred Arms, and assigned the contract to Hight. Ominously, the sinking continued even while the repairs were being done. By August 5, 1848, when Hight announced that he had finished his work, the south wall of the aqueduct had settled a full six feet, creating a lop-sided effect. Improvised wooden supports on the south side kept the trunk of the aqueduct even. When Hight asked for more money than originally agreed to, the Commissioners rightly refused.[12]

The Canal Company proved to be no help in managing the canal. The city was the largest stockholder and the sitting mayor was routinely elected chairman of the board. However, the mayor and the city council left the operation of the canal to the Canal Commission. The arrangement was awkward and confusing. The Canal Company was made up of citizens who financed the original $100,000 and thus became stockholders who theoretically owned the canal. The City Council invested $30,000 in 1846, another $30,000 in 1850, $10,000 in 1851, and $30,000 in 1852, thus becoming the largest stockholder.[13] Although the city virtually owned the canal it allowed the Canal Commission established by the 1844 legislation to continue to manage the canal. The unpaid Commissioners stayed on far longer than any of them had intended. Because he depended on the city for funding, Cumming had to beg the Council for more money as the canal costs escalated above $200,000. On several occasions Cumming reminded the City Council that it owned the canal and urged it to take over its operation. On September 1, 1848, he addressed the problem of the aqueduct in his report to the City Council, "Let the Council consider the present state of the...Aqueduct which now conveys a full supply of water for all the purposes of manufacturing and furnishes an easy and cheap mode of transporting rock, cement, and all other materials required for its repair, and then contrast this with what would be the state of things if but a single pier should fall, suspending all manufacturing operations below and all navigation on the whole line of the canal."[14]

While everyone wondered how long it would hold up, the tilting aqueduct lasted throughout 1849, though leaking badly. On October 2 of that year the Commissioners heard the bad news that the earthen bottom of the canal had collapsed at its junction with the wooden floor or trunk of the aqueduct. The good news was that James Coleman had come to the rescue by extending the wooden trunk over the gap. Better still, he asked for no remuneration.

The strain of waiting made Henry Cumming irritable. Twice, on September 13, 1849 and again on November 1, he urged the City Council to assume control of the canal. On the latter occasion he told the council that the Canal Company, composed of stockholders expecting profits, "seems wholly unfitted...to the purposes for which it was created." A new, permanent aqueduct was imperative "in lieu of the defective work now standing at that place."[15]

The City Council finally agreed that the Board of

Managers of the Canal Company was not the proper agent for operating the canal, and supported the measure enacted by the state legislature at the December 1849 session, allowing the Canal Company to transfer the canal to the city.[16] However, the City Council had no intention of taking on the myriad problems associated with the canal until Cumming and the Canal Commission had worked them out.

Cumming invited Frederick A. Barton of Springfield, Massachusetts, to come to Augusta and look over the situation. On June 11, 1850 Barton arrived in town with an experienced quarry man, a master mason, and a contractor. After an initial inspection, Barton became ill and returned to the North without signing a contract. Cumming took the expensive step of sending William D'Antignac and William Phillips to New York to draw up a contract with the ailing Barton. As President of the Augusta Factory, D'Antignac was especially anxious to secure a reliable flow of water, doubly so because the factory intended to build a second mill next to the first one. William Phillips later revealed that D'Antignac convinced Barton to build a larger and longer aqueduct than he had originally intended.

The Augustans returned with the contract and the plans. Barton would build a structure ninety-five feet wide, nearly twice as wide as the first aqueduct. Rae's Creek would flow through two huge arched culverts, each with a thirty-foot span. The stone structure would be a hundred feet in length. The earthen canal would have to be widened in its approaches to the aqueduct to accommodate the new width. The banks would be raised to permit a seven-foot depth in the waterway. The entire work would be fixed with the best quality Rosendale cement and would cost $28,000.[17] The friends of the canal hoped that Barton could get the job done before the old structure collapsed completely.

Barton's master mason, Putnam, arrived in Augusta in

mid-September 1850 and began the careful selection of stone from the quarry on the Skinner plantation. His tools arrived a month later and work actually began in November. The fifty hand-picked laborers had to build barges to convey the quarried stone to the site, and then excavate the soil on the western side of the old aqueduct down to solid rock.[18]

Just as Cumming tried to encourage the City Council, William Phillips in his long monthly reports to the Commission put a positive spin on the progress. Yes, the cost kept going up, $245,000 by the end of the year 1850, but look at Lowell, he argued. That system cost $560,000. "It is to be hoped," said Phillips, "that the friends of the enterprise will not relax their energies or fail to urge it forward until every drop of water in the Savannah has contributed to the welfare of Augusta."[19]

By February 26, 1851 the south abutment and part of the north had been carried up to the beginning of the arches, but it was slow, costly work. Phillips hoped that the project would be finished by July. However, on April 9, 1851, the subcontractors walked off the job, complaining that they had not been paid, and also of the chronic absence of Barton, the chief contractor. Henry Cumming had to promise that he would pay them himself if they went back to work. The City Council made good Cumming's pledge. The Commissioners drew up a new contract for the completion of construction with engineer Charles McClellan at the end of May, raising the total cost to $360,000.[20]

Phillips' hoped-for deadline of July came and went. McClellan blamed the slow progress on the lax discipline of the previous contractor. So much for the "hand-picked" crew. McClellan fired those he thought were the poorest workers, but found that it was not easy to secure replacements in the heat of an Augusta summer. In September a master mason and a gang of workmen arrived from the north and McClellan promised to finish by December. He was wrong. The work turned out to be harder than he thought, he told Phillips. By March 1852 the aqueduct was not finished but he was. McClellan declared bankruptcy. Phillips had to finish the job himself with a city crew.[21]

The old structure had held together longer than anyone thought possible. Inevitably it began to come apart. On May 8, 1852 the south wall bulged fourteen inches, snapping the retaining rods. Phillips put in new rods and braced the wall as well as he could and hurried work on the new aqueduct. At last on July 25, 1852, Phillips was able to report to Cumming that the job was finished, "Water is now in the new work." He could not be blamed if his report carried a note of triumph. However, if the commissioners were inclined to celebrate, they had no time to do so. Incredibly and tragically, on July 26th, the entire northwestern wall of the *new* aqueduct – not the old – fell

Figure 18. The old wooden aqueduct below the newer one.
(Drawing by Michael White.)

down! The supposedly permanent structure, with stone so carefully selected, and so painstakingly grounded on solid rock, had
collapsed while the tilted old structure still held. It was a stunning blow to the friends of the canal. Poor William Phillips tried
to find something positive to say. At least the two great arches
and the central portion still stood.[22]

Nothing could be done during August because a rising
river endangered the riverbank of the canal, and water backed
up through Hawk's Gully, broke loose all the bridges over the
third level and overflowed into town.[23] Not until October was
Phillips able to concentrate his crew on cleaning up the debris
caused by the failure of the northwestern wing. Then the work
of rebuilding and buttressing the wall began. A new man,
Patrick Whelan, was hired for this phase of the work. By mid-
April 1853 the construction had advanced far enough for a test
to be conducted. Phillips let the water run through the new
aqueduct while Cumming and his friends anxiously watched.
Surely this time nothing could go wrong. Nothing went wrong
for precisely one month, then on June 8, 1853 cruel fate struck
again; the same newly repaired wall fell again![24]

The state of mind of Henry Cumming and his fellow
Commissioners can only be imagined. Cumming had
announced his resignation in 1850, but stayed three years
longer to attend to the problems caused by the third level and
aqueduct. For the indefatigable Phillips, work was the best cure
for discouragement. He hired additional masons and worked
them feverishly all summer. Finally, on September 5, 1853 he
let water in again. This time the structure held, and on
December 27, 1853 Phillips diverted the entire flow of the
canal to the new aqueduct to a depth of six feet.[25] By now, the
friends of the canal were too jaded by previous failures to celebrate. In fact, attendance at Commission meetings during the

last year fell off. At times only Cumming and James Harper attended.

With the end in sight, Henry Cumming's strong sense of duty allowed him to resign. He had given almost ten years to the canal to the neglect of his law practice. His farewell remarks to his colleagues were low-keyed. He thanked them for supporting "a work we deemed of great public utility." The commissioners accepted his resignation and resolved that the object for which they had been appointed was "very near being accomplished and the Board stood ready to surrender the trust confided in them." The Commission met for the last time on November 5, 1853, with Andrew J. Miller in the chair. James Harper, Leon Dugas, Lewis Ford, and William D'Antignac attending. They deserve posterity's gratitude. So do the other three members of the Commission who were not present at the final meeting, John Bones, John P. King and Thomas Metcalf. The only action taken at the meeting was a resolution of tribute to their leader. To Henry Cumming, more than to any other individual, was due the credit for "the great work that has been achieved." The commissioners also passed a resolution of thanks to William Phillips for "the constant, faithful, and skillful attention he has given to the duties of his office." The Board then dissolved itself.[26] Whether they liked it or not, the City Council undertook the management of the canal.

As he took leave of the management of the canal, it might be noted that few, if any, Augustans have contributed in such a significant and lasting way as did Henry Cumming in conceiving and carrying out the building of the Augusta Canal.

The saga of the "defective" old aqueduct was not quite over. For one thing, the new aqueduct continued to give trouble all during 1854 with further settling and intermittent leaking, so the much-criticized old works continued to serve while the

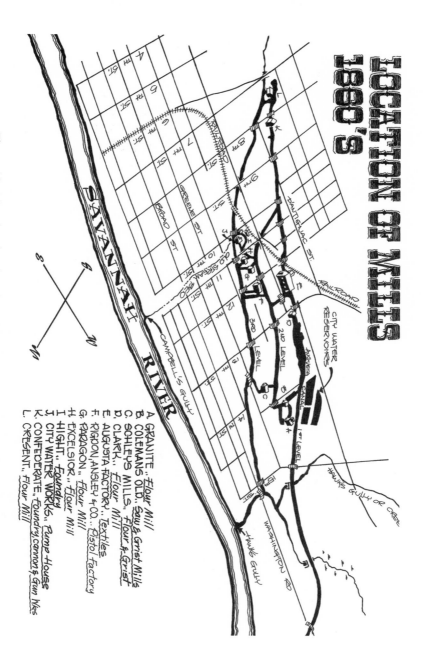

Figure 19. Map showing location of first buildings along the first level of the canal. *(Drawing by Bill Blackard according to research by Michael White.)*

new one underwent repair. For another, the original aqueduct served one of its original functions extremely well, and mention should be made of that. From its opening in February 1847 until September 5, 1854, Petersburg boats and barges had transported the following produce through the first level into the basin at 13th Street: 140,000 bales of cotton, 3,184 barrels of flour, 1,286 bushels of corn, 3,556 cords of firewood, 27,700 pounds of bacon, 89 bushels of peas, 20,500 staves, 1,638 bales of yarn, 226 bushels of wheat, 8 bales of wool, 8 cords of hickory bark, 758,020 feet of sawed timber, 117 casks of manganese, 1,500 hoop poles, 56,500 shingles, and 55,000 laths.[27]

In March 1855 William Phillips began the careful surgery necessary to sever the old aqueduct from the new and on July 2, 1855 he announced that the deed was done. Water no longer flowed through the old aqueduct. The dismantling began. The stone from the old structure was used to line the sides of the new trunk in place of the wooden walls.[28]

CHAPTER SEVEN

The Canal During Wartime

<hr>

A ugustans believed that their city was "the heart of the Confederacy." Early in the war Mayor Robert May campaigned for the capitol of the Confederate States to be located in his town.[1] His reasons seem logical: Augusta was centrally situated; railroads running through the town connected the eastern and western states of the Confederacy; its distance from the front lines afforded security; the Augusta Canal provided power for manufacturing the tools for war; and not least the great Confederate Powder Works was located in the city. Colonel George Washington Rains saw the advantages of Augusta after President Jefferson Davis gave Rains the responsibility of building a factory for the production of gunpowder, a staggering assignment for a man who had no experience in such work. Rains bravely assumed the task. On July 10, 1861 he left Richmond for a tour of the southern states, seeking a likely site. His reasons for selecting Augusta included the canal and the rail

Figure 20. The genius of the Confederate Powder Works, Colonel George W. Rains. *(Courtesy of the Augusta Museum of History)*

connections.[2] He might have added that the Augusta Arsenal had facilities for manufacturing small arms and cartridges.

The seizure of the federal arsenal on the Hill by forces of the independent republic of Georgia could have provoked a general war before the firing on Fort Sumter. Georgia seceded on January 19, 1861 and Governor Joseph E. Brown immediately called upon Captain Arnold Elzey, commandant of the arsenal, to surrender. When Elzey declined to do so, Brown called out all the militia units in the vicinity of Augusta: the Clinch Rifles, the Oglethorpe Infantry, the Irish Volunteers, the Montgomery Guards, the Washington Artillery, the Richmond Hussars, Companies A and B of the Minute Men, the Burke County Sharpshooters, the Greene County Volunteers, and finally the Piney Woods Rangers. Over a thousand men under the command of Lieutenant Colonel Alfred Cumming began marching up the Summerville Plank Road (Walton Way) on January 24 in high good spirits. Captain Elzey decided that discretion was the better part of valor and surrendered the arsenal with the promise of parole for his eighty-man garrison. Georgia thus gained 22,000 muskets and rifles, two twelve-pound howitzers, and two cannons. Augusta's Washington Artillery went up to the Arsenal and fired a salute as a white flag with a red star representing Georgia was raised.[3] The flag is now a valued possession of the Augusta Museum of History.

Not all Augustans showed the same enthusiasm for secession. In the elections of November 1860 a large majority of Augustans voted for Stephen Douglas, who favored allowing the people of the new territories to decide whether they wanted slavery, over John Breckenridge, who ran on a platform that would have guaranteed slavery in territories. In general the conservative members of the Whig Party that had supported the canal and the promotion of business opposed immediate seces-sion. Henry H. Cumming, Charles J. Jenkins, and John P. King opposed the secessionist slate of John Phinizy, Dr. Ignatius Garvin, and George Crawford.⁴ Augustans sent the secessionists to the state capital at Milledgeville largely because Georgia's sister states had seceded and it was clear that there would be a new confederation.

The political division between Whigs and Democrats affected William Phillips and the canal in a curious way. The Whigs on the City Council championed the construction and expansion of the waterworks, while the Democrats objected to the money spent on the project. Led by councilman Stephen Heard, the Democrats on the Council pushed through a contro-versial ordinance providing for the erection of an iron-frame tower in the middle of town. A large bell hung in the tower would be sounded by a watchman when he sighted a fire. The editor of *The Chronicle* expressed the opinion that the tower "would be an eyesore and that not one in ten wanted it."⁵ Nevertheless construction of the tower went on apace with that of the waterworks. On May 13, 1860, amid considerable excitement, the huge bell arrived in town. Nicknamed "Big Steve" in honor of its sponsor, it was paraded around town by the firemen's band. A reporter noted, "It is quite a monster and looks as if it might speak in thunderous tones."⁶

On February 1, 1861, with the euphoria of secession still exciting the city, William Phillips held a public testing of the fire-fighting capability of the new waterworks. Whig Mayor Foster Blodgett had the honor of handling a fire hose attached to one of the new fireplugs. He could scarcely control the hose as a jet of water shot over a hundred feet high. Everyone applaud-ed and *The Chronicle* pronounced it a "noble stream."⁷ On the other hand Big Steve's inaugural proved a disappointment.

Instead of speaking in thunderous tones, the bell emitted a sound more like a "clank." A caustic critic submitted these lines to the newspaper, "respectfully dedicated to the city council"

> Of all the humbugs now extant
> On this side of the Atlantic
> There's none that knows, but will declare,
> "Big Steve's" the most gigantic!
>
> Tis true he cost our City
> A mighty heap of dollars,
> But what's the use! He never rings
> Till everybody hollers!
>
> And that long-legged skeleton
> So bare and melancholy,
> That tower in which he hangs on high -
> A monument of folly -
>
> There's not a stranger comes along,
> But wonders what it's made for,
> And when that question's answered, he
> Still wonders if it's paid for?[8]

A self-advertised expert claimed that he could make the bell resound properly; instead he broke it. Big Steve was replaced with a smaller bell, but it, also, gave out a weak chime. The introduction of an electric fire alarm system in 1887 ended the dubious career of Big Steve. In 1894 the bell was sold to a company in St. Louis.

William Phillips attempted to avoid politics, but he could not help mentioning from time to time how a single fire

Figure 21. "Big Steve," located on the corner of Greene & Jackson Streets.
(Photo courtesy of the Augusta Museum of History)

hydrant was of more utility than all the city's fire engines. All during the war years, in addition to his additional duties with the canal, he continued to expand the waterworks throughout the city. As of July 1861, he listed the number of water permits he had issued: 152 "wash pavements," twenty-nine hydrants, ten baths, five wash sinks, one six-horsepower steam engine, fourteen wash basins, one fountain, five water closets, and one wash tub.[9] It is thought that one of the houses with the new water closets and perhaps the wash tub, was the home of Rev. Joseph Wilson on the corner of Telfair and McIntosh (7th) Streets. The house, constructed in 1861, was the boyhood home of Woodrow Wilson.

Mayor Robert May, elected in April 1861, praised the waterworks system in his annual address. "No improvement could have been executed by the city government of greater advantage" than the waterworks, he said.[10] Fires were extinguished more efficiently, insurance rates were lowered, streets were less dusty, and more water was available for household use. The one drawback was that the water, though fit for drinking, was more cloudy than that of the old Turknett Springs system, so the latter system was maintained for years together with the new system.

Phillips had more than one man could handle with responsibility both for the waterworks and the canal, but the war forced other duties upon him. After the Union troops landed on Tybee, people in Augusta expected Yankee gunboats to come up the Savannah River and bombard the city. Colonel Rains consulted Phillips about the best way to obstruct the river passage. Phillips assigned the canal crew to go down to Shell Bluff, a narrow stretch of the river, and construct fortifications, including a chain across the river and a platform for a Columbiad cannon half way up the bluff. Colonel Rains maintained a company of militia on watch at Shell Bluff, but they soon lost interest when the threat failed to materialize. On May 22, 1862 the steamer *Edisto* conveyed an excursion party downriver to see the defenses. The ladies were allowed to fire the great cannon and were thrilled at the sight of the huge ball crashing through the woods. The trip home was beguiled by band music and dancing.[11]

The ladies did more serious defense work. They conducted a drive to raise money for a Confederate gunboat and the city contributed $20,000 to the cause. The gunboat *Georgia*, built in Savannah, proved to be too heavy to move away from its berth, and remained in place throughout the war. When Sherman's troops marched into Savannah, the authorities, for some reason of their own, ordered the immobile vessel to be scuttled. So it rests today on the bottom of the Savannah River.

If Augusta could be called the Heart of the Confederacy, the canal was its muscle. Along the canal a remarkable industrial growth occurred that boded well for Augusta's post-war future. The most important of these new plants without question was the great Confederate States Powder Works factory. On August 29, 1861 *The Chronicle*, unconcerned about enemy spies among its readers, announced, "A Powder Factory and an Armory for the Confederate Government, established as they are to be in our midst will help to give Augusta that prominence to which eligibility of position entitles her."

Colonel Rains described his challenge, "Without plans, without machine shops, without powder markers, without mechanics, I was required to erect somewhere a gigantic works" to supply the Confederate army with ammunition.[12] He was lucky or shrewd in his choice of subordinates. C. Shaler Smith, his architect and engineer, worked with him to design buildings that were functional as well as handsome in the currently popular neo-gothic style.[13] Rains hired William Pendleton of the Tredegar Ironworks in Richmond, Virginia, as his superintendent. The firm of Denning and Bowe did the construction. Rains was fortunate to locate in Nashville a man named Wright who had worked in the British gunpowder plant at Waltham Abbey, and who possessed a pamphlet that explained the powder-making process. But there can be no doubt that Rains was the genius who learned every facet of gunpowder production and conceived new methods of manufacturing.

A British visitor referred to George Washington Rains as "a very clever, highly educated, and agreeable officer."[14] A native of North Carolina, he graduated from West Point in 1842, then taught chemistry and geology at the same academy. He served with distinction in the Mexican War. In 1856 he retired from the army and became president of the Washington Iron

Works in Newburgh, New York. He made Augusta his home after the war, served as headmaster or "regent" of Richmond Academy and taught chemistry at the Medical College of Georgia. His best known achievement was the construction and successful operation of the Confederate States Powder Works.

Figure 22. Rare photograph of the Confederate States Powder Works. The tall chimney still stands as a memorial to the Confederate dead. *(Courtesy of Joe Lee)*

Rains decided to locate his principal building, the Refinery, on the old United States Arsenal tract. He purchased 200 acres above the Arsenal tract from Judge Ebenezer Starnes for $2,000.[15] From Benjamin Warren he bought a mile and a half of land between the canal and river for $10,000.[16] Rains paid $90,000 to Henry H. Cumming, Lambeth Hopkins, Robert Y. Harris, John W. Walker, and Harris D'Antignac for the Foundry and Machine Shops along the second level between Jackson (8th) and Campbell (9th) Streets. The purchase included 28 buildings of various sizes that were used for the production of small arms as well as the production of cannon and large machinery.[17]

Figure 23. Drawing of Confederate States Powder Works
Refinery and Warehouse Building and Chimney.
(Courtesy of the Augusta Museum of History)

The raw materials of gunpowder were saltpetre, sulphur and charcoal. Rains issued a pamphlet explaining to farmers and others how nitrates could be used to produce saltpetre and he established a nitrate plant near Augusta to help furnish salt-petre, but most of his supply came from Europe through the Union blockade. He devised a way of making charcoal from cottonwood and obtained sulphur from Louisiana sugar planters. The three basic ingredients were refined by a process

Rains invented and reduced to black, moist "cake" ready for the next step in the process. This first step was done in the Refinery, a crenellated three-sided brick building fronting the canal. Four square towers at each corner were used as offices. In the central building the refining process took place; drying pans three feet above the floor were heated by a hot air furnace from below. The east wing contained a saltpetre and sulphur storehouse; the west wing was used for storing charcoal, and it also had a steam engine. Rains took special pains with the chimney in the three-sided enclosure, "a grand monumental structure" he called it, rising 150 feet. He conducted a ceremony of dedication by placing "the usual documents" into a cornerstone in one of the top corners of the square base of the obelisk.[18]

Behind the Refinery stood a building called the Laboratory. Like the Refinery it was crenellated; its dominant feature was a central tower seventy-five feet high with a four-sided clock. The interior was never finished because the work intended to be done in it was more easily conducted at the Arsenal on the Hill. Twelve connected "Incorporating Mills" extended up the canal beyond the Refinery. The walls of each unit were four to ten feet thick, and twenty-eight feet high. The fronts were made of light wood and glass and the roof sheet zinc. Alternate units faced away from the canal. An engine room in the center of the twelve mills housed a steam engine that turned a shaft running under all the units and capable of turning five-ton rollers in each unit. The rollers ground and compressed the "cake" into half-inch thick coagulated powder. Rains described each of the twelve mills as "a mortar of seventeen feet wide and twenty-four feet long." Any one of them could blow up, and for that reason he made sure that each would blow upward and outward and not affect the mill next to it. In fact, only three explosions occurred in these potentially dangerous places and only one was powerful enough to blow out the front and roof. Two workers were slightly injured.

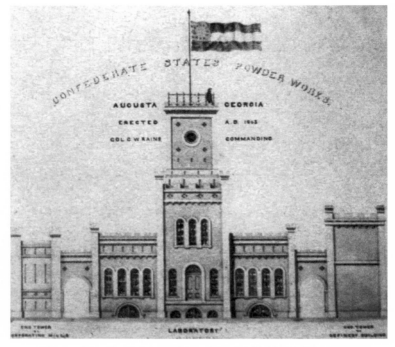

Figure 24. Confederate States Powder Works Laboratory.
(Courtesy of the Augusta Museum of History)

The compressed cake was taken across the canal to four shallow clay pits and allowed to dry and harden. A brick build-ing called the Press House stood on the same side near the clay pits for further pressing and thinning the cake. The hardened material was transported back to the river side of the canal, to the next building beyond the twelve Incorporating Mills, the Granulating Mill, a brick structure with thin walls and a light roof where the cakes were ground into powders of different grain. As a precaution in the event of an explosion, Rains sepa-rated the Granulating Mill from buildings on either side by a distance of a thousand feet. Across the canal was a second granulating mill constructed of wood. In August 1864 the worst accident in the short history of the Powder Works happened here. Three tons of granulated gunpowder, awaiting delivery, exploded with incredible force, throwing up a column of flame and smoke five hundred feet high and shaking the ground for a mile around. The seven men working in the building were blown to bits, as was a boy in an adjoining shed. Rains described the accident this way, "The bodies of the seven men and the boy with the debris, were carried up with the ascending column, and by its revolving action, reduced mainly to small fragments and dispersed."[19] A sentinel standing guard nearby was also killed, but not dismembered. Rains assumed that the explosion was caused by one of the men smoking while the supervisor was away.

After the granulation, or breaking up of the cake, the powder was transplanted by boat 2,500 feet up the canal to a building for further drying, dusting and glazing by a process Rains invented that involved blowing steam-warmed air over

Figure 25. The long spillway near Rae's Creek. The Dusting, Drying, Glazing Division of the Confederate States Powder Works can be seen in the upper left corner. *(Courtesy of the Augusta Museum of History.)*

the material. Two hundred yards farther along was a boiler house that supplied the steam. For safety, Rains placed the chimney of the boiler another hundred yards up the canal and connected the two by an underground flue. Rains reasoned that a spark would have to drift three hundred yards to reach the roof of the drying and glazing building. The dried gunpowder was then taken to still another building fifteen hundred feet beyond the boiler house where it was weighed and put into boxes designed by Rains. The boxes were floated three-quarters of a mile still farther up the canal to a fenced warehouse capable of storing a hundred tons of gunpowder. The canal was the thoroughfare for the transportation of the powder up to the storehouse and down to the basin to be loaded upon railroad cars in the special containers devised by Colonel Rains.

The Powder Works became famous, not only in the South, but internationally. British Colonel James Fremantle stopped in Augusta specifically to inspect the Powder Works.[20] Confederate authorities vied with one another in praising the works. President Jefferson Davis toured the facility and commented that the *Alabama* could have beaten the *Kearsarge* if Admiral Semmes had the Augusta powder. Confederate Chief of Ordnance General Josiah Gorgas expressed the opinion that Rains had built a "superb powder mill" that was "wonderfully successful." Rains calculated that from April 10, 1861 when the mill went into production until April 18, 1865, the works produced 2,750,000 pounds of gunpowder. Rains took satisfaction in the knowledge that no Confederate army lost a battle for want of ammunition. If the Augusta Canal had never served another purpose it would have achieved historical significance by its association with the great Confederate works. Rains paid the canal this accolade: "The safe, economical and ready means of transportation by the canal were invaluable;

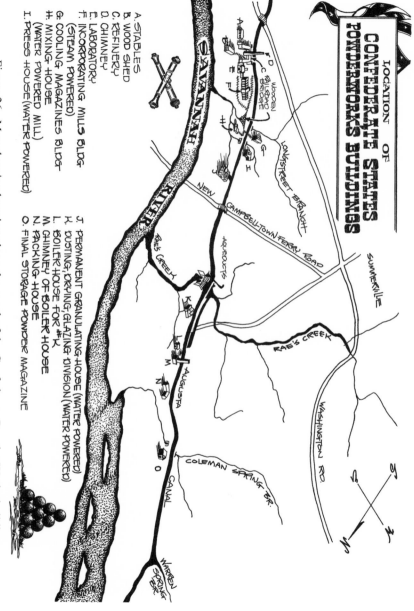

A. STABLES
B. WOOD SHED
C. REFINERY
D. CHIMNEY
E. LABORATORY
F. INCORPORATING MILLS BLDG
    (STEAM POWERED)
G. COOLING MAGAZINES BLDG
H. MIXING HOUSE
    (WATER POWERED MILL)
I. PRESS HOUSE (WATER POWERED)

J. PERMANENT GRANULATING HOUSE (WATER POWERED)
K. DUSTING, DRYING, GLAZING DIVISION (WATER POWERED)
L. BOILER HOUSE FOR #K
M. CHIMNEY OF BOILER HOUSE
N. PACKING HOUSE
O. FINAL STORAGE POWDER MAGAZINE

Figure 26. Map showing location along the canal of the Confederate Powder Works buildings. (*Drawing by Bill Blackard according to research by Michael White*)

no accident ever happened, notwithstanding the immense amount of combustible material – over two thousand five hundred tons – which had passed to and fro over it during the three years of operations."[21]

Colonel Rains assumed control of the Augusta Arsenal in April 1862. A large brick building at the eastern end of the property had been erected in 1861 by the then commander, Captain W.C. Gill, and 300 persons worked in it to make cartridges, cartridge bags and knapsacks. Rains expanded the Arsenal operations. He built a harness and equipment shop in the 1861 building, for the manufacture of equipment for field artillery. The Arsenal stepped up production of cartridges, signal rockets, time fuses, primers, percussion caps, and hand grenades. On several occasions Rains appealed to the women of Augusta to volunteer to help pack cartridges. They willingly obliged. He put up other wooden buildings for other uses, one a chemical laboratory, and another a factory for production of the boxes he needed to pack gunpowder.

War-related industries mushroomed in Augusta. S.S. Jones and Company produced buckles, canteens, and buckets for the army. George R. Dodge's shop dyed bolts of cloth for Confederate uniforms. Jesse Ormond removed his Savannah workshop to William Hight's empty machine shop and manufactured railroad cars, ordnance and wheelbarrows. The Georgia Railroad Machine Shops sold a locomotive and several freight cars to the Confederate government. Charles Rigdon, Jesse Ansley, Andrew J. Smith, and Charles R. Keen began making pistols in the Confederate Machine Works and turned out 2,359 "Confederate Colts" during the course of a year. Rigdon organized his sixty workers into a home guard unit.[22]

The Confederate government established a naval supply shop in Augusta and manufactured shoes and uniforms for navy personnel. *The Chronicle* praised Colonel Rufus B. Bullock who installed a leather-cutting machine at the naval supply shop for his enterprise. His machine expedited the manufacture of shoes and clothing.[23] (The newspaper would change its opinion of Bullock in 1868, when he became the Republican governor of Georgia.) In 1864 the Navy Ordnance Department opened a shipyard on the river. The Confederate Quartermaster Office employed hundreds of seamstresses, as did the Confederate Clothing Bureau. In addition the Georgia Clothing Bureau gave employment to 500 women. A Confederate Shoe Factory made shoes for the army. There was even a Confederate Bakery on the second level of the canal near Thomas Stovall's Excelsior Flour Mills, originally Alfred Baker's 1859 mill. A unique industry, not directly related to the war effort, was Captain Camille Girardy's Ice Factory, perhaps the first in the country. Emily Tubman, the prominent Augusta businesswoman and philan-thropist, ordered the machinery from France; a blockade runner brought the cargo safely to Savannah, and it came upriver by barge. Girardy obtained a patent for the ice-making process, and turned out a ton of ice a day.[24]

The Augusta Factory won a contract from the Confederate government to supply cloth at very favorable prices. In 1863 the factory earned $3,100,192 for the sale of 4,200,384 yards of cloth. Its 750 workers were mostly women who lived in company-constructed brick row-houses near the factory. President William E. Jackson won praise from Mayor May for donating cloth to the Augusta Purveying Association, an organization formed to give assistance to Augusta's poor. Augustans were not the only ones impressed at their progress. On May 13, 1864 *The Chronicle* quoted the Columbia *South Carolinian*, "No city in the Confederacy...are congregated more manufacturing interests, wealth and enterprise than in Augusta,

Georgia." The reporter was particularly impressed at the output and size of the Augusta Factory, surrounded by "a little town of its own." The Augusta Factory produced the Augusta canal's first mill village.

William Phillips worried constantly about the danger to the canal caused by the increased traffic and the demand for water for industry and for the ever-expanding waterworks system. At the outset, Colonel Rains had agreed to use only the water spilling over the Rae's Creek wasteway. Phillips could therefore reassure William Jackson of the Augusta Factory, and Francis Cogin the Superintendent, that the factory got all the water it contracted for. Jackson complained that it was never enough. The greatest danger was that of a sudden flood or freshet. On December 28, 1861 the earthen wall adjoining the chronically troublesome Rae's Creek Aqueduct gave way. Phillips mobilized a hundred workers to repair the breach.

On February 6, 1862 heavy rains caused Reed's Creek to flood the canal and break open the newly repaired wall. On the next day Phillips met with Colonel Rains, William Jackson and Henry H. Cumming. Rains suggested constructing a framework of 12-foot square wooden sills that could be filled with earth, instead of a simple wall of earth.[25] A dam at Reed's Creek kept water out while the new approach to the aqueduct was constructed. Finally, on March 2, 1862 the turbines of the Augusta Factory resumed operations, as did the pumps of the waterworks. Warren's Mill (formerly Coleman's Granite Mills) worked by day and Carmichael's (formerly Cunningham's) Mill worked by night. The Excelsior Mill, and the Confederate Machine Works, also on the second level, resumed work on March 25th, and on the 26th the canal was opened for navigation along the entire length of the first level. Contractors Denning and Bowe went to work constructing a wall of stone between the old and new aqueducts after they finished the Powder Works. The maintenance of the canal was Phillips' most important contribution to the war effort.

On June 19, 1862 Phillips led his canal crew down to Shell Bluff to work on the defensive fortifications there. After that bit of excitement the crew returned to the pedestrian routine of repairing the banks of the canal near the Powder Works. The towpath, used to haul boats and barges along the two-mile stretch of the Powder Works, needed constant attention. Phillips fretted about the lack of security along the canal, and continually complained about casual bathing in the canal by boys and men during the hot weather. He took up residence in the Carmichael Flour Mill office to better monitor the safety of the canal. He prodded the city council into passing an ordinance on March 6, 1863 forbidding the throwing of dead animals, garbage, trimming from trees, or anything else into the canal. Bathing was banned under penalty of a fine of $100. If a slave or free person of color were to be caught swimming in the canal, the punishment would be 39 lashes. The ordinance helped somewhat, although clandestine swimming never really stopped. A greater problem was caused by the fact that the city drains emptied into the third level with the result that the canal gave off an offensive odor. Phillips suggested various ways to flush out the system, but nothing came of it then and the third level became more noxious as the years passed.

If Phillips had a fault it might have been that he was overly protective of the canal, even to the point of chastising the wealthy and influential William E. Jackson. When the Augusta Factory cut into the canal to irrigate its gardens (the Factory was something of a showplace in those days) Phillips objected, contending that there were several plantations along the canal; if the Factory was allowed to tap the canal, so would the others. He wrote a sarcastic note to the effect that he was glad that the Factory had so much water that they could afford to water their flowers with it. This was a sore spot with Jackson, because despite the pre-war raising of the banks, and erecting waste-boards on the aqueduct, the Factory seemed to be chronically short of waterpower. Francis Cogin, the superintendent, asked Phillips to raise the wasteboards two inches to get more water passing through the aqueduct. Phillips thought the request unwarranted. He wrote a lengthy report to Mayor May filled with calculations illustrating the fact that by contract the Factory was entitled to 257.48 cubic feet of water per second and it was getting 351.83 cubic feet per second. May felt obligated to Jackson for his generosity to the poor of Augusta, and suggested to Phillips that they raise the boards as a favor, not as a precedent.

Phillips was anything but gracious in his acquiescence. He wrote to Superintendent Cogin that the Factory was wasting precious water. The Factory's "so-called" improvements could not compensate for inefficiency. "You have no right to demand an increase in supply," he wrote. But, because the mayor wanted to help the Factory, he said that he would raise the boards.[26] William E. Jackson nursed a grudge, and when he was in a position to do so, he struck back at William Phillips.

Phillips became involved, reluctantly one suspects, in the city's argument with the military authorities about providing hospitals for the sick and wounded Confederate soldiers. Railroads brought wounded men from both the eastern and western theaters of the war to Augusta. The city hospital was quickly filled. Surgeon Lewis D. Ford asked for the city hall to be turned into a hospital. The city council deliberated and concluded that the city hall was too important a place to be used for that purpose.[27] As more casualties arrived in 1863, the city council suggested that they be put in public buildings such as

Concert Hall, Lafayette Hall, Campbell's Infirmary, and the Newton Orphan Home. Colonel Rains lost patience with the city council and upon his orders the surgeons took over the Presbyterian Church and used it for a hospital. This prompted a meeting of churchmen with the city council.[28] The Reverend Mr. Hilliard challenged the right of the military to seize church property. The Reverend Mr. Clarke warned that "the impression had got out that Augusta was derelict in her duty to the sick and wounded." The council decided to construct temporary housing on the racetrack on Turknett Springs Road (today's Wrightsboro Road) between Marbury (12th) and McKinnie (13th) Streets, well removed from the settled parts of town. The Medical Director of Hospitals replied curtly to the mayor, "Your suggestions do not meet with my concurrence."[29] For one thing, the location was too far from the railroad.

The mayor replied that he had consulted William Phillips, "Civil Engineer and Surveyor of the City of Augusta" who lived near the race track and "from an intimate acquaintance of more that twenty years with the locality can speak with an approximation of accuracy that the distance from the railroad crossing...at the Augusta Factory is half a mile."[30] The Medical Director was unimpressed with Phillips' ability to measure half a mile. While the city fathers continued to argue for a race track location, Colonel Rains decided to build housing on Richmond Academy parade grounds. The Academy was closed and it too was used as a hospital. St. Patrick's Church (Most Holy Trinity) with its new church nearly completed, offered the old church building as a hospital. St. John's Methodist on Greene Street and St. Paul's Episcopal Church on Reynolds, all city hotels, and finally private homes were opened to receive the flood of wounded.

The journal of Gertrude Clanton Thomas reveals the

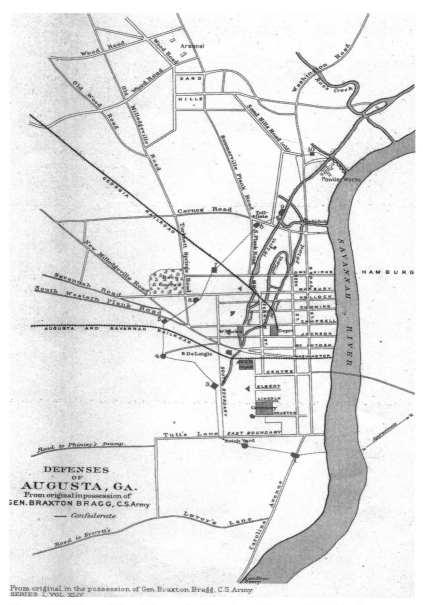

Figure 27. Map of Confederate fortifications. From original in the possession of Gen. Braxton Bragg, C.S. Army, Series 1, Vol. XLIV. *(Augusta
Canal Authority Archives)*

tragic condition of many of the wounded men. She went to the Catholic Church on Telfair Street to minister to the soldiers and found "laying on the floor upon beds hastily filled with straw were wounded men, wounded in every manner. Some with their arms and legs cut off, others with flesh wounds, two men in a dying state, another poor fellow with the ever present thought of home mingling in his delirium as he sits up and gathering his coarse shoes proceeds to put them on saying, I am going home..."[31] Across the street, at his home on the corner of 7th and Telfair Street, six-year-old Tommy (Woodrow) Wilson absorbed his first impressions of war.

On New Year's Day, 1864 the river backed up the third level lifting off bridges at Hawk's Gully and at McKinnie (13th) Street. Water filled the second level and caused a break in the canal bank. Phillips' crew, with some of the Powder Works hands, repaired the damage.[32] Bad weather during the winter muddied the much-used towpath, and Phillips spent several months repairing and raising the banks.

Mayor Robert May's annual address delivered on October 7, 1864 had an air of unreality about it in that he hardly mentioned the war, and the war in the autumn of 1864 was going badly for the Confederacy. He pointed with pride to the industry along the canal, "We have arrived at a point where we may be fully justified in manifesting a high degree of pride and predicting – unless crippled by unexampled reverses – a still more fortunate future."[33] He cited as reasons for his good report that the canal was working properly, and the city police force maintained order despite a rapidly swelling population of black and white refugees from the war.

In November General William T. Sherman unleashed his 60,000 "bummers" upon the land and optimism disappeared. All available Confederate troops were directed to

Augusta to defend the city and its precious Powder Works. A fortification of cotton bales was raised around the city and the people prepared for the worst. The November 24, 1864 *Chronicle* reported that the city "has the appearance of a vast military camp. Stores are closed and owners are shouldering muskets. Streets are quickened by the sound of martial music and the tramp of soldiery." Sherman was fooled by fake Confederate telegrams into believing that there were far more troops in the city than there were.

The Chronicle played its part in the game of disinformation by reporting that the Powder Works, arsenal, armories and machine shops had been dismantled and the valuable machinery removed to a place of safety. None of that was true. The greatest danger to the town came from the Confederate generals who wanted to set fire to the thousands of cotton bales warehoused in the center of the town. Mayor May found one reason after another to delay firing the cotton until the danger passed. Some students of history believe that Sherman made a mistake in not taking Augusta, because the Powder Works continued to turn out munitions and the war lasted five months longer.

The city escaped the danger from Sherman and from fire, but could not escape severe damage from the river. On January 10, 1865 the river flooded and backed up the third level again. The second level overflowed and the third level banks broke in three places. Downtown bridges were again carried off. *The Chronicle* of January 13 called it the most destructive flood since that of 1853. The entire town of Hamburg across the river was submerged. All of Broad Street was under water, and gaping holes were gouged in the streets. Phillips' men made some progress in repairing the breaks, but on January 22, the river swelled again and overflowed the third level. Then on March 20, 1865 forty feet of the Rae's Creek wasteway that provided water for the Powder Works gave way and caused more flooding. The recurring floods further eroded city streets and filled cellars. As a result the city presented a sorry spectacle to the Union General Emory Upton when he received the surrender of the city on May 3, 1865. Colonel Rains permitted his subordinate Captain W. H. Warren to surrender the Powder Works and the Arsenal to General Upton. On May 5, 1865 Union troops under General Edward L. Molineux occupied Augusta. Mayor May received a message from Molineux calling attention to the condition of the streets, lanes, yards, out-buildings, cesspools, water in cellars and other problems and directed the Mayor to clean up the city at once, or his men would do it and charge the cost to the city. The three floods had done more damage to the city than enemy soldiers.[34]

General Molineux won the respect of the community by the time he left Augusta in June. He wrote to a friend, "My city is clean, and matters begin to run smoothly."[35] Martin Calvin, principal of Houghton School, could write in September, "The close of the late bloody struggle left our merchants and businessmen generally in perfect darkness... Stores, whose shelves were then empty are laden now with the choicest goods. Merchants have been North acknowledging and liquidating the debts contracted by them before the war, (and) have found creditors. We witness stores undergoing repairs, business houses and dwellings Phoenix-like, rising out of the ashes... The flutter of wheels and the song of the saw on the canal are responded to by the lumbering of heavily laden drays along the streets... For from the boundaries of Dublin to the Banks of the Savannah, rises an unceasing hum - telling us that we live in the midst of an enterprising and industrious people."[36] The bally-hoo of the "New South" had begun even before the nostalgia for "the Lost Cause" set in. The canal would be key to Augusta's realization of the promise of the New South.

CHAPTER EIGHT

The Great Enlargement

———⟫●⟪———

N o one would be surprised to learn that the year 1865, the year of Confederate defeat, was a traumatic one for Augustans. Sherman's rowdies spared the town because their leader did not want a fight on his way to Savannah, but Augusta did suffer severe damage from, of all things, the canal. Before, the canal flood waters would course through Hawk's Gully and Campbell's Gully into Beaver Dam Ditch and flow into the Savannah River below Augusta near New Savannah. The canal now funneled the overflow down the first level and up the third level into the heart of town. Two bad floods had devastated the downtown by the time Union troops marched into the city. But that kind of damage did not cause lingering anger. Nor was the economy at the root of unpleasant memories. A *Chronicle* editorial on December 21, 1865 explained, "When the war ended Augusta was perhaps in better condition than any of the cities of this section of the South." The population had doubled, the summer trade was lucrative, and the town attracted new merchants. In fact, the federal officials found more hard currency in the town than they had seen elsewhere. When a statewide convention met in Milledgeville to draw up a new constitution, acting governor James Johnson had to borrow money from Augustans. Thomas S. Metcalf loaned the state $20,000 in gold at seven percent interest, William E. Jackson loaned $5,000, E.M. Bruce $10,000, C.F. McKay $5,000, and J.M. Newby $2,500.[1]

The city also relied on local businessmen in its return to solvency. Josiah Sibley went to New York to sell Augusta bonds to investors. William E. Jackson loaned the city $7,500. So the money was there to finance recovery, and there was never any lack of business acumen. The trauma that caused later generations to get angry just thinking about the reconstruction era was mainly psychological. In addition to the very real tragedy of lost lives and lost fortunes by some, for many the shock was the loss of the antebellum social philosophy. Augusta's prolific diarist Gertrude Clanton Thomas noted in her journal that Lee's defeat made her doubt the Bible; she had been convinced that God was on the side of the Confederacy.[2] It was not easy for a people reared in the belief that natural law divided society into classes to change their convictions. It would take several generations to get used to the idea that all men were equal under the law. Not even the male population of the victorious North was ready to acknowledge the fact that women were equal to men.

Insecurity, born of submission to new masters and a new social order, was aggravated by an over-crowded city. Federal troops kept reasonably good order, as most everyone admitted, but there was sporadic violence. It seemed that every man, black and white, went about armed. *The Chronicle* complained about the indiscriminate and casual shooting that went on. The most serious episode occurred on August 31, 1865 when three Augusta men shot Captain Alex Heasley, a white officer of a black regiment. The trial attracted intense interest and a local jury returned guilty verdicts against two of the men. William Phillips himself became a casualty when he was mugged by several white hooligans. A black man came to his rescue.[3] The January 1866 Grand Jury complained about the "reign of lawlessness" that prevailed and blamed it on the uncertainty as to who was in charge, the civil government or the military. Georgians had reason to hope that the restoration of state government in December 1865, and the election of Augustan Charles J. Jenkins as governor, would restore a sense of order.

Henry H. Cumming might also be regarded as a casualty of the war. He took his own life on April 14, 1866. His friend and neighbor Governor Charles J. Jenkins said that Cumming had accumulated heavy expenses during the war and moreover "the troubles of our suffering country also affected him."[4] His son Major Joseph B. Cumming was more explicit in his memoirs. He blamed the "procrastination" of William Cumming, the co-executor of Thomas Cumming's will, and the nephews who held Henry Cumming responsible for the loss of Thomas Cumming's legacy when the Bank of Augusta failed during the war. He faced a lawsuit from his nephews, and the prospect of leaving his wife in poverty was too much for his nervous system worn down by chronic melancholy.[5] The editor of *The Chronicle* spoke for most Augustans, "He was the soul of chivalry - sacrificing convenience and interest and lending the influence of his name to succor the weak and aid the friendless."[6]

On April 5, 1866 *The Chronicle* editors Henry Moore and General A.R. "Ranse" Wright called for the observance of a Confederate memorial day. The idea had a general appeal and on April 25 the city conducted a ceremony honoring the dead.

If not the first, it was certainly one of the first such memorial days. In honoring the fallen they laid the foundation for the tradition of the "Lost Cause." As the yearly celebrations were repeated, orators accentuated the positive virtues of the Old South and mentioned slavery less and less. By the Twentieth Century the antebellum South became in retrospect a land of plantations, chivalric gentlemen, gracious ladies, and happy black folk. Such things as factories, mill workers, and businessmen vanished from collective memory.

The post-bellum era in Augusta has been called the "Janus" era after the Roman god who had two faces, looking back and forward at the same time.[7] The individual who pointed the way forward was George W. Rains, as much a war hero as any of Augusta's fighting generals such as Lafayette McLaws, Ranse Wright, William Gibson, or even James Longstreet from Edgefield County across the river. On August 1, 1866 Mayor Abner Robertson invited Rains to speak to the City Council about the problem of recurring floods. The only logical way of preventing inundations, Rains said, was by building a levee along the riverfront. His suggestion showed how far ahead of the times he was. He would add a handsome esplanade along the top of the levee for people to enjoy. Then he added significant advice. The key to prosperity would be the enlargement of the canal. He believed that it could be done at a reasonable cost.[8]

William Phillips had said on several occasions that doubling the size of the canal was important, but he had to make do with raising dams and banks, and putting makeshift wasteboards on the aqueduct walls. Phillips had such a long list of improvements that needed to be done that the Council had stopped paying attention to his requests; however, they could hardly ignore Rains. John Foster, elected mayor late in the year

1866, acknowledged that Rains was right. Canal enlargement was "no doubt practicable and would result in great good to the city – but the present heavy drains on the treasury" prevented anything being done for the time being.[9]

William E. Jackson of the Augusta Factory, a hometown hero for his wartime donations of clothing and money to the poor, continued to feud with William Phillips about the lack of water in the canal. Phillips blamed the factory's inefficient machinery; Jackson blamed Phillips. Jackson persuaded the city council to give him the management of the canal for the year 1867-1868 as an experiment. Phillips was temporarily relegated to waterworks engineer. As it turned out, Jackson could not coax power out of the canal any better than Phillips could.

Political events took a turn for the worse during 1867. The Republicans in Congress hated the idea of the reconstructed southern states sending unrepentant Democrats to Washington. Their leaders felt that if they could guarantee the vote to black men, those voters would elect Republicans. So the House effectively removed President Andrew Johnson by the process of impeachment on a trumped-up charge. (The Senate failed to convict by one vote.) Then the leadership pushed through a harsh Reconstruction bill subjecting the former Confederate states to military occupation until the states ratified the Fourteenth Amendment conferring citizenship on all persons born or naturalized in the United States. In January General George Meade removed Governor Charles J. Jenkins from office and the military took control of the state. General John Pope appointed Foster Blodgett mayor of Augusta, and Rufus Bullock and Benjamin Conley, among others, to the Council.

The new administration retained William Phillips as waterworks engineer, and named P.S. Holden canal engineer, though William Jackson retained control during the experimental year. Phillips continued to worry about the canal. In February 1868 the Augusta Factory let the water out of the canal without informing Phillips. He warned the Council that the city water supply was thereby endangered, and if a fire had broken out, there might not be enough water in the system to fight it. "I mention this," Phillips said, " that in case of a failure the censure, if any, may be fixed in its proper place."[10] He meant William E. Jackson. Phillips kept busy with the extension of the waterworks. When Col. D.W. Flagler informed the city that the powder stored in the Powder Works had to be removed, Phillips volunteered to build a powder magazine. His plans were accepted and he constructed the magazine at the then city limits, Carnes Road (15th Street) and Summerville Plank Road (Walton Way).

Unfortunately, the apolitical Phillips became a victim of politics. At first, it seemed otherwise. When the Augusta Factory's contractual year expired, the Blodgett administration took over the management of the canal and restored William Phillips to his old job as canal engineer. Furthermore, the Council went on record on August 8, 1868 with the following resolution, "Resolved that in consideration of the faithful services of Mr. William Phillips for the last twenty years in the care and management of the Augusta canal, it is proper that the Council, in restoring him to the charge of that work, acknowledge in a substantial way their appreciation of his services."[11] By substantial acknowledgment they meant the gift of the canal office (the old office of the Cunningham Mills) for him to use as his place of residence. The restoration, the resolution and the residence all had the effect of identifying Phillips with the Blodgett administration.

During the year 1868 Foster Blodgett had become one of the city's most unpopular persons. Over four hundred citizens addressed a petition to General Meade, the military commander, asking him to remove Blodgett from office. Among other charges, the petitioners accused him and his Council of illegally lengthening their terms from one year to four years, raising the mayor's salary from $2,000 to $5,000, all while Blodgett retained the Postmaster's job and salary.[12] Perhaps worse in the minds of many, Blodgett chaired the Republican convention in 1868 and secured the nomination of his friends Rufus Bullock and Benjamin Conley as candidates for governor and lieutenant governor. They were subsequently elected. However, the Democrats retained control of the legislature and they pushed through a bill over the governor's veto setting municipal elections for December 1, 1868.

Blodgett's opponents formed "the People's Party" and chose Henry Russell as their candidate. Several prominent citizens stood for Council including William E. Jackson, J.V.H. Allen, William Tutt, James Gardiner, W.S. Jones, William H. Goodrich, and Josiah Sibley. Blodgett's supporters campaigned as "the Workingman's Party." Amid tension and excitement, with soldiers from the arsenal standing by in case of trouble, voters turned out on December 1 and elected Russell over Blodgett, 2,005 to 874. That night the victors celebrated with bonfires, fireworks and drum-beating.[13] Blodgett went off to Washington, complaining to Congress that the election had been stolen from him and asking for the return of federal troops.

On December 3, 1868 Judge Claiborne Snead administered the oath of office to the new mayor and councilmen. The first question facing the administration concerned the canal. Who controlled it? William Phillips was on hand to say that the last Board of Managers belonged to Mayor John Foster's administration prior to the appointment of the military government. To be safe, the Council entered upon the minutes of its meeting the December 19, 1849 act of the Georgia legislature giving the City Council control of the canal.

The first indication that William Phillips was in trouble occurred in a called meeting of the Council on New Year's Day, 1869. Phillips had hardly begun to give his usual lengthy report about the canal when he was curtly interrupted by Councilman William E. Jackson. The report was too long, Jackson said, Phillips could sit down.[14] That humiliation was outdone by a worse one on January 9th. Phillips was fired from his dual responsibilities at the canal and the waterworks. P.S. Holden was named Canal Engineer and Thomas Cumming, son of Henry H. Cumming, became Waterworks Engineer. The Council evicted Phillips from the house he had been given by the previous administration and charged him rent for the time he had spent there.

Perhaps William E. Jackson was not a vengeful man, but it certainly seems so. William Phillips had devoted his professional life to the care and maintenance of the canal. He did not deserve such cavalier treatment. A few years earlier he had suffered a tragic personal loss, ironically involving "his" canal. His wife Mary, only 38 years old, but sight impaired, drowned in the canal. It was thought that she had fallen while walking along its bank. Phillips, 64 years old when he was forced out of office, had only the love of his daughter Isabella to comfort him in the twilight of his life.[15]

With Phillips out, the fate of the canal itself hung in the balance. Councilman John U. Meyer emerged as the chief critic of the canal. He argued that the waterway cost more than it earned in water rent, and listed the expenditures over revenue since 1860. The Council posted a notice putting the canal up for sale to the highest bidder.[16] Thomas P. Stovall, proprietor of the Excelsior Mills, informed the Council on April 2nd that he had

Figure 28. After the accidental drowning of his wife, William Phillips' daughter Belle was the companion of his later years. *(Historic American Engineering Record)*

lined up a consortium of northern investors who were anxious to purchase the canal and invest a million dollars in enlarging it.[17] It was widely believed that a leading figure among those interested was Rhode Island Senator William Sprague, a notorious war profiteer. The thought that outsiders might control the canal and charge who knows what rent to the Augusta Factory alarmed William E. Jackson. The Council decided not to sell to Stovall's group and to screen other potential purchasers. The mayor appointed William Tutt as Chairman of the Committee for the Sale of the Canal.

Tutt's first action was to critique the canal operations, "After the completion of the canal at a cost of half a million dollars it was found inadequate to the wants for which it was intended, and only a limited amount of power could be obtained, thereby preventing the extent of manufacturing interest which is so important to the welfare of the city."[18] In other words, he blamed the canal, the catalyst for Augusta's industrialization, for hindering that same industrialization. Tutt's committee recommended opening competition for the immediate sale of the canal on the condition that it be enlarged so as to produce power for 80,000 spindles, and continue to supply water to the city. However, a growing number of Augustans objected to the sale of the canal. It did not occur to the Council to investigate the cost of enlarging the waterway until Col. George Rains suggested that such might be a good idea. He forwarded to the Council a bid from an engineer named Charles Mahone for a survey and an estimate of the cost for a fee of under $400. William Phillips, now referred to in the Council minutes as "ex-canal engineer," offered to do the survey. On the motion of William E. Jackson, his bid was received as information and ignored. Tutt's committee proceeded to contract with Charles

Mahone to draw up a plan for enlargement, and engaged an engineer named J. S. Williams to measure the flow of water.

The reports of Mahone and Williams were ready by November 1869, as was their request for an additional $700.[19] Their plan called for raising the dam and banks four feet and widening the canal by a hundred feet. The discharge would thereby be increased from 472 cubic feet per second to 1,690 cubic feet per second. Horsepower on the first level would go from 586 to 2,079. A seven-foot depth could be achieved for $384,093; eleven-foot depth for $395,236. Mahone's plan would have retained the Rae's Creek Aqueduct. William Tutt and his committee liked the plan, thought the cost acceptable and recommended that the city do the work rather than sell to outsiders. Mahone's plan, Tutt calculated, would provide power for thirteen more factories and give employment to 7,500 persons. However, it was already November with the Russell administration nearing its end. Tutt recommended that the incoming administration take action on the proposal. As a reminder and an incentive, Mahone's plat was framed and hung in the Council chamber.[20]

The new mayor did not need a reminder. Joseph Vicessimus Henry Allen had served on the previous Council and had heard all the arguments. A veteran of the war, he had served on the staffs of Generals W.H.T. Walker and Ambrose R. Wright. He was only thirty and proved to be popular with all segments of the population. On April 27, 1870 four thousand mostly black Augustans paraded to celebrate Georgia's ratification of the Fifteenth Amendment that conferred upon men of all races the right to vote. They carried a banner reading "Georgia Our Native State With All Thy Faults We Love Thee Still." The crowd stopped in front of Mayor Allen's house and gave him three cheers.[21]

The second occupation of Georgia by federal troops, pending the ratification of the Fifteenth Amendment, distracted attention from the canal, but on April 1, 1870 Allen recalled the Council's attention to the proposed enlargement, " I have long given the matter constant and serious reflection and deem it of primary importance to the best interests of every inhabitant of our city...we have within our reach the only means of adding to our personal wealth and population." He noted that the number of operatives at the Augusta Factory was 501 and estimated that their families added up to 2,000 persons. The city had an obligation to provide more work for the people of Augusta and the enlarged canal could do that. Besides, he said, the city was already threatened with lawsuits by mills that did not get a sufficiency of water. He reappointed William Tutt as chairman of a committee comprised of one person from each ward to move ahead on the project.[22]

The eager Tutt lost no time in carrying out his assignment. He had already made useful contacts in New York, so he had little trouble finding a contractor who would follow Mahone's plan for an estimated cost of $507,126. Furthermore the contractor would take city bonds at a reasonable eight percent interest in payment. Tutt showed the plan to William H. Grant, the engineer who carried out Frederick Law Olmsted's design for Central Park in New York City, and Grant thought the plan and the price were right. Tutt was buoyed by the congratulations of leading New York businessmen; "I am forced to believe that a prosperity unknown in the South is awaiting us if we carry on works of this character," Tutt told Council members. "The Manufacturers of the North are already looking with a jealous eye to the probability of the removal of...manufactories to the South."[23] Those northerners were prescient but premature. Tutt's canal committee voted unanimously for the proposal and recommended that on July 4, 1870 the question be put to a popular vote.

With so much momentum behind canal enlargement, it is difficult to understand why the movement came to a sudden halt. Perhaps Mayor Allen thought the risk too great. In any case he did not use his influence to promote the project any further. The initiative was seized by councilman James C.C. Black, chairman of the finance committee, who stated flatly that the city could not afford to undertake the project just then. The Council voted against the Tutt proposal.

William Tutt, a relentless entrepreneur (he later led the drive to build the Bon Air Hotel on the Hill), turned his energy into a campaign to bring the "Cotton States Mechanics and Agricultural Fair" to Augusta. Promising that the fair would bring "an immense throng" to the city, he asked for the Council to approve a donation of $15,000 to the project. Major James C.C. Black said that the city could not afford it, but this time was outvoted by the Council. The fair, not the canal, was the crowning achievement of the Allen administration. Every state from Maryland to Texas, and from Florida to Utah had an exhibit when the fair opened on October 26, and the expected throngs attended.[24]

It fell to Charles Estes, the new mayor, to resurrect the canal project. By accident of birth and by early experience he was well qualified to be the sponsor of the canal improvement. He was born in Jefferson County, New York, in 1819. As a youth he headed a construction gang working on the Genesee Valley Canal, a section of the famous Erie Canal. He moved to Augusta in 1844, the year that marked the genesis of the Augusta canal, and conducted a successful grocery business.[25] In his December 8, 1870 inaugural address he expressed his determination to increase the volume of water in the canal.

However, he disagreed with the estimate Tutt brought home from New York. Estes thought that Mahone's plan would cost nearly a million dollars, too much for the city to afford.[26]

Figure 29. Mayor Charles Estes.
(Courtesy of the Augusta Museum of History)

The issue rested for several months. Then on May 1, 1871 Councilman Thomas Barrett moved a resolution instructing the mayor to undertake a new study of canal enlargement. Estes welcomed the opportunity and took the well-traveled road to New York. Likely, he met the contacts William Tutt had made on the previous forays into that metropolis as well as some of his Erie Canal associates. One of these friends directed him to Charles A. Olmstead, another Erie Canal engineer; Estes liked him and hired him on the spot. The mayor returned to Augusta to tell the Council that Olmstead was "an engineer of fine abilities and large practical experience."[27]

Olmstead was also a remarkably fast worker. He arrived in Augusta on June 26, 1871 and toured the canal in the company of Mayor Estes and P.S. Holden.[28] Estes explained that the enlargement had to be done in such a way as to permit the continued operation of the existing canal. William E. Jackson and the other mill operators insisted on that. If the enlargement succeeded, Jackson promised to build a third mill adjacent to the first two. In addition Estes could report that a new company headed by James J. Gregg, son of Graniteville Mill founder William Gregg, was prepared to build a factory on the canal.[29] By August 7, Olmstead presented his complete report and a detailed estimate of the cost to the City Council. The work could be done for $371,610.56, even less that the Tutt Committee's estimate. Olmstead's contractor, John A. Green and Company, was ready to start work at once.

Mayor Estes was delighted; the councilmen caught his enthusiasm and set the first Wednesday in October for a public vote. Meanwhile Estes went back to New York and showed Olmstead's plans to some of his engineering friends. Everyone he spoke to thought the plan sound and the cost fair. Upon his return, his report helped win over some skeptics. The public vote on the issue was 781 to 147, an overwhelming endorsement of the mayor as well as Olmstead.

Estes asked Major Joseph B. Cumming, Henry Cumming's son and Speaker of the Georgia House, to introduce a bill authorizing the widening of the canal by the city. Cumming did so, and the bill became law on December 12, 1871. The Council instructed the mayor to bid for the Confederate Powder Works property when the government put that confiscated tract up for auction. Estes paid $10,000 for the Refinery site with its great chimney.[30] In recognition of all this good work Augustans reelected Estes for another term by a vote of 929 to one. Opposition had disappeared - for the time being.

Hikers along the canal today might wonder how Olmstead accomplished the feat of widening the canal while it continued to operate. He explained in some detail in his report to the Council. He divided the work into six sections. The first section extended 5,300 feet from the headgates. The new cut was entirely on the river side, its bank higher than the old parallel bank. When the water level was raised, the canal would overflow the old channel into the new. Where the bank came close to the river it would be protected by rip rap and stone walls. The second section was the same length and also independent of the existing canal. The third section was also the same length, but at 4,000 feet (the Rock Creek culvert) the new cut crossed the old canal; the remainder of the third section and 3,000 feet of the fourth section remained on the land side. At Warren Spring the new cut crossed back to the river side. For the last 700 feet of this section Olmstead said that there was nothing to be done because a hollow trench from a previous excavation would be used.

The fifth section of 5,300 feet followed the river side, at Warren Culvert the cut was on both sides, and from Warren's Creek the new ditch was on the land side. Near Rae's Creek the new line crossed back to the river side. The sixth and last section was the longest at 10,665 feet and was on the land side. Olmstead reckoned on a depth of eleven feet that would necessitate a higher dam and headgates. Another Erie Canal engineer, Byron Holley, designed the dam, headgates and locks. By May 1872 nearly 400 workers, almost all of them black, labored on the canal.

Curiously, Olmstead's original proposal did not include his best idea, that of using Rae's Creek Aqueduct as a dam. Only after beginning the new cut did he decide that it would be cheaper to block up the aqueduct rather than enlarge it, thus creating a new lake that would spill over into the canal.[31] The City Council approved the idea and honored the engineer by naming the lake after him. Plugging the huge culverts in the aqueduct required skillful stonework and for that Olmstead brought in experienced Italian stonemasons. A *Chronicle* reporter commented that Italians "are much preferred for this kind of labor than any other class of workmen."[32]

So far Estes could do no wrong. The government auctioned off additional Powder Works property on October 31, 1872, and the city bought it for $32,000. The mayor sold the machinery to a Tennessee businessman and planned to sell the estimated four million bricks to the builders of new factories. On November 4, the mayor invited Colonel Rains to come before the Council and relate the history of the Powder Works. Rains did so in his usual clear and articulate manner, then repeated an earlier request to the Council. He asked that his masterpiece, the tall obelisk chimney "be allowed to remain forever as a fitting monument to the dead heroes who sleep on the unnumbered battlefields of the South."[33] The Council was pleased to do so. Today the only extant structure built by the Confederate States of America is that majestic chimney.

Estes had no opponent in the 1872 elections. In his inaugural he said he would have retired except for his deep interest in "the one great work now in progress."[34] By the end of the year 1872 one-third of the estimated cost had been spent, and Estes predicted that the final tally would be within $50,000 of the original bid. On June 2, 1873 the first of the expected new industries applied for canal waterpower. Former mayor Henry Russell and C.W. Simmons of Rhode Island bought a portion of the Powder Works property from the city, and an additional ten acres across the canal for workers' cottages. They also bought 300,000 bricks from the city and began construction on July 1, 1873. The Russell and Simmons Factory began turning out cotton rope, yarn, and twine on January 1, 1874.[35]

Another cheering development in 1873 was the flooding

of Lake Olmstead. The lake began to fill in late April of that year. On May 7, *The Chronicle* enthused, "The lake affords the finest racing grounds for aquatic sports to be found in the South, and we doubt not that it will soon be dotted over with pleasure and race boats by our clubs and others who will not be slow to discover its beauties."[36] The first sailboat was canal engineer P. J. Kenny's "Home Made," launched in June. In July it was joined by the "New York Clipper" and the "Sallie." Indeed, the lake soon became dotted with pleasure craft.

Another development in that year titillated locals. The word went around in October that Chinese workers were coming to Augusta. Very likely no one in the entire region had seen a Chinese person. China had shut itself off from contact with the rest of the world until the British began trade in 1844. The first Chinese workers had been brought to this country during the Civil War to work on the transcontinental railroad. The famous railroad was finished in 1869 and the agents of the Chinese workers looked for other projects. Undoubtedly, the men coming to Augusta had first worked on the railroad. On October 24, 1873 *The Chronicle* announced that the canal contractor had engaged the services of about 200 Chinese men. In an understatement, the news item read, "Their presence will be a novelty in our community." A crowd gathered at the depot to gawk at the curiously dressed men wearing their hair in pigtails when they arrived on November 4.

Olmstead put the first contingent of thirty-five at work on the headgates. Despite their small stature, they carried heavy loads and worked quickly. On November 14 a reporter interviewed a worker named L.A. Sam. The man had been in this country only four years, but he spoke English "wonderfully well." By November 15 about 250 Chinese were on the job. The foreman of the crew asked a reporter to let him see the daily paper. "I see currency is going up and gold is going down," he said. The man, Ah Sin, had managed to save enough of his seven dollars a month salary to invest in gold shares. In addition to the new arrivals Olmstead used convict labor, mostly black, who wore striped uniforms and were chained together at night. In all over 400 men worked at the enlargement as the year ended.

There is no doubt that some of the Chinese men remained in Augusta after their work on the canal ended. In 1881 a *Chronicle* reporter referred to the Chinese Exclusion Bill then before Congress and subsequently enacted, and commented that an Augusta Chinese man would not be bothered by the law. Willie Loo Chong was already a prosperous merchant with a shop on Broad Street and in 1881 he married Miss Denise Fulcher of McBean, Richmond County. When another Chinese man, Thomas Willy, married white Anna Niece in the same year, *The Chronicle* noted that while white and black marriages were forbidden by law, the law was silent on the subject of Chinese marriages. The men married both white and black women. By 1886 the *Atlanta Constitution* ran a feature story on the Augusta Chinese. "Augusta is their paradise," the account ran, "and they seem to thrive there." Lee Ting, an Augusta merchant, said that the newspaper's estimate of hundreds of Chinese in Augusta was "picturesquely inexact." *The Chronicle* estimated that there were about thirty shops, mostly grocery stores in town. Some merchants were alarmed at the competition and asked the City Council to turn down future licenses. The Council refused to do so.[37]

Although Estes was again elected, the first public criticism was voiced in January 1874. The Second Ward Democratic Club made a formal request to the City Council asking for the total estimated cost of the project, and if there were any legal limit on the amount of money the city could spend. The Council took the request seriously and promised to publish the costs within two weeks. Olmstead was put in a bind. He was asked for the figures on January 10th and told that they were needed by the 14th. He did some quick arithmetic, and concluded that the cost would probably be $496,886, an amount equaling the Mahone estimate. City Attorney James C. C. Black gave his legal opinion that because the people had voted approval, and the legislature had conferred authority on the city to do the work, that in effect the city could spend whatever it took to finish the job. The "blank check" opinion alarmed many taxpayers.[38]

James J. Gregg secured the backing of several British businessmen, as well as Augustans including Charles Estes, and organized the Augusta Land Company. The company bought the land opposite the Schuetzenplatz, the new park built by Augusta's German community. The purchase included land between the Summerville Plank Road (Walton Way) and Washington Road. The company proceeded to divide the area into lots in anticipation of new mills to be built along the canal. The section came to be known as the West End though parts of it were popularly referred to as Rollersville and Hicksville from neighborhood property owners. A Boston newspaper took notice of the development and marveled that the new canal would be the largest in the country in volume of water; it could run all the mills in Lowell and Lawrence combined.[39] Estes' participation in the land company caused his critics to complain about his profiteering.

However, most Augustans stayed with Charles Estes and reelected him in 1874 for the following year. In his inaugural address he announced that the enlargement would be completed in 1875; only the bulkhead and the dam remained to be finished under Byron Holley's supervision. The stone headgates had seventeen slide gates that could be worked by a single person operating the iron gears. The lock featured mitre-swing gates similar to those on the Erie Canal. In 1875, with the work nearly complete, Holley left to oversee construction of the Vaucluse Mill in South Carolina.[40]

The new channel had been tested, some weak places discovered and repaired. Estes presented a report from an engineer named W.W. Thomas whom he had engaged to study the possibility of steamboat navigation on the upper Savannah River. Clearing the river for large craft would be impossibly expensive, Thomas reported. Instead he recommended widening openings in the rapids at a few points to facilitate the passage of Petersburg boats. At the time there were about eighteen such boats on the river, averaging forty feet in length and six feet wide. Each could carry 20,000 pounds of cargo. It usually took two days to make the dangerous run from McCord's place at Lisbon through the rapids, then three days of grueling poling by the six-man crew to return upriver.[41] The fact that Estes even thought seriously about running steamboats on the upper Savannah reveals much about his bold ambitions for the city and the canal.

Though boats ran on the canal, and the Augusta Boat Club held races on the wider course in July 1875, the work on the headgates and dam was still not finished as the year 1875 ended. On October 23, 1875 a party in opposition to the Estes administration was formed. The group included prominent individuals such as former mayor J. V. H. Allen, *Chronicle* editor Henry G. Wright, Houghton School principal Martin Calvin, Louis A. Dugas, Jr., and an old critic, John Phinizy. The cruelest cut was delivered by Henry Wright who called Estes "another Blodgett." The meeting adopted the resolution that "the administration of the present Mayor of Augusta is an emphatic failure."[42] As the annual election neared, the comments grew nasty.

"Citizen" wrote to the editor of the newspaper to assert that the Erie Canal had been a swindle and that Estes brought Erie engineers to Augusta to do another swindle.[43]

On November 1, 1875 Estes defused at least some of the criticism by disclosing that the canal improvements cost $750,000. In reality, all expenses were covered by city bonds and no additional taxes were needed. The expense placed no burden on the business or labor classes of the city. "It is just as if the money had been paid by the Bank of England," he said. He refused to blame Olmstead who by now had left Augusta to assume the position of Western Division Engineer of the Erie Canal, saying that the engineer had done his best to keep the cost down. He stressed the positive; two small mills and a large one had been started already. He looked forward to the day "when will be awarded the credit due to every citizen who has favored the project."[44] Estes was reelected over Lewis D. Ford, but it would be a while before he received the credit due him.

Estes had called for increasing the term of mayor from one to three years and the legislature finally obliged. He did not stand for the first election under the new regulation in 1876 and it did not bode well for him that a leading critic of canal expenses, John U. Meyer, won over wartime mayor Robert May, 1,562 to 1,410. Out-going Mayor Estes wished Meyer well, "I believe you will be able to perform the duties of the Office with greater satisfaction to the Citizens than it has been my lot to do."[45] In retrospect it seems a shame that Estes, who had done so much for the public good, left office feeling a failure.

The recriminations began almost immediately. On January 1, 1877 Councilman Wilberforce Daniel opened the Council meeting with the statement that "there had been much dissatisfaction expressed by the community in regard to the actions by the late mayor with reference to canal enlargement."[46]

He called for a detailed review of the whole process. Some objected to the insinuation of wrong-doing by Estes, and the vote split six to six. Mayor John Meyer broke the tie by voting for the investigation. Daniel was named chair of the committee to look into the matter.

Of course, Charles Estes took offense at the implication of malfeasance and said so in a letter to Daniel. Daniel replied that "Mr. Estes had certainly treated the Citizens of Augusta with great Disrespect...in retiring from office without making a detailed report to the people."[47] Now his committee intended to find the true cost "from the incipiency to the end of the Estes administration." Actually, the committee began not with "the incipiency" but as recently as the Allen administration. Meyer was made to look good by the committee's finding that, as a Council member, he had voted for enlargement only if the cost did not exceed Olmstead's estimate of $371,610. In the end, the committee had to accept Estes's statement of direct costs of $725,389, and add all the indirect costs they could find, including the cost of damages and repairs, real estate purchases, commission fees, losses on the sale of city bonds, and losses on city stock in the Macon and Augusta Railroad. They arrived at a grand total of $972,883.

Having found nothing wrong, the committee voiced only a mild disapproval, "We are constrained to believe, however, that the people voted for this enlargement under the impression that it would not cost any large sum." The committee put a positive spin on their report by expressing the hope that "this great work may be speedily utilized, and that the people of our city may obtain a rich return from their investment."[48] Charles Estes was left to wonder whether he was being held responsible for something wrong or given credit for something good.

As this chapter on the enlargement ends, it is appropriate

Figure 30. New headgates, lock and dam, constructed as part of the 1875 enlargement of the canal. *(Courtesy of the Augusta Museum of History)*

to take note of the career of the canal's most loyal caretaker, William Phillips. Mayor Estes helped Phillips financially by hiring him for specific jobs. In April 1874 Phillips completed a report for the city entitled "Report upon the Topography and Hydrography in the Vicinity of Augusta, Ga." The paper, not published until 1892, contained much useful information about drainage and flood protection, two topics that would continue to plague Augusta. He proposed, as Col. Rains had done, the construction of a levee of approximately six miles, costing about $1,500,000. An alternative would be the building of a series of reservoirs in the upper Savannah River. His first recommendation would be acted upon in 1913, the second would wait upon the construction of the Clarks Hill, Russell, and Hartwell reservoirs.

Phillips' unfailing good nature showed through the technical report. He wrote, "As an engineer, I can raise no question with Providence - for three score and ten it has dealt fairly with me, and I am now, as ever, perfectly willing to accept its decrees."[49] Those words would have been an ideal valedictory, but in September Phillips again needed work and approached Estes with a proposal to do a new map of the city. The Council failed to act on the proposal until March 1875 when it authorized the mayor to have a new map made "by a competent engineer." Fearing that he might be overlooked, Phillips sent Estes a petition that must have caused him some humiliation, asking the city to help him in his old age, either with work or with a donation. The Council accepted Phillips' bid of $2,612 to do the map.

The resulting map of Augusta in 1875 is a masterpiece and a legacy to students of Augusta history. For example, the map shows the factories along the downtown portion of the canal in 1875. The Granite Mill (later the Enterprise) is across the canal from the city waterworks. Schley's flour mill lies between the second and third level and its raceway flows into the third level near Sacred Heart Church. The many buildings of the Augusta Factory sprawl out between 13th and 12th Streets. The "Old Machine Works" is between the second and third levels at 8th Street, and the Crescent Mills are at the terminus of the second level and the beginning of the third level. On the third level at Calhoun Street (later Walton Way) is Coopers Foundry adjacent to the Gas Works. The waterworks pump house lies between the second and third level near 10th Street, a nearby foundry faces 11th Street. Two flour mills, the Excelsior and the Paragon, are between the second and third levels bounded by 11th and 12th Streets. Across 11th Street and between the second and third levels is the Southern Cross Mill.[50]

Phillips approached the Council once again. On February 5, 1877 he asked the city to employ him in selling his maps. He offered to return two dollars out of every five to the city.[51] He did not have much time for this latest venture. He died on November 13, 1877. He would be remembered for his maps, and for his long service as caretaker of the canal, but his most important contribution to the people of Augusta was the waterworks system, a system that he correctly predicted would never be finished.

CHAPTER NINE

The Big Boom, 1875-1890

<hr/>

T he boom years following the enlargement of the canal were the canal's most productive, and in many ways, most exciting. Robert Spude, a historian working for the Historic American Engineering Record, concluded that the Augusta Canal "contributed to making Augusta an envied manufacturing center. Indeed, during the 1880's the canal and the mills along its banks served as example for the rest of the South."[1] New factories mushroomed, farm families flocked into the "mill villages" to find work, the city's population more than doubled from 15,389 in 1870 to 33,300 in 1890. The canal vindicated its boosters and silenced its critics. The boom brought new issues to be solved, from social concerns such as workers' rights to practical problems such as water supply.

The rise of the Enterprise Mill is perhaps the most interesting story of the boom period, not only because of its transition from a flour mill to a textile factory, but also because of its

Figure 31. The mighty looms of the Enterprise Mill symbolize Augusta's industrial boom. *(Courtesy of Historic American Engineering Record)*

remarkable transformation at the end of the Twentieth Century into one of Augusta's showplaces. Its history encompasses that of the canal itself. It will be recalled that James Coleman's gristmill was the first to begin operating on the canal, in 1848. Coleman also constructed a stone building on the site and called it his "Granite Mill." *The Chronicle* hailed it as an "elegant structure" in 1850. The unlucky Coleman had to mortgage his mill, and his brother-in-law Benjamin Warren bought it at a sheriff's sale, to the immense annoyance of Coleman. Warren operated the flour mill for a decade, then sold it to George T. Jackson, brother of William E. Jackson of the Augusta Factory. Jackson enlarged the mill and diversified its uses. An 1874 letterhead of George T. Jackson and Company lists some of the company's products: flour, meal grits, middling fine feed, bran and pea meal.[2]

The Calvert Lith Co Detroit.

Figure 32. Sketch of Coleman's Granite Mill after acquisition by George T. Jackson. *(Courtesy of the Augusta Museum of History)*

In 1876, George and William Jackson decided to take advantage of the increased waterpower afforded by the enlarged canal. They contacted Jones Davis, a mill superintendent in Holyoke, Massachusetts and a rare individual who promised much and improved on his promises. He said that he had built up four towns in Massachusetts and could do the same for Augusta. The Enterprise and Sibley Mills are a lasting testimonial to his ability as an architect. With Davis under contract, the Jacksons organized the Enterprise Manufacturing Company on March 10, 1877 with a capital of $150,000. Major stockholders other than the Jackson brothers included Charles Estes, H.M. Clark, James A. Gray, and Francis Cogin, the superintendent of the Augusta Factory. George Jackson as president of the Enterprise Mill purchased the Granite Mill from himself as George T. Jackson and Company.[3]

Jones Davis designed a three-story brick building with a central stairwell tower in the fashionable French Second Empire style. Wisely, Davis installed two vertical turbines for twice the immediate need. Work began on March 22, 1877, a tribute to the swiftness of the Jacksons' planning process. The first floor held 242 looms, the second had 14 British carding machines, and ten "mule" spinning frames of 13,892 went into the third floor. The mill began operations on March 2, 1878. Davis the architect became Davis the manager. Under his supervision the mill delighted its stockholders by producing sheeting valued at $42,303 in the first six months. On February 23, 1881 the stockholders voted a 10% dividend and increased the capital stock to $500,000. The new subscription was quickly bought by investors from New York and Boston. An addition, nearly identical with the original section, doubled the size and capacity of the factory. Jones and Dutcher's history of Augusta, published in 1890, said that the Enterprise produced the finest cloth made in the South and sold it to markets in the North. During the fiscal year 1884 the mill employed 466 hands and produced 31,295 yards of cloth per day.[4]

The year 1884 brought a stunning surprise to all those connected with the Enterprise. George T. Jackson and Company declared bankruptcy in October, and in December the Enterprise stockholders learned that their company was well over $200,000 in debt. George T. Jackson blamed the losses on the national slowdown. However, he could not account for the delinquency. His trial in May 1885 created a sensation, locally and throughout the state. Jackson employed a team of Augusta's best lawyers, J.C.C. Black, H.D.D. Twiggs, and Joseph R. Lamar (the future Supreme Court Justice). Representing the prosecution were an equally talented team, Major Joseph B. Cumming and Boykin Wright. The jury might have been swayed by Jackson's pleas of innocence except that the bookkeeper N. W. Armstrong testified that he had not destroyed Jackson's fraudulent checks as he had been ordered to do. He produced the damaging evidence that Jackson had embezzled $271,000. The jury promptly delivered a guilty verdict and Jackson was sentenced to six years in the penitentiary. He was pardoned after serving two years.[5]

Francis Cogin took over management of the mill during the emergency. The company issued $250,000 in new stock to cover the losses and most of it was taken by Augustans Alfred Baker, Boykin Wright and George Lombard. The stockholders elected James P. Verdery president. In 1888 Verdery added a weaving room to the factory, allowing for a total of 904 looms and 33,000 spindles. The mill soon regained its profitability.[6]

Figure 33. The Enterprise Mill after completion. Notice the Granite Mill to the left. *(Augusta Canal Authority Archives)*

The Enterprise was the most visible example of the upgrading of antebellum canal structures, but there were others. William M. Hight operated the 1852 machine works during the Civil War and sold out to Lufburrow and Timmons in 1865. The new owners did business under the name Forest City Foundry. In 1869 George D. Lombard gained control of the company. Although George D. died the following year, his son

Figure 34. The George R. Lombard & Company Foundry, established in 1870, cast various machine parts and specialized in boilers. *(Photo courtesy of the Augusta Museum of History)*

George R. Lombard maintained the company under his own name, George R. Lombard and Company. The number of employees increased from fifteen to forty by 1878 and to 125 by 1887. The factory turned out various kinds of machinery but specialized in boilers. The company absorbed another early foundry, the Pendleton and Boardman. William Pendleton, who served Colonel Rains well as supervisor of the Confederate Powder Works, went into business with a man named Boardman as his partner in 1867 in a shop on the second level of the canal. The foundry produced turbines, gears and farm machinery. In 1882 Charles F. Lombard bought control of the company with Pendleton as superintendent. As business increased the plant expanded to employ forty-eight workers. In 1894 Charles F. and George R. Lombard united their foundries under the name Lombard Ironworks.[7]

The Augusta Machine Works, the first operation to be built on the second level of the canal, attained its greatest significance as the Confederate Machine Works during the war. The

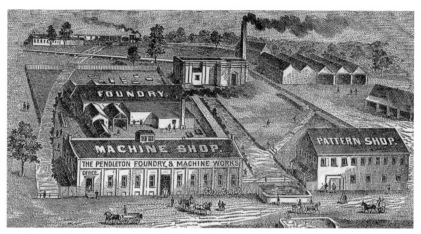

Figure 35. The Lombard Ironworks acquired the Pendleton Foundry in 1894. *(Augusta Canal Authority Archives)*

property was confiscated by the United States government after the war and auctioned to James A. Gray. Gray obtained a charter to operate the plant as a cotton factory under the name "Dublin Mills," but failed in his efforts to finance the company. In 1889 a lumber company headed by William Stillwell bought the property and did business as the Augusta Lumber Company.[8]

Figure 36. The boilers at Enterprise Mill. Manufactured by Lombard Iron Works in 1905. *(Courtesy of Historic American Engineering Record)*

The same James A. Gray who failed to attract investors to his Dublin Mills bought out the Russell and Simmons Mill, with his partner George P. Curry. The Russell and Simmons claim to distinction rests solely on the fact that it was the first to operate upon the enlarged canal, commencing on January 1, 1874. Gray changed the name to Summerville Mills, and added a third story to the main building as well as two shops in the back. The improved facility had 4,000 spindles and 150 looms. A hundred workers turned out checked and striped cloth. After Gray's death in 1880, Curry bought out Gray's interest, but could not repay his loans during the slowdown of 1884. He had to sell the mill to Stewart Phinizy, who happened to be president of the Augusta Factory at the time. The change in ownership brought on another name change, this time the works became the Algernon Mill. It happened again in 1894, when new owners changed the name to the Iasetta Mill.[9]

Alfred Baker's 1859 flour mill was operated during the war by Thomas Stovall as the Excelsior Mill. Jones and Dutcher described it as a five-story building "of honorable age, highest repute, and admitted excellence."[10] Robert Thompson of Nashville, Tennessee, converted the Paragon Flour Mill just west of the Excelsior into a cottonseed oil plant and it functioned as the Augusta Cotton Seed Oil Mill well into the Twentieth Century.[11]

The Dartmouth Spinning Company was incorporated in 1886 with a capital of $100,000, all of it northern money. Charles A. Maxwell designed the three-story building, which was located immediately to the east of the Enterprise Mill and constructed in the same year. The mill employed a hundred workers turning out yarn in various sizes. The usually effusive *Chronicle* congratulated the new arrival on the canal, "No mill is more perfectly built and equipped than the Dartmouth Yarn

Mill." The Dartmouth changed ownership in 1893 when it became the Sutherland Manufacturing Company. It was destined to participate in the renaissance of the Enterprise Mill in the 1990's.[12]

The largest of the new mills, the Sibley and the King, the two giants that line the canal as Augusta enters the 21st Century, stand as testimony to the daring of the businessmen of the New South era. The simultaneous construction of two such plants, when more nervous citizens wondered if there was enough of a demand to support one, was a venture in boldness seldom equaled in Augusta's history.

On March 10, 1877 Josiah Sibley applied for a portion of the old Confederate Powder Works tract. Later that same year, the Cumming Manufacturing Company also applied for

Figure 37. Josiah Sibley.
(Courtesy of the Augusta Museum of History)

the tract, specifically for that section on which the great chimney stood. Charles Estes, whose name appears in several enterprises of the era, assured the City Council as president of the Cumming Company, that his company would allow the chimney to remain, and perhaps even incorporate it into the company's new plant.[13] Estes and Sibley were too practical to quarrel over which company should occupy the site. They combined forces as the Sibley Manufacturing Company and dissolved the Cumming Company.

Josiah Sibley engaged Jones Davis, superintendent of the Enterprise, to design his new building. The resulting sketch delighted all who saw it. *The Augusta Chronicle* described the proposed factory as "one of the handsomest affairs that we have ever seen."[14] With interest running high, Wallace T. Wheless chaired a public meeting soliciting investors. He suggested that the mill be named after Josiah Sibley. An invitation was sent to "gentlemen of financial strength" to purchase stock. Investors who met on January 13, 1880 included a who's who of business leaders: Charles Estes, Patrick Walsh, Wallace Wheless, H.H. Hickman, John S. Davidson, Z. McCord, Edward Porter Alexander, Thomas G. Barrett, William C. Sibley, Charles H. Phinizy, R. A. Fleming, Robert H. May, H.H. Steiner, George T. Jackson (not yet fallen from grace), E. R. Schneider, A. Backer, George R. Sibley, William H. Barrett, Marcellus A. Stovall, James G. Bailie, H. Allen, John Wallace and Jones Davis. They elected Josiah Sibley president. Patrick Walsh's *Augusta Chronicle*, as much a cheerleader for Augusta as Henry Grady's *Atlanta Constitution* was for Atlanta, hoped that all the $500,000 initial issue of stock would be subscribed in Augusta, "Let us stop calling on Hercules for help when we are able – if we are willing – to help ourselves." However willing Augustans were, they could only manage $160,000, and that with the help of some investors in Savannah and Charleston. Josiah and William Sibley secured the rest from New York and Cincinnati. The Cincinnati investors were treated to a ride up the canal by barge and a barbecue at the pavilion.[15]

At a stockholders meeting on May 26, 1880 Josiah Sibley yielded the presidency to his son William. Construction proceeded rapidly under architect Jones Davis. He broke ground on June 1, 1880; on October 13 William Sibley's daughter Pearl laid the "corner brick" in lieu of a cornerstone. Sibley and Davis went to Lowell to buy the latest mill machinery. On October 27, 1880 a reporter had a preview of the interior of the factory and sounded the proper "booster" opinion that the Sibley was the "finest single mill in the world." He admitted that there were some grumblers who thought that money had been wasted on unnecessary decorations. However, most took pride in the neo-gothic building with its crenelated roofline that they said resembled the Houses of Parliament in London. The mill built houses for its workers along Pearl Avenue, an avenue named for Sibley's daughter.

Figure 38. Jones Davis' masterwork, the Sibley Mill.
(Augusta Canal Authority Archive)

Workers flocked into Augusta, driven from the farm by low yields on cotton and drawn by the promise of work for every member of the family. The grand opening of the mill on February 22, 1882 was an occasion for a civic celebration, with hundreds of curious townspeople touring the mill.[16]

The Sibley drew visitors from out of state, especially from New England. The cost of waterpower from the canal at $5.50 per horsepower per year was far less than anywhere in the North, a fact that intrigued potential investors. The Boston *Journal of Commerce* carried an interesting story about the Sibley construction. It reported correctly that the grounds on which it stood were historic, that a revolutionary battle had been fought there. As mentioned previously in this narrative, Lt. Col. Thomas Brown, the King's Ranger, had withstood a four-day siege by Elijah Clark's Georgians in a house on the same grounds. The Boston paper reported that the remains of British officers had been excavated on the site, their insignia of rank still on their uniforms. According to the article, a hospital had also been located on the tract and bodies of two nurses had been unearthed. The old United States Arsenal had been located on the tract, and it had an infirmary, so there may have been some truth to the Boston report. However, no one in Augusta seemed to have heard about the discoveries.[17]

The Sibley had disappointing returns during its first few years, posting its first dividend in 1887. After that the mill returned handsome profits to stockholders. Historian Robert C. Jorgensen wrote that "The last fifteen years of the 19th Century saw the Sibley Manufacturing Company grow into one of the best operated and managed mills in the country."[18]

After the dissolution of the Cumming Manufacturing Company, Charles Estes was not content to play the role of passive stockholder in the Sibley. In a city of boosters, he was both a booster and a doer. He had managed the enlargement and was determined that the canal would live up to the expectations he had set for it. The June 2, 1882 *Chronicle* reported that Estes had obtained a charter for a new mill and that he and James P. Verdery had left for New York – familiar territory for Estes – to interest investors in their project. Estes' contemporaries, Charles C. Jones, Jr. and Salem Dutcher, complimented him in their 1890 history of Augusta, "When this enterprise was inaugurated there were those who doubted whether the mill would ever be built, but with Mr. Charles Estes, to whom, by universal consent, the work of organizing the company was entrusted, there is no such word as fail, and in an incredibly short space of time the John P. King Manufacturing Company was an accomplished fact."[19]

Estes paid John P. King the compliment of naming the mill after him even though King was not involved in the project. However, as head of the Georgia Railroad Bank, King had a significant role in the industrialization of Augusta, and King was one of the most admired men in the city. After graduating from Richmond Academy, King had the good fortune to study law under Mayor and U.S. Senator Freeman Walker, and to inherit Walker's lucrative law practice. King traveled in Europe and on the return voyage struck up a friendship with the Marquis de Lafayette. King later welcomed the hero to Augusta when Lafayette visited the city in 1825. After serving eight years in the United States Senate, King accepted the presidency of the Georgia Railroad and Banking Company in 1841. He formed a friendship with engineer J. Edgar Thomson and helped Henry Cumming secure Thomson's services for the first canal survey. King retired from the bank in 1878.

In his generous gesture to King, Estes attached a highly respected name to a risky venture. At the April 15, 1882 cornerstone ceremony the 83-year-old Judge King thanked his audience but acknowledged that the credit for the enterprise belonged to Estes.[20]

Either because he had heard some complaints about the money spent on ornamentation of the Sibley, or because of his natural conservatism, Estes instructed engineer John D. Hill to design a functional but unpretentious building. Hill, superintendent of the Eagle and Phenix Mill in Columbus, Georgia, obliged. King Mill's row of wooden houses for its operatives, and Sibley's brick townhouses, transformed the area around the 1897 Ezekiel Harris House, known at the time as the Walker House. "Once the Walker House stood alone," noted a *Chronicle* reporter, "today it is surrounded by dwellings and stores and several churches."[21]

Mayor Robert May, the wartime mayor who returned to office to succeed John U. Meyer, warned his Council that the village of Summerville might be tempted to annex Harrisburg. "Immense factories are springing up like magic along the banks of our grand waterpower, the Augusta Canal, and with them comes a large and increasing population," he urged that

Figure 39. The John P. King Mill, one of the largest southern cotton mills, had fewer architectural trimmings than its neighbor, the Sibley. *(Augusta Canal Authority Archives)*

Augusta, rather than "a rival government," embrace the mill community. The State legislature approved the Council's request and in 1883 Augusta's limits were extended to include Harrisburg, Rollersville, Hicksville, and Woodlawn, creating a Fifth Ward.[22]

The King Mill was unlucky in that it began operation during a national depression in 1884. The Summerville Mills failed that year, and George T. Jackson's peculations almost brought down the Enterprise. The Jackson scandal was followed by another. The Bank of Augusta failed and its president, William S. Roberts, was charged with grand larceny. When the Grand Jury returned an indictment, Roberts cut his own throat in a suicide attempt. He recovered but faced a jail sentence. The *Atlanta Constitution* commented on the mood in Augusta as the year 1884 ended. The article stated that a few months previously no city in the South, presumably including Atlanta, gave "a brighter promise" of prosperity than Augusta. Now, it described an air of "stagnation" that seemed to have settled over the city. "The cavalier blood of the old regime, fiery enough on a point of honor, but sluggish in the channels of trade, still courses through southern veins."[23]

The remark calls for a moment's reflection. It indicates that the cult of the "Lost Cause" had begun to settle upon the southern psyche. The desire to become gentlemanly planters and aristocratic ladies was as real as any aspiration could have been in the old South. The myth of the "Lost Cause" simply took the aspiration as fact and depicted the antebellum South as a land of cavaliers and ladies, with everyone happily in the proper place. The Lost Cause was nostalgia for a way of life that very few attained. However, a corollary of the Lost Cause, the notion that the pre-war men in power were planters and the post-war leaders were businessmen, has taken root even among historians. The respected C. Vann Woodward represented the thinking when he wrote that the term "Bourbon," meaning the restoration of the old leaders after the Reconstruction, was as much a misnomer as the term "Indian" for Native Americans. The history of the Augusta Canal demonstrates that the same men occupied positions of civic and business leadership before, during and after the war. The *Atlanta Constitution* reporter had it wrong. The blood of Augustans had never been sluggish in the channels of trade. The canal and the great mills still stand testimony to that fact.

The social changes that accompanied the mill explosion in Augusta has drawn the attention of historians. Lee Ann Whites has questioned the assumption that mill owners were paternalistic towards their workers. She notes that much of the good work attributed to the male executives was actually per-formed by their wives. She asks the interesting question, if the mill managers assumed the mantle of paternalism, where did that leave the male mill workers? Traditionally women and children dominated Augusta's labor force. Whites quotes an Augusta Factory spokesman as saying, "The men do very little work except to watch the others and take care of the labor of the machinery. The actual operatives are nearly all female."[24] However, corresponding to the rise of the new mills, the pro-portion of men increased. In the case of the Augusta Factory the number of men went from 23% in 1880 to 39% in 1890. Her answer to her own question was that the male workers joined the union aptly named the Knights of Labor, thus claiming the right to protect their families even as did the knights of old.

In a study of public education in Richmond County, this writer touched on the efforts of Superintendent Lawton B. Evans to open schools in the mill district. In his 1883 report to the Board of Education he chided members for operating all its schools in rented buildings. He persuaded the Board to erect its first school in the area serving the Augusta Factory and the Enterprise Mill, and gave it the name of the first Board President, John S. Davidson. Evans expressed frustration at the fact that the children who should have been in school were at work in the mills. Those who did attend school had to leave to take a lunch pail to their parents at work. Henry Hicks of "Hicksville," a section of Harrisburg, offered Evans a room above his saloon as a school. The teacher soon complained that the noise from below was so loud that the children learned more from below than above.

William Sibley provided a building for the Fifth Ward School near his factory and Evans named the Reverend W.E. Perryclear as principal. Evans said that Perryclear was not much of a preacher and not much of a principal, "Still he was a decent sort of fellow and needed a job and there was no reason why he should not have it in those days when anybody that needed work was fit for the classroom." As it turned out, Perryclear was not "fit" for the classroom. He applied the strap so liberally that his seventh grade students rebelled; they told him that they intended to beat him up when he left the building. The reverend principal decided to remain inside until dark. He then went home and sent his letter of resignation to Evans, who managed to find a person better suited for the job.[25]

The mill children remained a source of concern for Evans. The school taught the children and the children taught the parents. "It seemed to me pathetic," Evans recalled, "when I saw a little child nine or ten years of age on the porch Sunday morning reading out loud of a third or fourth reader to a mother and father."[26] When Lawton Evans complained publicly that children as young as seven could not come to school because they had to work, William Sibley defended his mill's policy.

Figure 40. Young operative at Enterprise Mill, typical of the children who worked in Augusta's factories. *(Courtesy of the National Archives at College Park, Still Picture Branch)*

The Sibley did not employ children under ten, he said, and none worked for less than 35 cents a day. Sibley, whose wife was a leading temperance crusader and who himself had sworn off drinking, blamed fathers who made their children work for whiskey money.[27]

Not many of Augusta's public figures criticized child labor or any other mill policy. Judge H.D.D. Twiggs was one who did. A brilliant lawyer who was not afraid to challenge prevailing opinion, Twiggs upset many in 1882 by announcing that he intended to run for a seat in the U. S. House of

Representatives because the Democratic candidate preferred to talk about white supremacy instead of real issues. He said that voters should have a choice between "the irritating issues of the past" and issues relating to a progressive future. He regretted that a spirit of intolerance threatened the growth of the region. Nervous Democratic leaders persuaded Twiggs to withdraw his candidacy in the interest of party harmony.

A year earlier Twiggs alarmed the establishment by introducing a bill in the Georgia legislature that would hold factories liable for injuries sustained by workers on the job. His concern, he said, was for the many women and for the children, "the helpless little waifs upon the sea of life." His action provoked an emergency meeting of mill executives at the Augusta Factory. Chairman H.H. Hickman, President of Graniteville Company, voiced the opinion that the bill would greatly damage Augusta. George T. Jackson proposed a resolution that the bill would be detrimental to the general welfare of the community. William Sibley seconded the motion. A committee of thirteen was named to go with all possible speed to Atlanta to lobby against the bill. Their efforts had the desired effect: Twiggs's bill failed to pass. Clearly, the executives wanted no outside interference in the matter of caring for the helpless little waifs.[28]

Historian Julia Walsh has studied the dynamics of the mill community with special attention to the role of religion. Churches mushroomed in the mill district more rapidly than factories. In 1880 William Sibley donated land for a mission church that later became Sibley Presbyterian. Berean Baptist (later Crawford Avenue Baptist) opened in 1881. Emily Tubman, who owned stock in most of the mills and 200 shares in the Sibley, subsidized the establishment of the Second Christian Church (later Central Christian Church) in 1882. The Episcopal Church donated a ready-made building. The 1868

Good Shepherd Church in the carpenter gothic style was actually rolled down the hill on logs to its place on Eve Street, there to become Christ Church. Julia Walsh notes that though actual church attendance tended to be spotty, interdenominational revivals were popular. When they gathered to listen to a preacher like evangelist Sam Jones, the workers had an opportunity to compare their situations and plan for joint action. It is worth noting that the organizer of local 5030 of the Knights of Labor was the pastor of Berean Baptist, Rev. J.S. Maynardie. Maynardie encouraged his people to assert their rights by organizing. It is not a coincidence that the first labor dispute involved men who were members of the Knights of Labor.[29]

The trouble started at the Algernon Mill on June 12, 1886. The weaving room operatives demanded that the overseer McGaw be dismissed. McGaw blamed the Knights of Labor for the unrest. The workers won two days later when McGaw resigned.[30] Emboldened by the small victory, workers at the Riverside Mill (located on the river at 12th Street) who had similar complaints, went out on strike. Then the King Mill workers accused the overseer of making them work extra hours without extra pay. Again, the workers won the skirmish when they were granted a ten percent pay increase. The Augusta Factory workers had been patient during a cut in wages in 1884, but with profits increasing they struck for a fifteen percent raise in pay. President Charles H. Phinizy told them flatly that there would be no raise until business improved. The workers' movement gained momentum when the Enterprise operatives joined the strike, demanding a fifteen percent pay hike. The Sibley workers, making ninety cents a day, asked for the same pay scale as those at the Enterprise. On July 14, 1886 the national Knights became involved when James Wright arrived in town as the representative of national president Terence Powderly. He attempted to mediate the strike, but his request of a ten percent raise was rejected by management.

Mill owners, concerned that the union might strike one mill at a time, formed an organization of their own. They agreed to a general closure of all the mills in Augusta and in the Horse Creek Valley of South Carolina. The strike then became a lockout. Francis Cogin, superintendent of the Augusta Factory, broke ranks with management by declaring that the lockout was unfair. On August 10, *The Chronicle* described the strike and lockout a calamity. Three thousand people were out of work and dependent on funds from the national union.

As the strike dragged on, another kind of calamity occurred. Augusta experienced its worst earthquake on August 30, 1886. Headlines screamed, "Terror All Around!" Walls swayed, chimneys collapsed. Lawyer Joseph R. Lamar left his living room just as the heavy plaster ceiling smashed to the floor. Black restaurateur Lexius Hensen rose from his chair as his brick wall fell into the chair. Thirteen shocks reverberated throughout the morning. The epicenter of the quake was near Charleston and that beautiful city was badly damaged. It says something about the generosity of people of the day that Augustans took up a collection to aid the suffering people in Charleston.[31]

The suffering in Augusta needed help also, as the strike lasted through September and into October. On September 8, 1886 the Augusta Factory resumed operations with non-union labor. The strikers jeered at the "scabs" as the police kept a watchful eye. Mayor May and Master Workman J.S. Meynardie moved among the workers, urging calm. The City Council met to discuss how to deal with the situation. The Council authorized the mayor to name two citizens, one representing the management and one the workers, to meet with him and reach a settlement. The Council agreed with May's request for $1,000 in aid to those most in need. As word of the Council's action spread, some grumbled that the Council meant to encourage labor unions. City attorney John S. Davidson gave his legal opinion that the city had a right to make charitable donations. The Council voted down a motion to rescind the $1,000 already granted and voted an additional $1,000.[32]

Charles Phinizy of the Augusta Factory named Major Joseph B. Cumming as his representative. Mayor May asked J.S. Meynardie to nominate a negotiator. Meynardie replied that he would be willing to meet with the Mayor and the Major, but the issue rested with the National Council of the Knights of Labor, meeting in Baltimore on October 5, 1886. "We have no issue with the mills," said Meynardie, "except for more meat and bread. Give the operatives this and the whole matter is at once settled." He indicated that the Knights might be willing to submit to arbitration in lieu of a 15% pay increase.[33]

On September 13, 1886, three strikers assaulted two non-union men outside the Augusta Factory. The next day only twelve workers showed up at the factory for work. The factory management then used its ultimate weapon: it posted a notice that strikers would be evicted from company housing. The Augusta newspapers disliked printing bad news, but the *Atlanta Constitution* had no qualms about publicizing Augusta's problems. *The Constitution* estimated that 8,000 people were out of work in Augusta. *The Chronicle* argued that most of those unemployed had moved away or found other jobs, and printed a sixteen-page special edition boosting Augusta as the largest inland cotton market in the country, excepting only Memphis.[34]

Master Workman Meynardie returned from the October 5th convention in Baltimore exhausted and near a breakdown, but he succeeded in bringing an emergency fund of $22,000 to pay the mounting grocery bills of the strikers. James A. Wright was authorized to work out a settlement with the mill executives. On November 5th the city learned the good news that the strike had ended. Patrick Walsh presided at a workers' meeting at the Masonic Hall where Wright revealed the terms. No worker would be fired because of membership in the Knights, the mills would forgive the accumulated rent due for company housing, future disagreements would be settled by a committee of two executives and two workers, failing an agreement, the dispute would be settled by an arbiter, and the overseers would not demand extra work without pay. However, there would be no pay increase. Walsh congratulated the workers for their restraint during the strike, and observed that the King and Sibley had each lost $400,000 as a result of the strike and lockout. As a gesture of "good will" the mills announced that the work day would be reduced from eleven and a half hours to eleven hours.[35]

The strike had a lasting effect upon the community. Henceforth, workers would be wary of challenging management. The answer to the question of who would speak for the women and children seemed clear. The mill would. The strike had a national impact, also. It broke the treasury of the Knights of Labor and that first major labor union soon declined into insignificance. The only good thing about the strike, in Lawton Evans's point of view, was that school attendance increased. When the strike ended, he lost over 200 students to the mills.[36]

During the "big boom" era the growth in population made possible by the canal threatened the canal in an unexpected way. The problem of sewerage and drainage became acute. The City Council on August 5, 1878 voted to deepen the Beaver Dam and DeLaigle ditches east of the terminus of the second level, and extend the ditching to Butler's Creek where the overflow would be returned to the Savannah River well below Augusta. The proposal had the consequence of creating interest in deepening the ditch enough so that steamboats could venture up to the second level of the canal. Thirty-two citizens asked the Council to entertain that notion. Anything seemed possible in that era.[37]

The Board of Health intervened on January 9, 1879. Although the Board included two distinguished doctors, Lewis D. Ford and Louis A. Dugas, the language was that of the third member, Colonel George W. Rains, now professor of chemistry at the Medical College. He used strong language to describe the existing situation. One sewer emptied into the river at 8th Street and its deposits flowed past the Bay Street residential section. Another sewer ran into the third level of the canal. A third, described as "an abomination," discharged into an open ditch and then into the third level. "Thus the upper part of the city from Dublin Bridge is surrounded by a cordon of the most dangerous filth," the Board report scolded, and noted that all this noxious material flowed out Hawk's Gully and joined the 8th Street sewage. After cataloging other evils of the system, the report achieved a crescendo of criticism, "Your committee do but justify their sober judgment in declaring their conviction that Malignity plotting mischief against the citizens of Augusta urged by disciplined ingenuity, could not have spent the large amount of money – the cost of these sewers – in any way better for its purpose, than in building them."[38] In other words the devil could not have done a better job of poisoning Augustans. To emphasize their displeasure, the three members of the Board of Health resigned.

Robert May, the Civil War mayor, reelected for a three-year term in 1879, secured the consent of Council to employ an engineer to recommend a new sewer system. Mayor May hired Colonel George Waring to do the study. When Waring handed in his report, Dr. Eugene Foster, the new chairman of the Board of Health, found it so "radically at variance" with established practices that he recommended a second study. Mayor May obliged by hiring Dr. Azel Ames of Boston. The new recommendations seemed to please everyone. The voters realized that there was a serious problem and voted approval of a bond issue on July 9, 1881. As is usual in any case in which tax money is involved, some citizens filed suit to block the bond issue. To the surprise and consternation of the Mayor, the Council and the Board of Health, the Georgia Supreme Court sustained the injunction against the bond issue. Some people would rather be poisoned than pay any new tax.[39]

Mayor May expressed disappointment, but noted that doing nothing was not an option. Repairing the present "vicious" system would cost $12,500. May turned for help to Dr. William H. Doughty of the Medical College. After studying the problem, Dr. Doughty suggested a minimal solution, the construction of a large underground sewer from Crescent Mills at the end of the third level through the city cemetery and down East Boundary to the river. Dr. Doughty explained that it would simply be an extension of the canal, and that it would do for the east part of town what the third level did for the west part of town. In time, the sewers running into the third level could be diverted into this big new sewer. City Engineer A. H. Davidson estimated that the project would cost $39,000. The Mayor proposed a special tax of one-fourth of one percent of property value, the voters approved by a two-thirds margin, and the work was carried out with dispatch under the capable supervision of Engineer Davidson.

In his final report to the City Council, Davidson was pleased to announce that the cost was $37,048, under his original estimate. The work began on September 26, 1884 by contractor John M. Poland. Objections to cutting through the cemetery delayed the project and Davidson had to plot a new route down Second Street. To Davidson's credit the task was finished on time, March 22, 1886, and under budget. The massive pipe, six feet in diameter, measured 8,542 feet in length from Crescent Mills to the river. Davidson commended John Cartledge, head of the chain gang, who ruined his health working in the sewer.[40] Gradually, as new sewers were connected to the big pipe, the third level was relieved of some of its garbage, but it would take time.

Figure 41. Power station site at 15th Street and Augusta Canal. *(Courtesy of the Augusta Museum of History)*

A little noticed adjunct of the canal at the time, with major implications for the future, was the first electric power plant on the canal at 15th Street. On October 3, 1881, the United States Electric Light Company of New York applied to City Council for a license to operate in the city under the title "Augusta Electric Light Company." Within a month they managed to rig up lights in John W. Clark's Globe Mills, constructed in 1876 on the site of an old tobacco factory on the second level of the canal between 12th and 13th Streets. Beginning on April 30, 1882 Augustans were treated to two weeks of electric lighting on Broad Street. *The Chronicle* called Augusta the first city in the South to receive full street length illumination.[41] The demonstration was temporary and it would be several years before a permanent lighting system was available. Augusta acquired a second electric company in 1886 when Charles Phinizy and others incorporated the Turner-Houston Company and competed with the Augusta Electric Light Company for the street lighting business.[42]

The remarkable transformation of Augusta during the boom period caused Augustans to boast that theirs was the pre-eminent city in Georgia. However, they kept a wary eye on upstart Atlanta. When in 1881 the City Council learned that northern businessmen were visiting Atlanta, they sent a message inviting the gentlemen to Augusta for a ride up the canal and a barbecue at the pavilion. In 1887 Augustans learned that President Grover Cleveland intended to visit the Atlanta fair. The City Council passed a resolution explaining that Augusta "is second to no city in the State politically, socially, intellectually, or morally" and that the President would do better to visit Augusta.[43]

It occurred to local businessmen that if they hoped to entice a president that they needed to put on a fair that would outdo Atlanta's. On November 7, 1887 the city granted a license to James Tobin and others to conduct a "grand Exposition and Encampment" in the Fall, 1888. At a public meeting the next day enthusiasm ran high and $75,000 was pledged to the newly formed "National Exposition Company." The usually stingy City Council caught some of the excitement and voted $21,000 to pay for water connections from the canal to the fairgrounds at Druid Park. Bridges over the canal at 9th, 10th, and 12th Streets had to be widened in anticipation of traffic. Rail tracks had to be extended to the fair grounds. New streets leading to Druid Park had to be opened. The Exposition Company, proudly sporting the adjective "National" hired New Yorker J. W. Ryckman as impresario for the event. A massive building with gothic spires rose on the fairgrounds.[44] Beginning in April, Patrick Walsh's *Chronicle* began to boost the Exposition as a testimony to Augusta's industrial progress. The Exposition was intended to be the city's grandest advertisement to northern investors.

Then, on September 10, 1888, one month before opening, tragedy struck. Following several days of heavy rain, a torrent of water swept down the first level of the canal and up the third level, and the river washed over its banks. Water reached a depth of ten feet in the Springfield area and five feet at the City Hall. The canal banks ruptured in five places; all its bridges floated off. Many people were stranded in their homes for two days, waiting for the flood to recede. When it did it left ugly deposits of mud, houses askew upon their foundations, cellars flooded, streets severely eroded, clogged sewers, and polluted waterworks.[45] The great mills, dependent upon the canal for power, shut down for three months.

On only one other occasion, that of the great fire of 1916, have Augustans been so tested. The exhilaration of putting on a national fair might easily have given way to despair, or a sober realization that the thing could not be done. Later generations can marvel that the men and women of that era chose to do the impossible; they would clean up their town with no outside help and merely delay the opening day of the exposition by one month. Mayor May called the Council into emergency session and spoke calmly, "In view of the very serious calamity which has befallen our beautiful city, I have called you together." The Council voted to impose a tax of one percent on property for two years. The voters approved the tax, 973 to 237.

The Board of Health announced that, contrary to rumors, there was no epidemic in the city.[46]

With the triumphal firing of cannon and the blare of trumpets the National Exposition opened on November 10th, 1888 and lasted over a month with trainloads of people coming and going. On November 12, local militia companies reenacted Civil War battles as 21,000 watched. On November 29, a parachutist jumped from a hot air balloon and landed ungracefully in a tree.

On another occasion thirty-four groups paraded from City Hall to the Bell Tower and back again as an estimated 50,000 lined the streets. On December 11th Augustans donned formal attire to attend a grand ball at the Exposition Hall. The fair closed on December 18th with more cannon fire, ringing of bells, and blasting of fireworks. It was estimated that the Exposition drew over 150,000 people to Augusta. Even Atlanta had to admit that Augusta had pulled off a coup. Henry Grady's *Constitution* congratulated Augustans for their "pluck" and admitted, "No better or more significant show was ever made in the South."[47]

The new canal gave Augusta something to boast about, but it nearly set back that progress by unleashing a flood upon the city. The Exposition demonstrated that the city that built the canal could manage its consequences. The *Atlanta Constitution* was right. They showed pluck.

CHAPTER TEN

Protest & Progress, 1890–1900

<hr>

T he canal made it possible for some Augustans to become
wealthy, as the handsome Victorian residences on
Greene Street still attest. The canal also created mill villages in Harrisburg and around the Augusta Factory. Inevitably,
new class differences manifested themselves. Antebellum
Augusta had its classes, but – with the notable exception of the
American Revolution – none of them banded together to gain
their objectives. Now both operatives and management formed
unions and associations to maintain their interests. The result
was increasing bitterness and political polarization. The workers' protest movements form one theme of this chapter. The
other theme follows the progress made possible by the canal,
electrification and a modern water supply system.

During the decade of the 1890's the people of the mill
villages became increasingly isolated and disillusioned with
their lot. Historian Richard German listed five reasons for the

deteriorating quality of life in the mill district. First, the sheer numbers of workers increased to the point that mill executives and operatives had little or no contact. The workers had to deal with overseers whose purpose was to exact a maximum work effort. In 1887 weavers at the Sibley Mill complained to the management that C.S. Googin, the overseer, was "inhuman." The petitioners claimed that Googin had caused the death of several workers by "his tyrannical rules and actions." The response from the management was that Googin was a good, reliable man from Chicopee, Massachusetts, and had come to the Sibley highly recommended. Googin stayed on the job.[1]

German's second reason for the declining quality of life consisted in the unpredictability of even the normal job. Workers never knew when the mill might shut down for any of several reasons, for repairs to machinery or to the canal, or for insufficient water supply in the canal, or for high water. The canal was key to continual work. The mills shut down for three months as a result of the 1888 flood and the resulting damage to the canal. There would be no pay during the shutdowns.

A third reason for workers' dissatisfaction was the steady decline in wages during the decade. Annual wages in the King Mill declined from $216 in 1880 to $181 in 1898; in the Sibley from $242 to $225. At that level, Augusta's pay scale was below the average for industrial workers in the South ($452) and well below the $518 northern average.[2]

Richard German's fourth reason for labor unrest was psychological. The residents of the Fifth Ward realized that they were not considered part of the wider community. Because they lived in a recently annexed section they had inadequate sewerage, unpaved streets, minimal gas lighting. Harrisburg would remain a neighborhood of privies until well into the next century. Residents attended their own churches, schools and stores.

They felt that the "silk-stocking crowd on the Hill" looked down on them.

German's final cause of malaise in the mill district concerned living conditions and the health of the residents. The canal overflow created a shallow pool opposite the Sibley Mill. Children used it for bathing, but clandestine dumping of garbage made canal water unsanitary. In 1897 the Board of Health insisted that the city put a sewer under the canal, and in the next year the city drained the pool on the "flats." The lack of sanitation remained a problem, and its effects told on the workers. German quoted a woman who worried about a child's health, "You ought to see that boy. His face ain't as big as my hand, he is so poor and thin. And yet that boy works all day in the mill. I would not be surprised to see them bringing him home dead any day."[3]

It is not surprising that some young women of the factory district turned to prostitution. In 1897 the Christian Union Mission made an appeal to the City Council on behalf of "an unfortunate class of people whose presence in our midst causes unhappiness in many homes and whose numbers increase at a fearful ratio. We mean the dwellers in houses of ill fame." [4] The women of the Christian Union wanted the city to allocate $1,000 for a settlement house and provide $25 a month for a missionary to staff the house. The Council pleaded that legal reasons prevented them from obliging the ladies. When the Christian Union delegation came back to plead their case, the councilmen reached into their pockets and donated $5.00 each to the good cause.

The ladies were not satisfied. On August 2, 1897 they again appeared before the Council and painted a dire picture of what was going on. By then they had purchased a house on the corner of 11th and Reynolds Streets for their mission. They achieved new levels of outrage in describing "houses of shame, dives of damnable sin, suffering, debauchery and prostitution that exist openly without effort of concealment contrary to the city code." Four houses of ill repute operated in the same neighborhood as their mission. The complaint continued, "Beer and whiskey are sold at all hours without a license – a common ground of debauchery for city 'swells' as well as the mechanic and the factory hand."⁵ The minutes of the City Council do not reveal the response, if any, to the anguished appeal, other than the five dollars per councilman already mentioned.

Drugs were another problem. *The Chronicle* disliked printing unsavory news items, but broke with tradition to decry evidence of "a terrible cocaine addiction" as well as the fearful spread of the use of morphine and opium.⁶ Revivalists joined the crusading Christian women in calling for reform. The famous preacher Sam Jones conducted a massive revival in the mill district. He knew that most of his listeners came from the country and he stressed country virtue over city vice. He blamed the dominant Democratic Party for allowing the abuses to continue. "Democratic soak and whiskey soak are running Augusta in her hellward bound course," he thundered. "Augusta needs cleaning up, but you are afraid to speak."⁷

After Sam Jones's first denunciation of liquor in 1892, the reformers demanded that the city adopt a prohibition ordinance. The City Council obliged to the extent of conducting a public referendum on the issue. On July 1, 1892 the voting began at 8:00 A.M. at the courthouse. A procession of women led by Mrs. William Sibley marched into the courthouse yard, bearing blue banners and singing hymns. Children dressed in white carried banners on which were written slogans like "Vote to save my Papa" and "I am a temperance boy." After parading about, the ladies and children knelt on the ground and began to pray. The opponents of prohibition had engaged a brass band and the band proceeded to drown out the sound of the women. The women shouted louder. Then the opposing sides reached a compromise and took turns with the singing and the band playing. Prohibition lost by a two to one margin. The immediate response of the reformers was to join the People's Party and challenge the Democrats for control of the city.[8] They found a champion in Thomas E. Watson of Thomson, Georgia.

The People's Party, or Populists, appealed to the farmers as well as the factory workers. They called for government regulation of railroads and banks, inflation of the currency by the free coinage of silver, popular election of United States Senators, and an income tax. All of this sounded fearfully socialistic to the Democrats, and they expressed outrage when Tom Watson, having been elected to Congress as a Democrat, announced that he decided to join the Populist Party and run for reelection on that ticket. On November 13, 1891 a chapter of the Populist Party was organized in the mill district to support the Watson candidacy. The local Populists acquired a voice when William John Henning of Gracewood, a community south of Augusta, began to issue a news sheet called *The Wool Hat*. In his first editorial on June 1, 1892 Henning outdid Watson in denouncing the Democrats, "In the mighty struggle which is now in progress between the oppressed and the oppressors, between the working masses who produce and the favored parasites who prey and fatten upon the toil of others, we feel the need in our midst of a paper which shall advocate the cause of the people."[9]

The story of Tom Watson and the Populist Movement has been told by several fine historians, notably by C. Vann Woodward in the classic *Tom Watson Agrarian Rebel*. It need not be retold here in the history of the canal. Suffice it to say that the Tenth Congressional District was bitterly divided between

Watson supporters and the Democrats. Watson was defeated in 1892, 1894, and in a special supervised election in 1895. The Democratic candidate who won all these elections, Major James C.C. Black, was a good man and a gentleman, but his supporters used fraudulent methods to defeat Watson. In retaliation, the Populists stuffed the ballot boxes in those polling places they controlled. In the 1892 campaign excitement, Fifth Ward Populist organizer Arthur Glover shot Deputy Sheriff Henry Head. In the 1894 elections Populist John Goss shot three black men coming in to vote Democrat, and shot Marshal George Heckle for good measure, before Heckle shot and killed Goss. The Fifth Ward Populists venerated Goss as a martyr.[10]

After defeats at the national and local levels, the national Populist Party declined to the point of insignificance. However, in the Tenth District, and in particular in Augusta's Fifth Ward, the workers found a political solution. Tom Watson delivered an attack on blacks, whom he accused of selling their votes to Democrats, and he attacked Catholics as agents of a foreign power. Until then, Catholics had enjoyed the same acceptance extended to members of other religious denominations. In denouncing Catholics Watson had Patrick Walsh in mind; everybody knew that Walsh was a devoted Catholic. Walsh had gone from success to success as Watson failed. Walsh headed the two successful expositions in 1891 and 1893, he was named by Governor Northern to the United States Senate in 1894, and he was elected mayor of Augusta in 1898.

Watson advised his followers to rejoin the Democratic Party, and to set up a separate organization within the party. They should establish a chapter of the American Protective Association in each ward, swear to vote for the candidate of the chapter, and also swear not to vote for a Catholic. They would work for elimination of the black vote, for prohibition, and for the abolition of street carnivals, roller-skating rinks, and theaters. Populist chairman Jim Barrett of Gracewood quit the party, accusing Watson of trying to gain control of the Democratic Party by attacking Catholics.[11]

Union organizers took advantage of the disaffection of the mill workers by sending national leaders to stir militant action. It made front page news when representatives of the National Textile Workers Union came to town and called a meeting. Public suspicion increased when the "outside agitators" refused to admit reporters. The first result of unionization was the appearance of a workers' delegation before the City Council in February to present a petition on behalf of 409 operatives. Arthur Glover, the same Populist organizer who shot Henry Head, acted as spokesman. He asked for the elimination of the $5.50 charge per horsepower for canal water. Mayor Patrick Walsh answered that the Council could not do that because the canal income had to pay for the new waterworks system. Glover asked for a reduction of city property taxes because property had declined in value by as much as fifty percent in the last five years.[12] The Council members listened but declined to lower taxes.

The mill executives played into the hands of the union leaders by their joint announcement that wages would be cut by ten percent as of November 21, 1898. That seemed a deliberate provocation, a test of strength with the union. On that day the Sibley workers walked out, the King Mill operatives joined them, and they paraded to Greene Street where the Enterprise workers came out. The crowd in a defiant mood paraded down Broad Street to the Confederate Monument where they were harangued by one of the national leaders, E.L. Cranfill. He told them that he had been at the Haymarket Riot in Chicago, and at Cripple Creek in Colorado and in fifteen other strikes. The secret to success consisted in staying together.

The Augusta strikers were the focus of workers across the country. If the mill owners succeeded in cutting wages in Augusta, the cut would spread across the country. Like Tom Watson, Cranfill sounded the racial note. If Negroes send their children to school, he said, while you have to send yours to work, the Negroes will get the upper hand. Mayor Patrick Walsh mounted the steps to address the workers, risking their displeasure. Instead they gave him their attention as he offered to mediate the dispute. The next day Walsh met with Charles Estes, John Chafee, James P. Verdery, and Thomas Barrett. They would not rescind the cut, but they agreed to pay the Augusta workers six percent more than those in South Carolina. That concession was not good enough for the union leaders.[13]

As the strike lengthened some workers drifted away. More came in looking for jobs. One farmer from Glascock County brought his wife and seven children to Augusta during the strike. He and his family were willing to work for a month free provided he and they would be hired at the end of the month.[14] On December 6, 1898 the mills not affected by the strike announced a lockout if the strike did not end by December 24. On that day, the Enterprise Mill, the Augusta Factory, and the Horsecreek Valley mills locked out their employees. Wholesale grocers refused credit to strikers.

On January 6, 1899 Charles Estes of the King Mill announced that strikers would be evicted from mill houses to make room for new people willing to work. After the deadline diehard strikers were forced out of their lodgings. Ironically, the Sibley Mill employed Arthur Glover, the workers' spokesman, as constable to enforce the evictions. Realizing that they were beaten and to save face, the union leaders sat down with the mill executives and agreed to the proposition that Augusta mills would pay six percent more that South Carolina mills. The union tried to organize the workers again in 1902 and conducted a short-lived strike for a ten percent wage increase. That, too, failed. Historian John S. Ezell wrote, "Textile unionism took its last big chance in Augusta in 1902 and lost."[15]

The mill workers turned to politics to improve their lot. First called the A.P.A. (American Protective Association), the ward-based organization later took the name of its Harrisburg chapter, the "Cracker Party." Some of its members, including Jim Barrett who has already been mentioned, disliked the direction the party took. William John Henning, the ardent Populist editor of *The Wool Hat* and later of the *Augusta Tribune* wrote editorially that "designing men had gotten control of the movement" and the Fifth Ward was their stronghold.[16]

Though it may seem that our story has strayed from its central theme, namely the history of the canal, the labor unrest of the Nineties stemmed directly from the industrialization made possible by the canal. The enlargement of the canal had other consequences for the entire city, one of the most obvious was that the canal powered the first electric plants and provided for electric lighting and electricity-powered transportation. The man who had the most to do with the electrification of the city was a flamboyant westerner, Colonel Daniel Burns Dyer, known by the locals as "Daniel Boone Dyer."[17]

D.B. Dyer made an immediate impression upon Augusta and Augustans when he arrived in the city in November 1889. He had lived among the Indians of the western plains for fifteen years, serving as agent to the Cheyenne and Arapahoe Nations and acting as attorney for various tribes in lawsuits against the government. One of his closest friends was "Buffalo Bill" Cody. Dyer was one of the estimated 50,000 "boomers" who raced into Oklahoma at high noon on April 22, 1889. In one day 10,000 people settled the town of Guthrie and

Figure 42. Colonel Daniel Burns Dyer (left) and his friend William F. "Buffalo Bill" Cody. *(Courtesy of the Western Historical Manuscript Collection-Kansas City)*

they elected D.B. Dyer their first mayor.

He might have stayed on as mayor when Guthrie became the capital of the new Oklahoma Territory in 1890; instead, this legendary figure decided to leave the Wild West and come to

Augusta. He came as the principal in a group of Kansas City businessmen who intended to invest in the electrical development of Augusta. Envisioning a street car line around Augusta he bought the Turpin Hill tract for $25,000, paid $16,000 for half interest in the Monte Sano tract, $23,000 for the old Lafayette Race Course, $12,000 for the Lambert place, $6,000 for the Lambert property, $9,000 for two places in Woodlawn and $11,000 for a power plant off the first level of the canal at 15th Street adjacent to the Turner-Houston power plant.[18]

Patrick Walsh, one of Augusta's premier entrepreneurs, dared challenge in court Dyer's right to build an electric trolley line. Walsh, as president of the Augusta and Summerville Railway, had a license to run an electric car from the Magnolia Cemetery to the Augusta Arsenal on the Hill. Walsh lost the court test and sold out to Dyer. A company called the Belt Line had obtained the right to run cars around the city, but had done

Figure 43. Patrick Walsh, president of the Augusta and Summerville Railway. *(Courtesy of the Augusta Museum of History)*

nothing else. Dyer bought it also. He further astonished every-one by ordering fifty cars for his Augusta line.[19]

Great interest and much excitement attended the run of the first car on May 29, 1890, with Dyer and selected dignitaries riding in it. All along the route people waved and cheered and the trolley gave out a happy clang clang in reply. A reporter aboard wrote that the ride from the Arsenal to the town was like "coast-ing on a fast sled." According to his watch, it took two minutes to go from the Bon Air Hotel on Walton Way to the Schuetzenplatz (today's Tubman School). If so, it was a record never bettered.

The mules that once drew the cars, with their colorful ribbons and jingling bells, now went into retirement. One par-ticularly conscientious old mule, grazing on the common, saw the car go by and trotted out to get in front of it in its accustomed pulling position. A Chinese gentleman who mar-veled at the sight of the horseless trolley was quoted as exclaim-ing, "No pushee, no pullee, but go like hellee, all samee."[20] Patrick Walsh's *Chronicle* paid a gracious and perceptive com-pliment to Dyer who gave the city "command of the territory that surrounds it." A businessman now could live farther away from his workplace and yet be closer to it. A number of Hill dwellers formed the habit of taking the two o'clock trolley for a leisurely dinner and nap before returning to town. Dyer pro-moted growth along his line by extending the rails around Monte Sano Avenue and down Central Avenue. He advertised 50 lots for sale for prices from $300 to $750. He set the tone himself by purchasing the historic early 19th century Bellevue Hall, recently the home of the nationally known writer, Octavia Walton Levert. Dyer preserved the house by building a ram-bling Victorian structure around it. He called it "Chateau Levert" and may have started the legend this writer heard as a child, that George Washington stayed there.[21]

On August 31, 1891 Dyer informed the City Council that he had even bigger plans. His power plant drew 500 horsepower from the canal; he asked for double that amount because he intended to provide electricity for lighting city streets and houses. The Turner-Houston Company furnished electricity to factories, but Dyer proposed cheaper rates available to more people. The City Council gave Dyer everything he asked for, over the objections of the gas company. He put up his poles and wires and on August 1, 1892, Dyer's lights illuminated Broad Street. Mayor James Alexander called it "one of the greatest improvements in the city for many years."[22]

Dyer, whose pockets seemed bottomless, then built the city's largest office building on the northwest corner of Broad Street at 8th, a five-story structure complete with an electric elevator. In 1895, Dyer announced that he intended to provide trolley service to the mill district. In order to increase traffic through the Harrisburg neighborhood, he built recreational facilities at Lake Olmstead at no expense to the city and called it Lake View Park. When Dyer asked the city for $500 to help him entertain 1,300 guests from northern cities who might invest in local businesses, the Council quickly gave it to him.[23]

During the Spanish-American War in 1898 Dyer did his part by donating his Turpin Hill tract for a camp for the black Tenth Infantry. In his honor it was named Camp Dyer. The Reverend Charles T. Walker gave a stirring talk at a review of the troops, telling black listeners to be true to the flag, "whether it be true to us or not." Mayor Patrick Walsh paid a compliment to the soldiers of the Tenth, including the ten black Augustans who had charged up Kettle Hill in Cuba alongside Teddy Roosevelt's Rough Riders.[24] Dyer double-tracked his Central Avenue line to accommodate the soldiers stationed at Camp McKenzie on Wrightsboro Road. After the army camp closed Dyer constructed a new park between Monte Sano Avenue and the reservoir, put in a dance pavilion and announced that he would run a summer vaudeville program.[25] Daniel B. Dyer belongs in this history of the canal because he extended the potential of the canal to give the city better lighting, transportation and recreational facilities.

The specter of the terrible flood of 1888 haunted the city fathers. William Phillips had suggested a levee, so had Colonel Rains, but the Council considered the cost prohibitive. Mayor Robert May established a committee to study the problem in 1887, but they failed to agree on a solution. Immediately after the disaster, May appointed Patrick Walsh to the committee with instructions to make a recommendation. Walsh employed a Chicago engineer named J.F. Stones to survey the situation. Stones handed in his report to the commission on June 14, 1889. He, too, advised building a levee, but neither the committee nor the council wanted to hear that. Stones recommended raising the canal banks four to six feet above the high water mark. He also suggested deepening and extending the Beaver Dam Ditch to allow excess water to run out Rocky Creek.

After they had a second study done, the Council decided that the cheapest option would be to simply deepen the Beaver Dam Ditch. They set about securing the rights of way but became involved in litigation that held up the project. Residents near Beaver Dam Ditch complained to a Grand Jury on the lack of progress, causing the Council to resolve to complete the "Beaver Dam Outlet Canal" as soon as possible, and to allocate $6,000 to the project. As has frequently happened in this history of the canal, some citizens objected to the city spending the money and secured an injunction delaying the work. The city had to wait for an act of the legislature in December 1905 to begin the excavation. Presumably the much delayed project then got underway because we hear no more about it in the Council minutes. The 1908 flood demonstrated the inadequacy of the solution.[26]

The final problem regarding the canal during the Nineties concerned the increasing unpleasantness of the city's drinking water. With the increase in population William Phillips' waterworks had become overextended. Residents of the mill district insisted on dumping garbage into the canal above the pump house located off the second level at 11th Street. The solution suggested itself: put the pump station above the settled part of town. Leonard Phinizy, acting on behalf of a number of citizens, threatened to sue the city if nothing was done to furnish clean drinking water. The present system, said Phinizy, was "a fraud and a failure."[27] To outgoing Mayor James Alexander's credit, he had already scouted around for land on the top of the Hill above Summerville for a reservoir and had secured options on sixty acres of land.

William B. Young, Alexander's successor as mayor, persuaded the legislature to authorize the city to build a water system beyond its corporate limits and to use the right of eminent domain, if necessary, to secure the land. The measure became law in December 1895. Despite Young's urging that a site for a pumping station be selected on the canal, nothing was done until 1897 when Charles Estes was named to a commission to make specific recommendations. Estes, who has played such a prominent part in canal history, made another contribution by securing the services of a talented Atlanta engineer, Nisbet Wingfield. Wingfield proved to be as dedicated as William Phillips and as comfortable among city leaders as Charles Estes. On October 9, 1897 the City Council approved Wingfield's plans for a new waterworks system, complete with pumping station, pipelines, reservoir, and filter basin. On November 12, 1897 Estes' commission recommended the

Figure 44. Piston pumps in the 1899 Waterworks Building.
(Augusta Canal Authority Archives)

acceptance of the bids of C.H. Eglee and Company and A. J. Twiggs, for a total cost of $292,160. The city relied on the income from the canal to pay for the system.[28]

Nisbet Wingfield made such a good impression upon the members of the City Council that they created a new office for him, "Office of Commissioner of Public Works" and gave him control over the canal, waterworks, streets and drains. He offered to keep A.H. Davidson on as Canal Supervisor, but Davidson declined, perhaps disappointed that he had not got the promotion. Davidson had served the city well, especially in the construction of the big Houston Street sewer from the end of the second level to the river.

Wingfield went to work with dispatch; excavation on the reservoir basin on the crest of the Hill began in January 1898. By April Wingfield reported that the work was half done and he had begun laying the pipes from the pumping station site near the Augusta and Knoxville Railroad crossing of the canal to the reservoir. He had to wait on the specifications for the pumping machinery from R.D. Wood and Company before building the pumphouse. Meanwhile he repaired the pavilion, walkways and steps at the locks. In June he began construction of the pumping station, using stone from the excavation of the station's tailrace to the river. In August the river rose to the level of the pumping station, halting work there; Wingfield placed stone on the inner banks of the reservoir.[29]

In the larger world President William McKinley asked Congress to declare war on Spain to secure the liberation of Cuba. Some Augustans volunteered to go to Cuba, and, although the white volunteers got no farther than Ybor City, near Tampa, Florida, at least ten black Augustans saw action with the Tenth Infantry. The war intruded upon Nisbet Wingfield's pre-occupation with the waterworks project, but as it turned out, the waterworks caused him to become involved in the war. Mayor Patrick Walsh, who had recently served an unexpired term in the U.S. Senate, used his political connections to secure two military camps for Augusta, Camp McKenzie for white troops on the Hill on Wrightsboro Road, and Camp Dyer for black troops on Turpin Hill. The Army's condition was that the city must furnish a sufficient supply of water to the camps. Nisbet Wingfield had to work overtime to supply both camps. The new pumping station was not ready, of course, so Wingfield removed the old steam pump from Phillips' pumphouse on 11th Street to Turknett Springs, built a basin there and laid pipe to the Wrightsboro Road camp. The village of Summerville operated a pumping station at the foot of the Hill and the village authorities agreed to divert some of their limited supply to the camp.[30]

The crowning moment of Patrick Walsh's distinguished

career came when President McKinley accepted Walsh's invitation to visit Augusta. Never mind that the textile workers were on strike at that very time. John J. Cashin, as acting mayor, asked all Augustans to join in decorating the city for McKinley's reception. On December 19, 1898, the presidential party arrived at Wheless Station, toured Camp McKenzie, proceeded down Wrightsboro Road, across Johns Road to pay a courtesy call on the Augusta Arsenal, then down Walton Way, across Crawford Avenue to the mill district, and down Broad Street to the Confederate Monument. The 12,000 people who lined the way cheered the President but cheered louder for his companion, Augusta native son Major General "Fighting Joe" Wheeler, who fought against the Union in the Civil War and for the Union in the Spanish-American War. In an emotional moment, Wheeler greeted the sixty-two Confederate veterans in their old uniforms drawn up at the reviewing stand.[31]

Patrick Walsh died on March 19, 1899 after helping mediate the textile workers' strike. The City Council voted thirty days of official mourning. Thousands of grieving Augustans lined the funeral route from St. Patrick's Church (currently Most Holy Trinity Church) to Magnolia Cemetery. Even Tom Watson, Walsh's political enemy, contributed to the erection of a statue honoring Walsh. It still stands today in Barrett Plaza near the Federal Courthouse on Telfair Street.[32]

On June 5, 1899 Nisbet Wingfield reported that no one remained at Camp McKenzie. Camp Dyer had already been abandoned. He shut off the Turknett Springs connection and turned his attention to the completion of the new waterworks system. On August 28, 1899 Wingfield activated the pumps and water flowed from the canal across the Hill to the reservoir. Minor problems had to be worked out before Wingfield was satisfied. By March 29, 1901 the job was done. The total cost was about $320,000. Wingfield's plans called for a second reservoir adjacent to the first, but that would have to wait until the demand for water increased and the necessary funding became available.[33]

The people of Augusta benefited in a major way by a seemingly inexhaustible supply of clean drinking water. In a small, but important way they benefited from Wingfield's good idea to convert Phillips' old settling basin into a pond as part of Allen Park on Walton Way at 15th Street. Councilman Richard Allen sponsored the creation of the park in 1902.[34] With Dyer's Lake View Park and Allen Park the canal contributed to the leisurely pursuits of Augustans even as it supplied water, industrial power, disposal, and electricity.

Though it was not clear at the time, the end of the canal's industrial boom coincided with the end of the century. The last factory to locate on the canal was the Georgia Iron Works. Founded as the Warwick Machine Company in 1891,

Figure 45. Boat House at Lake View Park
(Augusta Canal Authority Archives)

Figure 46. Aerial view of the Georgia Ironworks, circa 1940.
(Augusta Canal Authority Archives)

and reorganized as the Georgia Iron Works in 1892, the company manufactured mill machinery in its shops on 11th Street. In 1899 the company moved its operations to the site of the defunct Sterling Cotton Mills between the second and third levels on 12th Street to take advantage of the canal's waterpower.[35]

From the turn of the century on, the canal's industrial future depended on its ability to supply electricity. During every decade of the Twentieth Century Augustans debated how it might best do that.

CHAPTER ELEVEN

Dealing With Disasters, 1900-1920

⟞⟩●⟨⟝

The dreaded four horsemen of the Apocalypse visited the city during the first two decades of the Twentieth Century: war, flood, fire and disease ravaged Augusta. The canal, that "bright arm" of the Savannah River thrown around the city by Henry Cumming, and the river itself, smote terrible blows upon the town and its people. While Augustans labored to build a great wall to fend off the river, a fire wiped out the finest residential section. Then war intruded and a major military encampment had to be provided for. Finally, an influenza epidemic paralyzed the community in 1918. Floods, fire and military camp all involved the Augusta Canal and form the theme of this chapter. The subject might equally be "the ascendancy of Nisbet Wingfield" because in his capacity as Commissioner of Public Works, he had to meet the many successive challenges.

Several other dramatic events during the period colored

the history of the canal. One earlier episode was the drowning of
Henry Cumming Lamar and his fiancée Louise King Connelly
in Lake Olmstead in 1891.[1] A marker near the outlet of the lake
at the "tin gate" commemorates the tragic event. An act of heroism stirred the feelings of the community on July 29, 1902. City
workers, including a young Irish immigrant named Dennis
Cahill, were busy repairing the wooden flooring on the steel
bridge over the canal on 15th Street, traditionally called the
"High Bridge" because canal boats had to pass beneath. No one
saw nine-year-old Dallas Kitchens wander onto the bridge. Her
scream as she fell through an opening in the floor alerted the
men. Cahill, an expert swimmer who had already rescued two
persons from drowning in the canal, responded immediately. He
dived into the canal, reached the struggling girl and began to pull
her to the bank. Then something happened, perhaps an attack of
stomach cramps, no one was ever sure, and the two sank into the
depths and drowned before anyone could help. Citizens contributed to a memorial to Cahill and his brave act. Like Cahill,
the stone monument at the southeastern approach to the bridge
is simple, rugged, and noble.[2] Judge Henry Hammond, grandson
of Henry H. Cumming, wrote the inscription, invisible to swift-
ly passing motorists, but arresting the attention of the occasion-
al pedestrian:

> "Dennis Cahill
> By a deed of self-sacrifice
> Such as all humanity claims
> And counts among its jewels,
> Hallowed this spot and rendered
> His name worthy of such
> Lasting Memory
> As these rugged stones and

This simple tablet can secure.
For here he gave his life
In a vain effort to save
From drowning a child, having
No claim for his sacrifice save
Humanity and Helplessness.
                    July 29, 1902"

Since events in the mill district are part of this narrative, the bizarre murder of Maude Dean Williamson in the weaving room of the Sibley Mill on October 19, 1906 belongs here. Arthur Glover strode into the weaving room at the mill, confronted Maude Williamson as she sat at her work, then fired his pistol several times into her body, killing her. He left the mill unmolested, went to a saloon for a drink, and then home to his wife and children at 1827 Ellis Street. His motive, as he revealed later, was that Maude Williamson was his mistress and she had been unfaithful to him. There was no question as to the facts; everyone in the weaving room had witnessed the deed. The jury returned a verdict of guilty, and Glover showed no signs of remorse as Judge Hammond pronounced the death sentence.

The matter might have ended there, except that Glover had recently worked for former Congressman Tom Watson. He has been mentioned in an earlier chapter as the Populist organizer who wounded a deputy sheriff, and as a constable serving eviction notices under orders from the mill executives. As the date of his execution neared, Glover decided that he would rather not die. He appealed to Tom Watson, saying that the Augusta people were trying to hang him because he had worked for Watson. Without investigating, Watson demanded that Governor Hoke Smith pardon Glover. When the governor told Watson he could find no grounds to issue a pardon, Watson helped defeat Smith in the next election. Glover went to his death as scheduled on January 13, 1908. His last remark was that Maude Williamson's murder was her fault, not his. Some persons in the Harrisburg neighborhood still remember the words of "The Ballad of Arthur Glover."[3]

The always interesting Daniel B. Dyer continued to influence events as the century turned. He sold his electric trolley system to James U. Jackson, the developer of North Augusta who ran the line all the way to Aiken, advertising it as the longest trolley line in the world. Dyer started a winter horse show for the entertainment of the increasing number of winter visitors at the Bon Air and Partridge Inn. In 1906 he unveiled his plans for a grand motor boulevard around Augusta, coincidentally using land he owned. The route capitalized on the scenic potential of the canal, beginning at Allen Park, circling around to the south of the city to today's Highland Avenue, past his Monte Sano Park on Highland between Wrightsboro and McDowell Streets, out to his Lake View Park, along the canal through a new park opposite the Sibley Mill called Chafee Park after John Chafee, President of the Sibley, and finally to Allen Park. A play at the Lake View Casino and a fair at Allen Park demonstrated the recreational possibilities of the canal parks. At the 1907 fair at Allen Park a feature attraction was Mademoiselle Therese who parachuted out of a balloon, aiming to land in the park. By a miscalculation, she landed in the canal and would likely have drowned as her chute settled around her except that she had taken the precaution of wearing a life jacket.[4]

Though it encompassed more than the canal, Dyer's vision might be considered the first master plan focusing attention on non-industrial uses of the canal. In fact, Commissioner Nisbet Wingfield borrowed Dyer's idea and in 1909 drew up plans for a boulevard up the canal and around Lake Olmstead.[5]

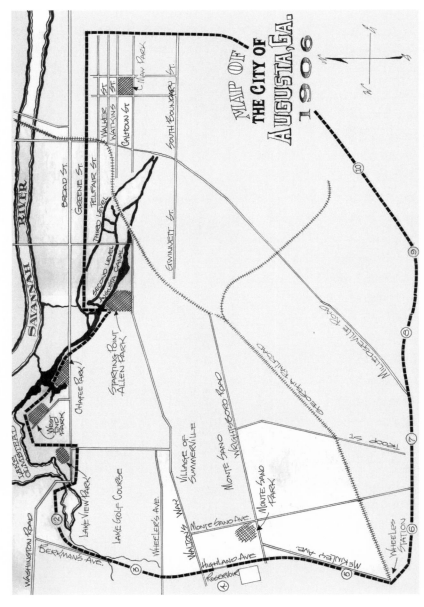

Figure 47. Colonel Dyer was the first to exploit the scenic and recreational uses of the canal. Map shows Dyer's proposed "Grand Boulevard," a motorway around Augusta. *(Map by Bill Blackard)*

Picnic barges to the locks were still popular, with barbecues in the pit and dancing on the pavilion.

Dyer entertained President William Howard Taft at Chateau Levert on January 21, 1909 when the newly elected president vacationed in Augusta. In November 1911 Dyer bade farewell to the city and his many friends here, and returned to the western plains to enter into a business partnership with an old friend of his, William F. "Buffalo Bill" Cody. Colonel Dyer died in Kansas City in December 1912, having left a lasting impression upon Augusta's history.[6]

We might notice what happened to his trolley system. James U. Jackson sold out to the famous Edward Harriman who at the time was engaged in a rail-buying competition with J.P. Morgan. Then Harriman and Morgan merged their lines until the Supreme Court dissolved the monopoly. The Redmond Company of New York bought the trolley line, and in 1911 allowed non-union car men to be employed. Richard Cornelius, head of the National Streetcar Workers Union, came to Augusta in 1912 and called a strike to protest the hiring of non-union men. The strike took an ugly turn when strikers began to tear up tracks and threaten damage to the power plant on the canal at 15th Street. At the request of Mayor Tom Barrett, Governor Joseph M. Brown called out the national guard, in this case Augusta's Clinch Rifles and Oglethorpe Infantry. The soldiers took up a position near the power plant and declared a no-trespassing zone on the immediate area. Anyone attempting to cross the High Bridge over the canal had to cross the zone and inevitably innocent persons became involved. Two citizens, Robert Christie and Alfred Dorn, who unknowingly trespassed, were shot and killed. Charles Wilson, riding in his buggy with his wife and child, was fired upon but managed to escape.[7]

Thirty-five hundred angry people gathered at the courthouse to demand the removal of the guard. The crowd began to march toward the power plant where soldiers waited with a Gatling gun. Dr. James R. Littleton, a popular physician in the factory district, mounted atop a car and appealed to the people not to risk certain bloodshed. His bravery saved a tragic confrontation and earned for him election to the mayoralty. Incumbent Mayor Tom Barrett helped end the strike by working out an agreement between the union and the company.[8] The power plant, much enlarged, occupies the same site today, but few Augustans associate it with the battle of 1912.

At the time of the strike, the Aiken-Augusta Railway and Electric Company was the only supplier of electric energy to the city, but in 1911 the Georgia-Carolina Company began to build a plant on the South Carolina side of the river at Stevens Creek above the lock and dam. J.D. "Pink" Wood, who had come to Augusta as an associate of Colonel Dyer, supervised the construction. At the dedication of the Stevens Creek plant on February 15, 1914, Judge Henry Hammond exclaimed, "The good old Savannah River is dammed forever, and in its damming we are saved." Governor John Slaton sent his greetings, "Lowell may now become the Augusta of the North."[9] The success of the Stevens Creek venture caused city fathers to seriously consider how they might extract more electrical energy from the canal. During the next two decades the idea became something of a fetish.

In 1912 the canal became forever associated with one of the great maritime disasters, the sinking of the British White Star liner *Titanic*. Native Augustan Major Archibald Butt went down on the supposedly unsinkable ship. Archie Butt was born in Augusta on September 26, 1865. He attended Summerville Academy on the Hill and the University of the South at Sewanee, Tennessee. He majored in journalism and worked as a reporter for several newspapers; some of his articles were published in *The Augusta Chronicle*. He also published a novel. He volunteered to join the army when the Spanish-American War began, served in the Philippines, and attained the rank of captain in the Quartermaster Corps. He later acted as depot quartermaster in Washington, D.C., and because he had charge of the stables, he met President Theodore Roosevelt, who enjoyed a morning ride. Roosevelt liked Butt and in 1908 made him his personal aide and chief of protocol. Butt had the responsibility of arranging White House functions without hurting important persons' feelings, a job he did to perfection.

Butt stayed on during the presidency of William Howard Taft. Butt's Augusta connections were instrumental in Taft's decision to vacation in Augusta. Taft promoted the Augustan to the rank of Major in 1911 and insisted that he had been working too hard and that he should go to Europe for a vacation. Butt took return passage on the famously ill-fated *Titanic* and died with more than thirteen hundred others. His friends remembered his calm heroism in the face of death. He wrapped Mabel Dodge in a blanket, smiled at her as her lifeboat pulled away and called to her, "Will you kindly remember me to the folks back home." President Taft came to Augusta to pay an emotional tribute to his friend at the Opera House on May 2, 1912. The tearful audience sang the song "Nearer My God to Thee." They had heard that Butt requested the band to play the song as the ship went down. Whether Butt did or not, and whether it was that particular tune or not, there were witnesses enough to testify that the ship's band played on as the ship began its final plunge. Survivors say they saw Archie Butt and John Jacob Astor arm in arm on the deck.

Augustans collected $20,000 to adorn the new High Bridge at 15th Street with memorials to honor Archie Butt. The four stone lions guarding the approaches hold shields bearing the coat of arms of the United States, the State of Georgia, the Temple-Noyes Lodge of Washington, D.C., and the Butt family. The multi-talented Nisbet Wingfield, whose activities dominate this chapter, designed the bridge and built it in reinforced concrete. Ex-President Taft returned to dedicate the Archibald Butt Memorial Bridge on April 15, 1914.[10]

Figure 48. The new Butt Memorial Bridge over the canal at 15th Street, with the Enterprise Mill in the background. *(Augusta Canal Authority Archives)*

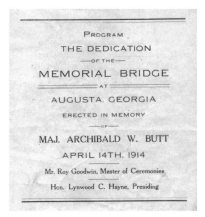

Figure 49. Butt Bridge Dedication Program, 1914.
(Courtesy of the Augusta Museum of History)

Dennis Cahill's modest monument and the majestic Butt Bridge reminded Augustans then and remind them now of heroic deeds, tinged with tragedy. Augustans harbor a special reverence for the bridge and that portion of the canal and rally to preserve the bridge when it is threatened by progress.

The history of the canal during the first two decades of the Twentieth Century is intertwined with the career of Nisbet Wingfield, introduced in the last chapter as the Commissioner of Public Works who built the new waterworks system with its reservoir on the Hill. He basked in that achievement during the first years of the first decade. Mayor Richard Allen referred to the waterworks in 1905 as "One of the best and most complete in the country, and the purity of our water is far-famed."[11] Wingfield improved it in 1909 by constructing a second building at the Pumping Station adjacent to the first to house auxiliary steam pumps.[12] Upon Wingfield devolved the problem of how to deal with recurrent flooding. Ironically his worst problem during the first few years of the new century concerned too little water rather than too much. During an unprecedented dry spell in 1904 Wingfield diverted the entire flow of the Savannah River into the canal and even that did not suffice. Water had to be rationed to the mills, the oldest having priority.[13]

Flow returned to normal in 1905 and the canal made a profit of $101,804, enough to pay the salaries of all the city employees from the mayor on down. A heavy rain caused a break halfway between the Pumping Station and the locks in 1906. Workers threw up a sandbag dam across the canal and repaired the extensive damage in only twelve days. In 1906 Wingfield anticipated the Stevens Creek project by recommending that the city build a power plant somewhere on the canal or on the river above the canal.[14]

Most knowledgeable Augustans, including Wingfield, knew that only a levee could provide flood protection, but officials quailed at the cost. The great flood of 1908 made them reconsider. One of the Jesuit priests at Sacred Heart Church provided an eyewitness account of the flood. Father L.G. Bashnall wrote a letter to a friend explaining that a hard rain had fallen for days, but otherwise town people had no warning that a flood was imminent. Animals sensed trouble before humans did. At 6:00 A.M. on the morning of August 26, 1908 a number of horses galloped wildly past Sacred Heart Rectory on their way to higher ground. Water began backing out of sewers. By 9:00 A.M. Ellis Street was covered with rising water. At noon as the nervous community sat down in the basement refectory for lunch, water began pouring in under the doors. The fire in the kitchen stove went out in a burst of steam. The frightened men retreated to the second floor and from their windows could hear a thunderous sound and see two torrents merging, one from the overflowing canal, the other from the river. Bewildered cows were lifted out of backyards and carried away down flooded Ellis Street. Two courageous men who attempted to rescue stranded people nearly drowned when their boat was dashed into a tree. They were swept onto the rectory steps and helped inside by the priests, exhausted and half-drowned.

That night Father Bashnall kept awake listening to the "uncanny gurgling, swashing and soughing of the water in the lower part of the house." The flood outside sounded to him like the rolling ocean surf. By the first light of dawn Bashnall saw a torrent six to seven feet deep rushing between the rectory and the old church building next door. Water had reached a depth of ten feet during the night and came within two feet of flooding the great church itself. When the flood receded a thick layer of mud covered everything. Many houses, especially those in the

Springfield Baptist Church neighborhood, were toppled from their foundations and the streets were badly eroded.[15]

Nisbet Wingfield reported that the thirty-six foot flood caused fifty fatalities and $2.5 million in property damages, in addition to the lost time incurred by the mills. Three and a half miles of the canal bank washed out from the headgates down. Working continuously for six weeks Wingfield's crew rebuilt the bank.[16]

Figure 50. The 1908 flood caused the public to support the building of the levee. *(Courtesy of Joe Lee)*

On August 28, 1908 Mayor William Dunbar called an emergency meeting of selected citizens including the aged Charles Estes, Thomas Barrett, F. B. Pope, and former mayors William B. Young and Richard Allen. Those present recommended the establishment of a Flood Commission empowered to find a solution and act upon it. The City Council appointed an eleven-man commission with Linwood Hayne as its first chairman. In 1909 the commission adopted the name "Canal and River Commission for the Protection of the City of Augusta," popularly known as the "Flood Commission." The commission hired Wingfield as a consultant and instructed him to draw up a plan to prevent a reoccurrence of the flood of 1908. With some trepidation on March 15, 1909 Wingfield presented his estimate for the cost of a levee – $1,500,000. The amount seemed prohibitive to the Commissioners. Augusta had other expenses, the annexation of Summerville, Harrisonville and Nellieville involved the extension of water and sewerage; also the City had to build a new hospital or lose the Medical College of Georgia. Tom Barrett argued for building the levee, but most of the Commissioners cringed at the cost. Wingfield later noted that "no one expected a bad flood like the one in 1908 for a long time and there was no use in getting hysterical."[17]

The Commission compromised by adopting the traditional method of dealing with floods, raising the first level gates and banks and deepening Beaver Dam Ditch. Wingfield began calling the latter the Beaver Dam Canal. The Commission invited Colonel Daniel Kingman, district officer of the U.S. Army Corps of Engineers, to look at Wingfield's plans. Kingman irritated the members of the Commission by reminding them that the Corps of Engineers claimed jurisdiction over the river and its banks. F. B. Pope, the second chairman of the Commission, inquired whether the Corps would contribute to flood protection. After Wingfield visited with Kingman in Savannah, the two agreed that the Corps would rip-rap the actual bank of the river if the City put up matching funds; the estimated cost totaled $250,000; the city's share would be half that. This cost-sharing agreement was the only contribution of the federal government to flood protection at Augusta.[18]

Wingfield's plans included a new spillway just above the Pumping Station. He believed that an outlet at that place was necessary because when the control gates on the canal near the mouth of Lake Olmstead were closed to prevent high water reaching the city, too much water backed up behind the Rae's Creek spillway. Curiously, the spillway was not built until the 1940's and then it was left incomplete and was finally abandoned. By 1911 the cost of raising the canal bank from the locks to the Pumping Station had risen to $59,813 and the excavation of Beaver Dam Canal to $40,000. Work began on dredging the third level of the canal.[19]

During 1911 Wingfield was distracted from flood protection to his other duties as Commissioner of Public Works. A watermain burst, a turbine at the Pumping Station blew out, the reservoir drained to a depth of eleven feet and water had to be rationed. Wingfield reminded the City Council that his original plan for a waterworks system called for a second reservoir on the Hill, and recommended immediate attention to its construction.[20] The second reservoir would not be built until 1928.

Nature again interfered in the Commission's plans. On March 16, 1912 a flood of 36 feet 10 inches visited Augusta. Water covered the town again, not so deep nor damaging, but infinitely discouraging. Wingfield noted that the people seemed demoralized, "There was evidence on every side to show that unless something was done Augusta would not only stop growing, but would go backwards." Tom Barrett, long a proponent of the levee, now occupied the Office of Mayor, and he insisted that the levee now be built. Few could argue; the second flood was persuasive. First, the constitutional provision barring cities from incurring indebtedness had to be amended by a statewide referendum that permitted the city to issue bonds based on fifty percent of the city's assets. The value of the canal and water works was put at $3,500,000. Therefore, the city could issue bonds in the amount of $1,750,000. The levee could not have been funded but for the equity in the canal and its water works.

The Canal and River Commission retrieved Wingfield's

1909 plan for a levee and adopted it on May 14, 1912. Colonel Kingman of the Corps of Engineers endorsed the plan as long as it did not impair the river banks and as long as the government did not have to contribute to the levee. The Commission invited two prominent engineers to review Wingfield's drawings, A.L. Dabney of Memphis and H.T. Corey of San Francisco. They gave their endorsements to the blueprints. The plan called for an earthen levee starting above the uppermost mill, the Singleton Silk Mill, passing behind the Sibley and King Mills to Hawk's Gully; from there following the river bank to East Boundary, then cutting across the wide bends of the river to Butler Creek. The mouth of Rocky Creek was closed, and the creek diverted into Butler Creek. All the sewers that emptied into the Savannah River had to be rerouted into Beaver Dam Canal.[21]

The Commissioners chafed at the amount of time required to obtain the right of way for the levee. An impatient Chairman Pope put it bluntly to his colleagues, "There are three courses open to us, one to go on as we have done, begging and pleading, going on our knees in our attempts to get people to grant us a right-of-way. I think it will never happen. Second, by a friendly arbitration; third, by a condemnation proceeding."[22] The Commission decided on a combination of the second and third alternative and hired Roy Goodwin as appraiser and arbiter. The Commission could play hard ball when necessary. The Charleston and Western Carolina Railroad wanted $381,552 for its land along the river. The Commission offered $81,014. The two sides settled for $100,000.

The Southern Railway estimated that changing its tracks at Hamburg and on Augusta's Sixth Street would cost $380,000 and asked the Commission for reimbursement. Wingfield answered that the rail company would have to pay it all because the public welfare required the changes. The Aiken-Augusta Railroad said that it could not use the 13th Street bridge with the new grade. The Commission answered, in effect, "too bad." The North Augusta Flood Protection Committee worried that the Augusta levee might cause the next surge of high water to wipe out Hamburg. In that case, who would pay, they asked. Fred Pope replied that the South Carolinians need not worry because the anticipated disaster might never happen, "We are the trustees for the City of Augusta in this great work, and it is not for us to discuss what might happen in the future."[23] The North Augustans might have wondered at that response, because, in fact the Commission was worried about the future, the future of Augusta. And the Carolinians were right to worry because the floods of 1928 and 1929 wiped out the old town of Hamburg.

Albert J. Twiggs, who had worked with Wingfield on the waterworks, was low bidder for the first three sections from above Singleton Mill to below East Boundary. His contract included a penalty clause for lateness. He constructed a railroad trestle and ran cars along the top, dumping fill from a pit above the Singleton Mill through the trestle and covering it up. Though not an original method, Augustans applauded its ingenuity. When Twiggs failed to finish the work on time, the Commission was inclined to forgive the forfeiture, but Wingfield insisted that Twiggs pay the penalty. In January 1915 Twiggs asked the Commission for $5,000; the balance of an advance already agreed upon. Wingfield said no, Twiggs had not progressed sufficiently. However, when Wingfield went to the Mississippi River to inspect its levee and recruit contractors, the Commission quietly awarded Twiggs the $5,000.[24]

In addition to his trip to the West and his several visits to the Corps of Engineers in Savannah, Wingfield traveled twice to Washington, D.C. to lobby for the almost insignificant funds for rip-rapping the river bank. Congressman Tom Hardwick had neglected to ask for the appropriation in a river and harbors bill. Only Wingfield's alertness and his testimony before the committee insured that the federal share of $125,000 be included in the budget.[25]

By mid-1915 Wingfield heard complaints about the way the levee was being constructed. He insisted that the Commission bring back the expert engineer A.L. Dabney to examine the work underway. Dabney came, looked around, and assured everyone that "the work is being handled in a capable and efficient manner." He promised, "You will have a substantial and efficient levee system." The Commission thereupon increased Wingfield's salary from $1,200 to $2,400 for the duration of the work.[26]

In 1916 Wingfield and Twiggs renewed what had become a feud. Twiggs asked the Commission for ten percent allowance for "shrinkage." He referred to the fact that the levee tended to settle about ten percent and he had to go back and add new fill. Wingfield refused, saying that the contract already allowed for shrinkage. Twiggs sent his attorney to ask the Commission for the money. When the attorney failed to get satisfaction, Twiggs sued the city for $135,954.[27]

Wingfield seemed to add insult to injury when he apparently denied Twiggs the opportunity to bid on building the Butler Creek gates. Twiggs appealed to the Commission, arguing that his work was the best along the canal, "While I was well aware of Mr. Wingfield's attitude towards us, I did not think he would assume the right to dictate who should bid on the public work of the City of Augusta." Wingfield was anything but apologetic. He pointed out that the bids were solicited in the press for two weeks and Twiggs missed the deadline. Besides, he had heard that Twiggs had threatened to run up the cost if he got the job. Finally, on February 18, 1917 Twiggs and his lawyer together with the Canal and River Commission members sat down with the City Council Finance Committee and compromised on a settlement of $50,000 for the "shrinkage" claim. That was not the end of it. Still smarting from Wingfield's snubs, Twiggs secured legal action to enjoin the city treasurer from paying Wingfield a salary for his work with the Commission while he received his regular salary from the city as Commissioner of Public Works. In his defense the Commission appealed to the Georgia Supreme Court, but that court agreed that Wingfield was not entitled to extra compensation for his work on the levee. Twiggs won that fight, but it was a hollow victory because the extra pay would have ended anyhow with the completion of the levee.[28]

The lower sections of the levee work were contracted to C.A. Teague, the Globe Dredging Company, and to the firm of Morris and Glover. Their work went without incident, except that Morris and Glover were painfully slow in their progress through the swamps at the end of the levee and the City had to take over the last portion of the works at Butler's Creek. On January 5, 1919 Mayor James Littleton pronounced the levee "practically complete."[29]

Nisbet Wingfield's final report on the levee appeared in *The Chronicle* on February 2, 1919. The total cost of construction came to a staggering $1,979,538.53. Total length of the levee was (and is) eleven and four-tenths of a mile, the Beaver Dam Canal was deepened five and six-tenths of a mile, and the canal bank raised a length of three and a half miles. Thirty-five contractors worked on the job. The levee included nine gates: six at Sibley Mill, five at King Mill, ten at Hawk's Gully, and six at Butler's Creek.

As though on schedule, the Savannah River tested the

new works on December 24, 1918 with a flood of over thirty-five feet. All levee gates closed properly. The excess water drained out of Beaver Dam Canal as planned. In short, the levee system passed the test with flying colors. Mayor Littleton told his fellow citizens, "Our city is now safe from flood waters of the Savannah River."[30]

The Flood Commission turned the levee over to the City Council of Augusta on April 29, 1919, but before doing so the Commission paid tribute to its chief engineer. Mayor William P. White entered into the minutes a resolution honoring Nisbet Wingfield, "Throughout he has proved himself courteous, persistent, courageous, capable, honest. His assiduity has never flagged; his loyalty never abated, now therefore: Be it resolved that the thanks of this commission which had in its charge the construction of the Augusta levee be extended to Nisbet Wingfield, for the excellence of his plans, for his conscientious fidelity, for his unswerving loyalty, for his fairness and honesty."[31] Never before, and perhaps never since, has the City Engineer been given such high accolades.

Any reader of this chapter must wonder how Nisbet Wingfield had any time for his other duties as Chief Engineer and Commissioner of Public Works. In that capacity he had to monitor the canal, waterworks, streets and drains in addition to his involvement in the levee project. Next to the levee, his greatest concern was with the increasing consumption of water caused largely by waste. He wondered if the waterworks could continue to supply the amount of water consumed by the community. In his 1915 report he wrote, "Water used in Augusta is out of all proportion to the number of consumers, being above normal by at least forty percent." The situation was worsened by several years of low water following the flood of 1912. Wingfield had to ration water to the mills. A more serious problem was voiced by Fire Chief Frank Reynolds in 1915. There might not be enough water to fight a serious fire.[32]

A year after Chief Reynolds warned the City Council about the danger of low water pressure, a terrible fire swept through Augusta. A community that had to bear the enormous cost of the levee and a new city hospital now had to cope with this disaster. Mayor James Littleton expressed the feelings of many, "While the administration was still gasping under this heavy load, and hoping that the worst had come, the City of Augusta was visited, on March 22nd, 1916 by a conflagration that swept away in a night taxable property aggregating several millions of dollars."[33] The blaze began in the Dyer Building on the northwest corner of 8th and Broad and tornadic winds carried the flames eastward, burning out twenty-six city blocks entirely and seven blocks partially, destroying 526 residences and 138 business buildings.

Historian Calvin Billman studied the causes of the fire and concluded, "On that day at least part of the terrible price Augusta paid was due to low water pressure and the local *Herald* admitted as much."[34] Nisbet Wingfield blamed the tragedy on the frightful waste of water, "On the night of the big fire while water was being delivered from the reservoir to the city at a rate of over eleven thousand gallons per minute, no pressure could be had sufficient to cope with the situation."[35] Wingfield pleaded with the City Council to install meters and charge consumers by the volume of water they used. Still the Council dallied until the threat of losing a major military encampment forced the issue, and they had to install meters or lose the camp.

By 1916 Wingfield figured that at least four million gallons of water per day were wasted. In February 1917 almost all of the water drained from the reservoir. Anticipating war with

Germany, Wingfield applied to the War Department for a training camp to be located in Augusta on Lake Aumond. He estimated that the camp would require three million gallons of water a day. The American declaration of war in April enhanced Augusta's chances of getting a camp, and the city had to choose between meters or the camp. Mayor James Littleton put it simply, "The use of water meters was adopted, which was the only recourse left."[36] On May 15, 1917 the City Council enacted an ordinance requiring the installation of meters to all water customers. Installation began in June and by November water consumption had decreased by 4,271,000 gallons over the previous year.[37]

Meanwhile, Wingfield prepared his specifications and on May 19, 1917 presented his case to the Army officials. He learned that they wanted more details showing the location of thirty-two regimental units. Back home, working almost without rest, he completed the plans and made maps showing the distribution of all units and submitted them to the Army by June 2nd. On June 21 he received the bad news that Augusta had been dropped from consideration because Lake Aumond was too remote from the city. Wingfield rushed to the Army's district office in Charleston to present a new set of plans, this one locating the camp adjacent to the reservoir and near the streetcar line. On July 6th Wingfield learned that the higher ups were interested and that he should come to Washington again to explain the details. Wingfield met with a general and his staff from 9:00 A.M. to 11:00 P.M. on July 12th, going over the plans. The Army officials seemed won over by the proximity of an adequate water supply.

Given the go-ahead, Wingfield had the whole camp surveyed by the end of July. He managed to secure pipes from a Birmingham foundry, laid them, and on August 15th turned on the water as hundreds of workers hurried to finish the buildings.

Wingfield quite properly boasted that Augusta was the last encampment to be authorized and the first to be ready for troops. The first detachment of a Pennsylvania division arrived on August 20, 1917.[38] The Pennsylvanians honored one of their Civil War heroes, General Winfield Scott Hancock, by naming the camp after him. In all, 60,000 soldiers occupied 887 buildings at Camp Hancock located on Wrightsboro Road west of Highland Avenue. By any standard the establishment of this huge military installation constituted a remarkable achievement, the more so because Augusta had to rebuild after the fire of 1916 and had to complete the construction of the levee.

Inevitably, there were problems associated with the massive infusion of men into the city. The streetcars could not accommodate the demand. Generals complained about illicit liquor sales (Georgia had adopted prohibition in 1909), and they blamed Augusta authorities for tolerating prostitution. Worst, the canal that had made the camp possible almost caused its failure. More accurately, the vagaries of the river brought on a crisis in the winter of 1918. Water flow was so low in January that the Stevens Creek power plant could not supply electricity, and the canal could not supply enough water to meet the demand. The bitter cold brought on a fuel shortage. All businesses were forced to close on Mondays to save fuel. The Pumping Station ran out of coal to power its auxiliary steam pump.[39]

Warmer weather in February and a return to a normal river flow eased the crisis. However, another scourge, the last of the terrible four, afflicted the community in the same year. An epidemic of influenza, "the Spanish flu," swept the nation and hit Augusta hard. Three thousand cases of the particularly virulent flu were reported at Camp Hancock. The Board of Health closed all schools, churches and theaters on October 8th and they remained closed until the danger passed on November 26th, 1918.[40]

The problems disappeared almost simultaneously. The World War ended in an armistice on November 11, 1918, the influenza epidemic subsided in the same month, and on December 24th the levee withstood a thirty-five-foot flood. In 1919 Nisbet Wingfield decided that the city could do without his services and he retired to private consulting with an office in the Lamar Building on Broad Street in downtown Augusta. He had served the city well for twenty years. The modern water works and the levee stand witness to his achievements.

CHAPTER TWELVE

New Threats to the Canal, 1920–1940

———————

The Clarks Hill project on the Savannah River twenty miles above Augusta saved the Augusta Canal in two ways. It ended the first effort to put a hydroelectric power plant on the canal that would have meant drying up the canal from Lake Olmstead down, and it did what the levee could not do, it protected the canal from flood damage.

The canal and the river did not dominate the news as they did during the first two decades of the century, but they continued to occupy the almost constant attention of the City Council. Except for the ever-flowing waterways, the '20s and '30s contrasted sharply. The '20s were exuberantly optimistic; the '30s discouragingly depressed.

The '20s emphasized advertising, promotion, and bally-hoo to such an exaggerated degree as to make the city boosters appear ridiculous. Never before and not since did Augusta advertise itself so frantically. The Chamber of Commerce took out a full page in the October 18, 1925 *Chronicle* to announce that "America is watching Augusta, the future playground of this country." The ad went on to say that Augusta was only twenty-four hours from Chicago and the West, and twenty-four hours from New York and the East, and that France with its chateau district could not match Augusta's charms. History was sacrificed to promotion: the lonely old market pillar became haunted; the 1797 Ezekiel Harris House became the 1756 Mackay House; Augusta had more pre-Revolutionary buildings than any southern city (unfortunately, we have none); George Washington stayed in Meadow Garden and Chateau Levert (he did not) and he planted a gingko tree in front of the Old Government Building where the state legislature met (the house was not built until after Washington's visit and after the state legislature moved to Louisville). Augusta was proclaimed "the wonder city of the South" and the "city with the golden future." The Chamber predicted that there would be five or six new luxury hotels constructed in the next five years. The Forrest Hills Ricker turned out to be the only one.

The Chamber also spent money on stunts designed to lure people downtown. Bill Strother, "the Human Spider," climbed up the outside of the Lamar Building and stood on his head atop the pinnacle. The Great Zarelli walked across Broad Street on a tightrope every day at noon for a week. Mabel Cody's flying circus did aerial stunts over Broad Street. Perhaps the most incredible and the most bizarre was an aerial demonstration of the strength of silk stockings. Eighteen-year-old volunteer Agnes Holloman, who had never been up in a plane before, hung from the wing of a biplane suspended by a rope of twisted stockings and waved to onlookers on Broad Street. Tourists still came to the Bon Air Hotel and the Partridge Inn, and there was a residential building boom around Lakemont, Lombardy Court and Forrest Hills.

Then came the Depression. Triple blows knocked out the optimism. On the international scene the rise of Hitler, Mussolini and Stalin threatened world security. On the home front, the stock market collapse, the bank failures, and the massive unemployment meant a loss of economic security. The floods of 1928 and 1929 broke through the supposedly impregnable wall of the levee. On all fronts people felt vulnerable. In 1932 Mayor William D. Jennings said that Augusta had just experienced "a year of stress and struggle" and predicted that "a sea of troubles lie ahead." The language of reality had replaced that of bally-hoo.[1] The old A.P.A. organization changed its name to "Cracker Party" and, with its control of the white primary voting lists, dominated city and county politics. Reformers complained about illegal liquor sales and big-time gambling to no avail. Richard Allen, Jr., the son of a mayor of the same name and the grandson of Mayor J.V.H. Allen, and a progressive mayor himself, took full advantage of the assistance offered by Franklin Roosevelt's New Deal administration. As a result, the canal, waterworks and levee received unusual attention.

The gravest danger to the canal during these two decades came from its owners, the City Council. Nisbet Wingfield, before he retired, suggested that the city could use the canal to produce electricity. In his report for the year 1907 he wrote, "At the time the present canal was constructed there was no such thing as commercial electric power." He went on to say that a power plant could be built at the lower end of the canal, or on the river above the canal.[2] Almost on cue, J. P. "Pink" Wood, mentioned earlier as an associate of Colonel Dyer, organized the Georgia-Carolina Power Company and constructed a dam across the river at Stevens Creek. Wingfield complained that the dam was lower on the Carolina side and at low river the main stream was diverted to that side. In 1911, the year the Stevens Creek plant began operations, Wingfield prepared plans for a municipally owned plant on the first level of the canal above the uppermost mill, the Warwick. The city set aside a plot of land for the project.[3] The 1912 flood and the construction of the levee put plans for a power plant on hold.

In 1919 as soon as the levee was finished, Mayor William P. White called the city council's attention to the need for a city-owned source of electricity. The current rate charged by the Augusta-Aiken Railway and Electric Company was "exorbitant and unreasonable."[4] He repeated the suggestion in each of the next two inaugural messages and before he left office had the satisfaction of signing a contract with "Pink" Wood, who offered to construct the plant for the city.[5] In his first message to the council, Mayor Julian Smith said he heartily agreed with "the plans for hydro-electric power on the canal... finally eliminating the canal altogether." If determination alone would have accomplished anything, Mayor Smith had enough to get the job done. "I deem this matter so important," he said, "I recommend that the city go about the development with all possible speed."[6]

The project met with an unexpected setback when the bill authorizing the city to build the plant failed of passage in the Georgia Legislature. Mayor Smith blamed the defeat on individuals, who "I do not believe understood the effect of the proposed legislation."[7] The issue continued to agitate the City Council. On August 18, 1924 the Council engaged in a heated debate not on whether to build a power plant and shut down the canal, but whether to own it or lease it. The Canal Commission of the City Council recommended that the charge for water be doubled, from the traditional $5.50 per horsepower rate to $11.00 per horsepower per year. The increased revenue would be put into a reserve for a ten-year period. After that, the city could afford to finance the construction of the hydroelectric plant.

The debate centered on whether to adopt the new rate and the ten-year delay, or to find ways to proceed with the lease with the Georgia-Carolina Power Company. Respected Judge Enoch Callaway asked to speak to the Council, "I am against allowing the canal to be leased to private operators who are thinking only of their profit and gain, and the moment you lease it to Mr. Wood, the Augusta-Aiken Railway and Electric Company, or anyone else, you will break faith with the people and you will get no more mills here." The judge asserted that the mills preferred to do business with the city and would willingly pay the increased rate. Water rental would bring in far more to the city treasury than the proposed lease to a power company. To the objection of Landon Thomas of King Mill, who had complained about the $11.00 rate, Judge Callaway answered that Thomas was bluffing, "When his present lease has expired, cut off his water supply and let him get his power elsewhere." Mayor Julian Smith cast the deciding vote for implementing the new rate with the implication of constructing a city plant ten years in the future. "I feel satisfied," said the mayor, "that if this policy is pursued, the Canal will become the most valuable asset of the City."[8]

Julian Smith had hoped that the canal power plant would be his legacy; instead he is remembered for the city's purchase of Colonel Dyer's Lake View Park from the Augusta-Aiken Railway Company. The casino at the park was renamed in his honor. Public Works Commissioner W.H. Wise supervised the erection of stone entrance gates and the repair of all buildings. He removed a water fountain from Greene Street and installed it in the park.[9] Wise also constructed a forty-foot wide

causeway across the northern end of Lake Olmstead that provided a road connection around the lake for the convenience of
the residents of the growing Lakemont community.

Julian Smith's tenure in office also coincided with the
city's involvement in river transportation. In order to demon-
strate the city's interest in the development of the Savannah
River, the City Council purchased an old steamer named the
Altamaha. As is often the case influential citizens went to court
to block the city's action. Mayor Smith testified before Superior
Court Judge David Franklin that unless Augusta used the river
it might just as well be in a desert. To Smith's dismay the judge
denied the City's right to go into the boat business. Smith
appealed to the Georgia Supreme Court and had the satisfaction
of winning. The Court decided on December 22, 1924 that the
city's charter was broad enough to permit the purchase of a
riverboat. The significance of the aged and practically useless
Altamaha is that the Corps of Engineers concluded that the city
was in earnest about river development and the Corps began
plans for a lock and dam at New Savannah that would insure a
pool of water at Augusta. The New Savannah Lock and Dam
would lead to the more important Clarks Hill Project.[10]

All the discussion about the electrification of the canal
caused the Enterprise Mill to convert canal waterpower to electricity. In 1920 the mill became the first in Augusta to install its
own power plant. Two huge turbines drove two "umbrella" type
generators. The mill entered into a contract with the city to
increase its allotment of water to four times the original
amount. In 1923 the Graniteville Company in the Horse Creek
Valley of South Carolina acquired controlling interests in both
the Sibley and the Enterprise Mills. In 1940 the two mills were
combined as the Sibley-Enterprise, and in 1954 the two mills
became units of the Graniteville Company. Graniteville also

Figure 51. One of the Enterprise Mill generators, installed in 1920, still furnishes electricity for the renovated mill today. *(Courtesy of Historic American Engineering Record)*

bought the Sutherland Yarn Mill and turned it into a waste factory, baling and storing cotton waste from the other mills.[11]

Mayor William P. White, Julian Smith's successor, died after two years in office and the City Council elected Raleigh Daniel to fill out the three-year term. Daniel is remembered because during his year in office the city purchased the old Camp Hancock airfield and named it Daniel Field. Councilman Jack Callahan sponsored the construction of a bridge over the canal's third level on Calhoun Street (now Walton Way) and the Council named the bridge in his honor.[12] Commissioner W.H. Wise took up important unfinished business in 1927, the excavation of the second reservoir on the Hill. Work began on the project before Wingfield left office in 1919 and every mayor after that urged that it be completed; Daniel managed to push the project through. Wise called Wingfield out of retirement to act as consulting engineer on the job. Water began to flow into the new basin (west of the first) on March 28, 1928.[13]

The appointment of Lester Moody as Secretary of the Chamber of Commerce on July 13, 1926 seemed relatively unimportant at the time, but Moody proved to be the city's most effective lobbyist in persuading Congress to develop the Savannah River. In the same year the Savannah River Electric Power Company applied to the Federal Power Commission for license to construct a power plant at Clarks Hill on the Savannah River. Moody became intensely interested in the project. He used his considerable influence to get the government to provide the electricity, rather than a private company.[14]

In 1927 the Georgia Power Company was formed out of the merger of several regional power companies. In July 1928 Georgia Power bought the Augusta-Aiken Railway and Electric Company with its old power plant on the canal at 15th Street. The power company had no use for the trolley line to Aiken and shut it down on July 8, 1929.[15]

The City Council could not resist the lure of having its very own power plant, and in 1929 took up the subject again, without waiting for the expiration of the self-imposed ten-year waiting period. The City employed a Kansas firm to advise it on the best way to go about constructing the plant. The consultants gave the wrong answer by suggesting that the city use diesel power instead of waterpower. The City Council disregarded that advice. In 1931 the Council introduced a bill in the legislature authorizing a bond issue to finance the construction of a water-powered plant. The measure passed in July 1931 and in November the Council voted to proceed with the electrification of the canal. It now seemed that the long anticipated project would become a reality. However, the City could find no purchasers for the bonds in the aftermath of the stock market collapse. The City could not show that the expected revenue would be sufficient to pay off the $2,500,000 bond issue.[16]

Having failed to secure financing from the private sector, the City turned to the federal government and applied for a loan from the Reconstruction Finance Corporation, an agency established by the Hoover administration to cope with the depression. However, not even that agency would take on such a risky proposition. With the advent of Franklin Roosevelt and the New Deal's generous loan policy, the City tried again. In June 1935 the City learned that the Public Works Commission approved the project. Mayor Will Jennings said, "With its promise of an asset of immeasurable value, the project now seems an assured fact."[17] Coincidently Lester Moody returned from a trip to Washington, D.C. to announce that President Roosevelt had taken a personal interest in the Clarks Hill Project. Now the city leaders could not decide whether they wanted the city power plant or the Clarks Hill plant. They could not visualize two power plants. Editor Tom Hamilton, a chief booster of river development, wrote editorially, "The whole future of Augusta and this section depends upon Clarks Hill." He called upon the city to defer its plant. However, the availability of federal funding presented too great a temptation to the City Council. That body voted to go ahead with the city power plant.[18]

In late December 1935 the City heard the disappointing news that the crusty and cautious Secretary of the Interior Harold Ickes imposed a delay on the city plant pending the report of a special commission. On the other hand, the March 18, 1936 *Chronicle* announced that President Roosevelt's commission gave a positive recommendation on the Clarks Hill

Project, setting an estimated cost of $21,244,000. Augusta had become involved in a contest between two factions, one for Clarks Hill and the other for the canal power plant.

Frantic at the thought of losing its power plant, the City Council entered into an agreement with the hitherto leading opponent of the municipal plant, the Georgia Power Company. Georgia Power consented to take on the project with the understanding that the government would provide an outright grant of $193,000 and also purchase City bonds in the amount of $630,000. When the federals seemed lukewarm to that proposition, the Power Company offered to buy the city bonds if the Public Works Administration would contribute $193,000. The offer was accepted and the issue seemed finally settled.[19]

The one consistent feature in the history of the canal is that no expenditure of the city has gone unchallenged by one or more of its citizens. In this case James L. "Uncle Jim" Cartledge and other taxpayers secured an injunction barring the city from proceeding with the canal plant. To the chagrin of the promoters of the municipal plant, Judge David Franklin granted the injunction. At this point the Georgia Power Company, never very enthusiastic about the project, and apparently satisfied that a competing power plant would never be constructed, withdrew from the arrangement.

The inauguration of the New Savannah Bluff Lock and Dam provided solace to the City boosters. *The Chronicle's* Tom Hamilton, one of the foremost proponents of the New Savannah project, wrote that the lock and dam made the Clarks Hill Project possible. He might also have said that the City's purchase of the *Altamaha* prepared the way for the lock and dam. In 1937 the ancient craft had been bought by a farmer from the City for $125; he intended to cut holes in the side and use the hull for a cow barn.[20] It had served its purpose in staying afloat long enough to attract the attention of the Corps of Engineers. In March 1941 the first barge passed through the New Savannah Locks. The Merry Brick Company's *Merry Queen* caused Augustans to anticipate a renaissance of river traffic.

In 1938 engineers began to survey the vast area to be covered by the Clarks Hill reservoir. President Roosevelt signed the bill authorizing construction of the dam and power plant on December 23, 1944.[21] The prospect of cheap electricity from the Clarks Hill plant put an end to the will o' the wisp notion of Augusta Canal electrification, at least for the time being. The massive dam, once completed, helped extend the life of the canal in another way; it provided flood protection from the river in a way the levee never could.

The successful test of the levee by the thirty-five-foot flood of 1919 had caused Augustans to feel confident that the city was at last safe from devastation by water. The City Council created an office of "Keeper of the Levee." That gentleman dutifully patrolled the banks looking for possible breaks, and, for nine years, reported none. The levee withstood a greater threat in 1928 when the river rose to forty feet six inches. *The Chronicle* credited the levee with "saving Augusta again" even though acknowledging that Hamburg across the river was inundated. However, the system could not cope with the monster forty-six-foot flood of 1929. The levee broke behind the Goodale House on Sand Bar Ferry Road and water backed into the city, covering a hundred residential blocks. Commissioner W.H. Wise opened the gates at Butler Creek to let the water out, and when that was not enough contractor W. F. Bowe dynamited a section of the lower levee, releasing water trapped behind the levee.[22]

On October 1, 1929 weatherman E.D. Emigh forecast a surge of forty-seven feet. Mayor William Bell urged town resi-

Figure 52. The 1929 flood waters reached the old jail located between the Canal and the River upstream of Sibley Mill. *(Courtesy of the Augusta Museum of History)*

dents to flee to the Hill. Fire trucks drove through the town at midnight warning people to evacuate the city. Volunteers worked alongside convicts piling sandbags on top of the saturated levee. The river crested at just over forty-five feet, tore away a span of the railroad bridge at Sixth Street and with it five loaded coal cars placed on the bridge for stabilization. Dangerous slides occurred in the levee banks; water in town reached the Union Station. On October 3rd the waters began to subside; the first light of dawn showed fish stranded on city streets. Later that day residents began returning to their homes.[23]

Much of the after-flood conversation concerned the levee, why it broke, who was at fault, and how a repetition could be prevented. Less public notice was paid to the devastating damage to the canal. The canal above Rae's Creek was virtually destroyed and would have to be rebuilt. Meanwhile, the Pumping Station could not function and the mills had to close down and lay off workers. It was a major catastrophe.

Commissioner W. H. Wise, who had no opportunity to

distinguish himself until then, rose to the occasion. He divided the work to be done into four sections and contracted with four different companies to get it done quickly. He determined the cause of the initial break was an unusually swollen torrent from Reed's Creek that washed out the bank opposite, and allowed the rising river to pour through. The river continued to rise, covering the canal banks and washing them down to a rubble of stone and sand. When the river receded, Wise put up sand bag dams at Reed's Creek, Rock Creek, and at the Pumping Station. Before he could start rebuilding the bank he had to dredge the tons of sand and construct a road along the land side of the canal for trucks use.

W. F. Bowe contracted to do the 6,875 foot section from the locks to Reed's Creek. Along the first 3,400 feet he shored the bank with a masonry wall. The Twiggs Company rebuilt 7,125 feet of the bank below Reed's Creek to Rock Creek. R.M. Mitchum worked on the section from Rock Creek to within a

Figure 53. After the 1929 flood the long spillway woodwork was replaced with concrete. *(Courtesy of Michael White)*

thousand feet of the Pumping Station. The Claussen-Lawrence Company shored up the bank from the Pumping Station to the beginning of the levee near Warwick Mill. The same company rebuilt the long spillway at Rae's Creek, tearing out the old woodwork and replacing it with concrete.

"We worked every day and most of the nights," reported Commissioner Wise. The cold, rainy winter weather, the slippery clay, and the mud made work more difficult. Wise credited his assistants, E.E. Pund and M.B. Cooper, with devotion above the call of duty. Wise hired twelve inspectors to keep careful track of the work, and several timekeepers to monitor the contractors.

Under the circumstances the fact that they rebuilt the canal in forty-five days is remarkable. Even so, Wise was criticized by some citizens for hiring too many timekeepers and for not laying off the contractors earlier than he did. Wise explained that the timekeepers helped keep the cost down. He did not dare stop work until the banks were raised three and a half feet above the latest flood-line. Wise said that he warned the City Council after the forty-foot, six-inch flood of 1928 that the levee and the canal were not secure from a higher flood but "City Council did not seem to realize the necessity of action until the recent high water."[24]

If not as dynamic as Nisbet Wingfield, nor nearly the public figure, Wise earned the city's gratitude for his services in the canal crisis of 1929. He had a new "dining hall" built at the lock and dam in 1932 and repaired the pavilion. After repairing a "blow-out" in the canal bank at Rae's Creek Spillway in 1933, he retired without fanfare later that year. E.E. Pund took his place as City Engineer and Public Works Commissioner.[25]

By 1933, the mood of the city, and indeed the mood of America, had changed. This was the period characterized by Mayor W. D. Jennings as one of struggle. Governor Eugene

Talmadge took pride in disdaining Franklin Roosevelt's relief measures and in refusing to cooperate with government programs, but Jennings and the Council took immediate advantage of all the opportunities offered. With federal relief money in 1934, the City put a thousand men on the levee, raising the banks. Mayor Richard Allen, Jr. followed the same policy. He told the council frankly that he intended to "take advantage of every bit of cooperation and financial aid that the Government can and will extend." He ignored the mutterings of the anti-New Deal people who predicted the triumph of socialism. Thousands of Augustans, black and white, who would have had no other jobs, went to work on the canal and levee. They dug trenches for sewers and extended the waterworks system. In 1936 the federal government supplied fifty trucks for the work on the levee. In the same year a new casino of stone and wood was constructed at Lake View Park; a pavilion and a barbecue pit were added in the next two years.[26]

When the forty-foot flood of 1936 caused a breach in the canal bank near the locks Commissioner E.E. Pund had hundreds of W.P.A. workers do the necessary repairs. He improved upon the opportunity to prepare a master plan for canal upgrading that included replacing all the gates, improving the Rae's Creek long spillway, raising the banks three feet above the 1929 flood, straightening the canal above the Pumping Station and building a new spillway above the Pumping Station to relieve pressure on the Rae's Creek spillway in cases of excess water. To initiate the first repairs the city borrowed $90,000 from the federal Reconstruction Finance Corporation, and then continued the work with a grant of $661,000 from the W.P.A. (Works Progress Administration). The work of raising the banks went on continually with new grants until 1942, as the canal received unprecedented attention.

Another W.P.A. grant of $685,000 funded the work on the lower reaches of the levee. Meanwhile the P.W.A. (Public Works Administration) financed waterworks improvements. In 1939 Mayor Allen reported that for a cost of two million dollars the city received ten million dollars from the government, that 3,600 Augustans were employed with W.P.A. funds, bringing $150,000 a month into the local economy, and that he was not the least bit ashamed of accepting federal aid.[27]

Throughout this canal narrative, the condition of the "canal people," the mill district residents, has been of interest. They welcomed the New Deal, especially the National Industrial Recovery Act, the one that set forty hours a week and forty cents an hour for mill workers, and banned child labor. The local mills asked for and received a grace period of five years to fully implement the program; meanwhile, they pledged to raise wages as low as $6.00 a week to $12.00 a week. They would gradually lower the seventy-hour work week to forty hours.[28] All stores that agreed to adhere to the new guidelines put a "blue eagle" emblem in their store windows, and Augusta was soon festooned with blue eagle signs.

In October 1933 Augusta mill workers conducted a two-week strike to prompt the local mills to adhere to the codes; at the time only the King Mill had begun to do so. The National Textile Union called for a general strike on September 1, 1934 to force the implementation of the codes. The Augusta mill workers again struck all but the King Mill. On the fourth day of the strike the police used tear gas to break up a demonstration at Sibley Mill. Mayor Richard Allen, Jr. circulated among the crowd of a thousand people urging calm. More serious trouble started at the Enterprise. Strikers scuffled with police, and the police fired into the crowd, critically wounding three men. Mayor Allen hurried to the scene, "I am sick at heart," he said when he saw the bloodshed. He felt that if he had come earlier, he might have prevented the violence.[29]

One of the wounded men, Norman Leon Carroll, did not recover. In an extraordinary outpouring of grief and solidarity 7,000 mourners crowded Jennings Stadium in Allen Park for the memorial services. A speaker said that "He died that others may be free." On September 9, 1934 the same thousands formed the funeral cortege to escort the body of Leon Carroll through the mill district to the West End Cemetery on the canal near Lake Olmstead.[30]

Georgia Governor Eugene Talmadge, who affected the attitudes of a man of the people, mobilized the national guard to keep the mills open. He had the guard arrest the strikers around Atlanta and put them in "internment camps." On September 22nd the national union terminated the strike. Local workers had suffered much and gained little.[31]

One other important way that the New Deal affected the residents of the mill district was the construction of modest but adequate housing. On July 2, 1938 the Augusta Housing Authority broke ground for the first of the Olmstead Homes residences in the Harrisburg neighborhood adjacent to Lake Olmstead.

Though the decade of the '30s was a time of depression, the New Deal proved to be generous to the canal and its people. City Engineer E.E. Pund summed up the progress in his 1941 report, "The condition of the canal system is far stronger than it has ever been prior to the time this work was done by the W.P.A."[32]

CHAPTER THIRTEEN

The Canal as a Nuisance, 1940–1980

———————>ɔ●ɕ———————

After it received so much attention during the '30s, the canal suffered from neglect during the next three decades. In 1960 when County Commissioner Herbert Elliott characterized the canal as a "cesspool" it was hardly an exaggeration. Mayor Lewis Newman managed to have the canal cleaned in 1974, and he voiced the opinion that it was the first time in its history that it had ever been cleaned. The neighborhood around the second and third levels had become blighted. The Augusta Factory, closed in 1937 because of a failure to modernize, loomed like a hulk, derelict and blackened with soot from passing trains.[1] The consensus opinion was that the ancient factory and the buildings surrounding it were beyond rehabilitation; they should be torn down and the canal covered up.

Progress meant closing the canal and developing the river. The completion of the great Clarks Hill Dam, the dredging of the river to create a nine-foot channel, and the construction of state docking facilities below East Boundary focused public attention on the river and its exciting possibilities. Lester Moody and other dreamers revived George Walton's idea of a canal linking the Tennessee River system and the Savannah River headwaters. Augusta forgot about Lowell and decided that it would be the Memphis of the East.

During the decades covered by this chapter Augustans were interested in issues other than the canal. In the '40s, Augusta coped with the war effort. After two decades of very little change, the war brought massive dislocations and remade the city. Camp Gordon became post-war Fort Gordon; the Oliver General and the Lenwood Hospitals merged into a larger Veterans' Hospital; Georgia Aero-Tech training school became Bush Field. Clarks Hill hydroelectric plant provided a plentiful source of energy and attracted the huge Savannah River Plant, the "Bomb Plant," to the South Carolina side of the Savannah River. In the '50s and '60s new factories rose up south of the city, taking advantage of the available electric power, the abundant river water and the comparatively low taxes.

The Cracker Party controlled politics during the '30s and into the '40s until the Supreme Court ruled the white primary unconstitutional in 1944. A reform movement swept the Crackers out of power in 1946. Chastened, the Crackers accepted the reality of black participation in politics and re-emerged as the "New Cracker" Party. The '50s witnessed the beginnings of black activism and the corresponding rise of opposition to integration, especially by politicians who expected to ride white supremacy into elected office. When the Supreme Court outlawed school segregation in 1954, the old guard in the state legislature reacted angrily with a barrage of laws opposing integration and for good measure inserted the Virginia battle flag into the state banner. (The Sons of Confederate Veterans and the

Daughters of the Confederacy opposed doing away with the old flag modeled as it was after the official flag of the Confederate States.) Paine College students sat at white-only lunch counters and in the front of city buses, got arrested and caused courts to outlaw segregation in lunch counters and on buses.

The more paranoid types viewed the Civil Rights movement as a Communist plot. In fact, the fear of Communism mounted almost to hysteria during the '60s. The Vietnam War raised passions to an unprecedented degree, with some arguing for an Armageddon-like stand against Communism and others convinced that the Vietnamese did not understand our worldview and a military attempt to win their hearts and minds was futile. The '70s brought a merciful end to the war abroad and a beginning of the effort to integrate schools at home. A flight of stores from downtown, begun in the '50s, climaxed with the opening of two malls on the outskirts of town in 1978.

Thus, World War II, the Civil Rights Movement, and the Vietnam War relegated any news about the Augusta Canal to the back pages. Though hardly noticed at the time, the canal actually played an important part in World War II. Public Works Commissioner Ernest Pund had to stop his work on the canal and hurry to lay pipes to the new army camp on Tobacco Road called Camp Gordon. In his 1942 report Pund noted that most of the projected W.P.A. work had been done except for a masonry gate at Reed's Creek. The long spillway above the Pumping Station remained to be finished, as did the proposed straightening of the canal above the Pumping Station. The Army paid for a new water main from the Pumping Station to the reservoir on Highland Avenue. The main crossed the canal on a bridge rather than along the bottom of the waterway. The Army also subsidized the enlargement of the filter station at the reservoir.

Mayor James Woodall told the City Council that the Army spent $300,000 improving the waterworks system.[2]

The incoming mayor in 1943, W.D. Page, reflected the attitude of his predecessors. To him, as to every mayor before him without exception, the canal was a major responsibility of the city and a priority concern. At the outset of his term he asked Public Works Commissioner Pund to recommend necessary improvements in the canal. Pund repeated the same suggestions he had made before: the Reed's Creek gate, and the long spillway, the straightening of the canal. Unfortunately for Page's good intentions, nothing could be done because the demands of the military for water created a crisis. The necessity to supply both Camp Gordon and the Army Air Base at Daniel Field depleted the water supply in the reservoir to the critical stage. Mayor Page negotiated with the Army to pay for a second 18-inch water main from the Pumping Station to the reservoir.[3]

Mayor Page was the last to inquire about the canal for over a decade. Commissioner Pund fell into a habit of recommending the same three improvements year after year. In 1944, '45, and '46 he repeated the need for a gate at Reed's Creek, the completion of the spillway, and the straightening of the canal. Pund retired in 1947 with none of the three projects done. His successor John Twiggs attempted to educate the City Council on the importance of paying attention to the canal. He told them about how much good work had been done during the heyday of the W.P.A., and how the work had not been completed, specifying the same three improvements. The long spillway above the Pumping Station, he thought, was especially important. "I strongly recommend its completion for the present spillways and control gates are inadequate to discharge flood waters should it be necessary to close gates across the canal near the city stockade." His recommendation fell on deaf ears.[4]

In 1948 the canal reminded the City Council of its presence when floodwaters caused a break in the canal bank at 13th Street. Engineer Twiggs fixed the break at a cost of $12,017. A growing population required more water, and in 1948 the voters approved a bond issue permitting the expansion of water and sewerage connections. In fact, the unglamorous waterworks expansion became a constant need during the next decades.[5] After eight years of pleading, the Reed's Creek gates were installed in 1950; in the following year gates at the locks were rebuilt with steel by the Columbus Construction Company at a cost of $12,200.[6] The long spillway above the Pumping Station was never completed. There is no evidence in the records that the straightening of the canal was ever done, either. Instead, the massive expansion of the city's population as the result of the 1951 construction of the Savannah River Plant and the resulting need to supply water engrossed the attention of Commissioner Twiggs and the City Council. Engineer Twiggs negotiated an emergency loan from the government and then a grant in the amount of $1,652,000. However, the city had to spend $3,000,000 to upgrade the water system. M.P. Phillips replaced Twiggs and supervised the installation of 6.53 miles of new sewers, the expansion of the filter plant, and the increase in capacity of the Pumping Station by the addition of a new station adjacent to the old one.[7]

The waterworks expansion did not attract public notice and the canal would have escaped newspaper mention entirely during the '50s except for a tragedy that had all the elements of a mystery story. On April 27, 1951 the body of seven-year-old Lois Janes was discovered jammed up against the Sibley Mill raceway. An autopsy revealed that she had been murdered. All Augustans, and especially the residents of Harrisburg, were intensely interested in the search for her killer. After a month of investigation the police arrested a homeless man, described as a fisherman, named Lovey Ivey. He incriminated the little girl's grandmother, Mamie Price, who paid him $5.00 to murder the child so she could collect the insurance money. Mamie Price was tried and convicted of the crime; she and Ivey were sentenced to life in prison.[8]

Mayor Hugh Hamilton's administration introduced fluoridation into the city's water supply in 1955, over the objections of some who thought it another Communist plot. The decade of neglect began to attract unwelcome attention to the canal. Engineer M.P. Phillips reported that Beaver Dam Ditch had become clogged causing sewage to back up into the city. During the next two years, the city attempted to improve drainage by dredging the ditch. In 1956 surveyors marked the point on the first level of the canal where the projected Interstate Highway 20 would pass.[9]

Under Mayors Hamilton and Millard Beckum (during his first term in office) Augusta enjoyed an industrial boom rivaling that of the 1880's. A $12 million Talmadge Hospital was dedicated in March 1956, and in the same month the Defense Department announced that Camp Gordon would become Fort Gordon, a permanent installation. The great expectations elicited by the completion of the Clarks Hill Dam and power plant were fulfilled by a procession of new industries to the area: E-Z-Go Car Corporation, Continental Can, Wilson Shirt Company, S. H. Kress Warehouse, General Electric Tube Plant, Procter and Gamble, Monsanto Chemical Company, Columbia Nitrogen, and dozens of lesser companies, all of whom located here to take advantage of the abundant water of the Savannah River, the climate, low taxes and non-union labor. Of interest to this narrative is that none of the new companies chose to make use of the canal. The same voices cheering for the new arrivals called for the dismantling of the canal and the old structures along its banks. The tearing down began in 1958.

Mayor Hugh Hamilton initiated the first urban renewal project in May 1957, and his successor Millard Beckum carried out the program. The first of several projects focused on the second level of the canal. The area from 13th to 11th between D'Antignac and the canal was targeted for demolition. A wider neighborhood south of the target area as far as Gwinnett Street (Laney-Walker) would be "rehabilitated." With a federal grant of $1,808,853, the city began the clearance in July 1958. Over a hundred citizens in the rehabilitation area brought a suit against the city, but Judge Fred Kennedy rejected their complaint. By the end of 1960 Mayor Beckum reported that 97 percent of the real estate parcels had been purchased, and 197 families or individuals relocated.[10]

No tears were shed for the demolition of the Augusta

Figure 54. The end of an era: the demolition of the Augusta Factory as part of the 1960 urban renewal. *(Courtesy of Tom Robertson)*

Factory and its attendant buildings, once the pride of the city and the seat of its industrial revolution. "Good riddance" summed up the public's attitude regarding the filling in of the second level. *The Chronicle* of January 28, 1960 called attention to the rest of the polluted canal; even Lake Olmstead had to be closed because of contamination. The reason for the attention to a filthy canal should have been obvious. The city's population had grown enormously and yet the old sewers still emptied into the canal. Ironically, some of the same persons who were responsible for the dumping blamed the canal for being dirty.

The second urban renewal project included 26 acres adjoining the Medical College and allowed for its expansion. The third prepared the way for the construction of the new University Hospital and involved the clearing of 96 acres of the old "Frog Hollow" neighborhood, where many factory workers had lived. Urban renewal continued throughout the three years of the Beckum administration and the three-year term of his successor, George Sancken, Jr. Margaret Twiggs, veteran reporter for the *Herald,* reflected the general opinion in her article, "Where once stood shabby houses – modern stores, plants and perhaps motels are expected to rise."[11]

Mayor George Sancken's term of office, 1964-1968, represented a nadir in the history of the canal. The mayor considered the lower portion a noisome nuisance. He applauded the filling in of the second level, "This eliminated a most undesirable and unsanitary situation in a heavily populated area. Additional projects of this nature should be continued until all like conditions can be eliminated." Mayor Sancken revived the old power plant idea, partly because, as he said, it "would eliminate the need for the Augusta Canal." The mayor led a delegation to Washington, D.C. to secure the Federal Power Commission's approval of the project.[12]

Norman Kaylor wrote an article in the Chamber of Commerce publication giving a description of the state of the canal in 1966. He wrongly assumed that there had been no changes on the canal in ninety years. Actually the canal had been rebuilt in 1929 and worked over for a decade after that. Four textile mills still used canal power to run their own generators: the King, Sibley, Enterprise, and Globe. The old picnic area at the locks showed rampant neglect, and danger signs warned visitors away. He described the third level as "a polluted stream flowing into the center of downtown, eventually flowing back in the river." The only positive note he sounded was the hope that the Georgia Power Company would soon build a power plant at Lake Olmstead.[13]

Objections by the King Mill delayed federal approval of the proposed plant until March 1969 when the mill acquiesced. It would purchase electricity rather than generate its own. *The Chronicle* welcomed the news as a Christmas gift, "The canal began with great promise which was fulfilled. Its prospective end comes with equal promise in meeting the demands of a new age." In December 1969 the Federal Power Commission gave the official go-ahead. Mayor Sancken called the announcement great news and stated that the canal's fate was "all but sealed." He referred to the proposed highway later called the John C. Calhoun Expressway and suggested that it be routed down the dry bed of the canal. When planners recommended that the Butt Memorial Bridge be taken down there was no public protest.[14]

However, the canal had some defenders. Sam Waller, the city attorney, was one. He asked a crucial question, "If the canal becomes a dry bed, who owns it?" In his opinion hundreds of legal deeds would have to be examined to find the original owners who granted the canal easement. He also noted that the canal brought in $129,922 in revenue, and that Georgia

Power would pay only $63,780 annually for the lease of the waterway. Besides, the power plant would require 4,500 cubic feet of water per second, and the city engineer could only guarantee a total flow of 5,000 cubic feet. Mayor Millard Beckum, elected to a second term, pondered these facts and concluded, "The margin was a little bit too close for comfort." He regretted the loss of the power plant, "It offered an excellent opportunity to get rid of the canal as it now exists, and to get rid of some unpleasant odors that people complain about."[15]

The canal had another friend in the person of Joseph B. Cumming, grandson of Major Joseph B. Cumming and great-grandson of the Father of the Canal, Henry H. Cumming. Some of the silver service presented to Henry H. Cumming for building the canal sat on Joe Cumming's mantelpiece.

Cumming also happened to be the chairman of the influential Georgia Historical Commission. Through his suasion, the Commission placed the Augusta Canal on the National Register of Historic Places on July 26, 1971. Cumming pointed to the fact that the canal was probably the only one in the country that was still used for power, transportation, and for water supply. The city could now apply for federal funds to clean out the canal and rid it of the bothersome odors. The listing proved to be a turning point in the recent history of the canal; it began a slow process of growing public appreciation for the canal as a unique feature of Augusta's heritage. The nomination would not have prevented the owner, the city, from closing the canal, but it complicated matters.[16]

The National Register nomination had several beneficial effects. The city fathers began to look upon the waterway differently. An immediate result of the listing was a recommendation by Governor Jimmy Carter's National Heritage Trust Commission to purchase land along the first level for a state park. Governor Carter agreed with the idea, and the state spent a million dollars acquiring 230 acres of land along the canal. The Department of Natural Resources contracted with the Eric Hill Associates of Atlanta to draw up a plan for the park. Meanwhile, Mayor Lewis Newman embraced the project whole-heartedly, "The potential of the park and attendant development is tremendous; it is not just day-dreaming to envision a great, permanent asset to the whole area in this program." The mayor assigned city crews to clean up the canal, now suddenly important. He assumed that it was the first time the canal had

Figure 55. Joseph B. Cumming, II.
(Courtesy of David Hugh Connolly, Jr., grandson)

Figure 56. The engraving on the silver ewer states: "Presented by the City of Augusta to Henry H. Cumming, President of the Board of Commissioners of the Augusta Canal under a resolution of the City Council adopted March 2, 1850." *(Courtesy of the Augusta Museum of History)*

ever been cleaned, and he hoped that it would be the last, because the state would have that responsibility in the future.[17]

On March 15, 1974 the consultants delivered their report to the state, the mayor and the chairman of the Richmond County Commission. They envisioned three component sections, the headgates to the end of the first level, Thirteenth Street to the Gordon Highway, and an ancillary park along the riverfront that would connect with the canal. The state declined to do so much, but did agree to develop a park from 13th Street to the I-20 crossing. It would be up to the city to do the rest. Mayor Newman continued to be the chief cheerleader for the project. The park, he said, "is going to be one of the biggest long-range benefits to this area of anything we've got going."[18]

The entrance to the state park would be at Chafee Park, across from the Sibley and King Mills. Mayor Newman sponsored the building of a substantial bridge across the canal at that point, connecting Pearl and Goodrich Streets. The 18th century house across Broad Street from Chafee Park would be the state's welcome center and staff office. Therefore, the office of Historic Preservation dispatched a recent graduate of the University of Georgia to do background research on the house in preparation for the park and for the nation's bicentennial. In the course of her research, Martha Norwood discovered that the house was not what locals thought it was. It was not the circa 1756 Mackay House, the site of a Revolutionary War battle and supposedly the place where thirteen American prisoners were hanged by the British after the battle. She found that the Mackay House had been destroyed during the battle, and that the standing structure had been built by a tobacco merchant named Ezekiel Harris in 1797, the same Harris who surveyed and laid out the 500-acre tract into lots and called the development Harrisburg.

The initial surprise and indignation of local history lovers gave way to a gradual acceptance of Norwood's findings. To buttress her conclusions the state brought to Augusta an archeologist from Colonial Williamsburg named Paul Buchanan. Norwood invited Heard Robertson and Ray Rowland of the Richmond County Historical Society (which had been founded in 1948 to preserve the house) and this writer to witness Buchanan's investigation. After crawling around under the house, and inspecting it from top to bottom, Buchanan testified that it had been built within five years of 1800. He had not known that Norwood's research gave it a date of 1797.[19]

Governor George Busbee declared that the state would not be party to a hoax, and immediately gave the house back to the city to be administered by a "Bicentennial Committee" and later by Historic Augusta, Inc. At that time, this writer happened to be President of the Richmond County Historical Society. A reporter relayed Governor Busbee's characterization of the house as a fake and asked me about it. I replied that it was not the fault of the house; we were to blame for getting the history wrong. Georgia has too few 18th Century houses to despise any of them. Indeed, the Smithsonian Institute in Washington, D.C. later said that the Harris House is the finest example of 18th century architecture in Georgia. We should have known its history; an article in *The Chronicle* in 1902 made it clear that the house was not the Mackay House, but in the hoopla of advertising during the '20s city boosters elaborated upon its history, adding that on occasion the groans of the thirteen patriots who were hanged could still be heard.[20]

Meanwhile, Mayor Newman continued to do his part. In anticipation of the new state park on the first level he focused on the lower canal system; he called it the "Lower Canal Development Plan." In 1975 the Augusta-Richmond County Planning Commission headed by Dayton Sherrouse asked consultant Sydney Carter, who had worked with the Eric Hill Associates, to draw up a plan for the rehabilitation of the canal. Carter's report referred to the state portion of the canal with its exciting features, the scenic upper stretch, the Confederate Chimney, the great mills, the Harris House, and Meadow Garden as the relatively easy part of the development plan. The city must address the lower portion in the inner city. He described the third level as in an "extreme state of deterioration." Low water levels created marsh-like conditions. The canal had become "the receptacle for trash and junk." What was most deplorable, he continued, was that raw sewage was dumped directly into the canal. Citing the overhead utility wiring, the billboards, the rail and traffic noise, he concluded with an understatement that there was "a relatively unattractive southern boundary to the downtown area." He called for an immediate end to the practice of dumping sewage into the canal and he cited the need for a city park at D'Antignac Street between the old second and third levels, using an abandoned fire station as anchor.[21] To his credit, Mayor Newman supported both these recommendations. The city leveled over a portion of the third level to create Dyess Park, named after World War II hero and Medal of Honor winner, Colonel James A. Dyess. The Dyess family had operated the Augusta Lumber Company on the site of the new park.

City engineers began realigning the sewer system to connect with a wastewater treatment plant at Phinizy Swamp. By 1979 the treatment plant, named after City Engineer James R. Messerly, began to make the "sludge," a by-product of the cleaning process, available to local farmers as fertilizer.[22]

Illustrative of a wider interest in the historic value of the canal was the 1976 research effort of a team working for the Historic American Engineering Record, a division of the National Park Service. The researchers made detailed drawings of the locks, gates and other mechanisms and completed histories of the various mills that had used the canal over the years. The members of the team deserve credit for their diligence and the quality of their work. However, whether intended or not, the studies had the tone of a requiem for a canal on the verge of dissolution. Robert L. Spude's fine study of the canal is almost a eulogy, "The construction of Clarks Hill Dam on the Savannah River above Augusta has relieved the residents of any fear of major flooding, and thus the canal has continued to deteriorate. Headgate arms have broken, gates have rusted fast, or fallen down entirely, and the once flowing second and third levels have become choked with overgrowth...The first level continues to power the city water works and hydroelectric units in the Sibley, King, and Enterprise Mills, but even this may end if negotiations with the Georgia Power Company transpire...The future of Augusta's power canal is indeed bleak."[23] The studies prompted the National Park Service to designate the canal and its mills a National Historic Landmark. Perhaps because they were concerned with the industrial uses of the canal, the visiting team missed the stirring of interest in the scenic, cultural and recreational uses of the waterway.

Public interest in canal preservation, tweaked by the outsiders' attention to the historic waterway, was also promoted by the awarding of "historic landmark" status to the Pumping Station by the American Water Works Association. For the first time perhaps ever, volunteers began to turn out to clean the banks of the canal. In 1978 the Young Adult Conservation Corps tidied up five miles of the towpath from Chafee Park to the Lock and Dam.[24] Still expecting great results from the state park, Mayor Newman gave his support to the restoration of the headgates and locks in 1978. The contract with the T.M. Nickles Company called for replacing eight hand operated wood gates with four square sluice gates, rebuilding the remaining nine wood gates, and renovation of the locks. The mayor assumed that this was the first time in over a hundred years that such work was done.[25] Actually it had been done during the W.P.A. era in the '30s.

The contract with the Nickles Company set a March 22, 1979 date for completion. By March 16, 1979 City Engineer James Messerly reported that the gates were still in disrepair and "the operation of the canal is in jeopardy." He recommended termination of the Nickles' contract. The city then engaged the Lee Turzillo Company to complete the project at a cost of $975,000. Unfortunately, the Nickles Company sued for wrongful termination, and an arbitrator ruled that the company had to be paid for the work it did, amounting to $378,292. The settlement raised the total cost of improvements in the headgate area to $1,486, 677 by 1980.[26]

Finally, in preparation for the canal park and to enhance the appearance of the canal area, the city allowed the vacant Singleton Silk Mill to be demolished in 1975.[27] What, then, happened to the greatly anticipated state park? This writer sat on the board of the Georgia Heritage Trust Commission from April 21, 1976 to the demise of the agency five years later. Although the Commission continued to advise the governor to proceed with the canal park, other priorities of the Department of Natural Resources took precedence year after year. As merely an advisory body the Heritage Trust Commission had no budget of its own. After five years of frustration the Commission dissolved. The state exchanged its land along the canal for some land owned by the city that the state needed for an extension of the Bobby Jones Expressway. The best that can be said of the state park idea is that it prompted the city to pay more attention to the waterway and its possibilities.

During the '60s Lester Moody revived the 18th Century dream of George Walton, and otherwise sane and responsible people began to talk about a canal connection between the Savannah River system and the headwaters of the Tennessee River. The completion of Clarks Hill Dam provided a steady river-level at Augusta for the first time in its history, and the Corps of Engineers dredged a nine-foot channel. In this case the "build it and they will come" theory failed. Except for the rare Merry Brothers barge and a barge used once by Cox Newsprint, there was no river traffic.

Lester Moody reasoned that if the federal government could be persuaded to connect the Tennessee and Savannah then boats from the Ohio and Mississippi Rivers might be induced to come to Augusta. Moody had manipulated the government functionaries so many times before that there were those who thought his proposal quite reasonable. One was Congressman

William Jennings Bryan Dorn of South Carolina who promised to introduce a bill in Congress for a study of a feasible route through the mountains. Another disciple of Lester Moody was the influential editor of *The Chronicle*, Louis Harris. Harris chided skeptics of the plan and promised that the canal's importance would "rival the St. Lawrence Seaway."[28] In May 1971 Congressman Dorn reassured the canal boosters, "It will be done." True to his word he introduced a bill on May 16, 1971 for a survey of the best route for the canal.[29] Anticipating a happy ending to the scenario, the city designated November 4, 1972 as "Lester Moody Day." Moody died a month later, greatly honored and much loved. Presumably he continued to visualize barges from the Ohio docking at Augusta's wharf until the last moment.

The arrival of a Swann Oil Company barge in 1974 caused the dream to linger in the mind of Louis Harris. He argued editorially for a twelve-foot channel in the event that the over-the-mountain connection became a reality. Scott Nixon of the Augusta Port Authority, whose enthusiasm for the project equaled Moody's, continued to lobby for congressional action on Dorn's bill until 1976. However, Swann Oil stopped using the river in 1978 and Col. Tilford Creel of the Corps of Engineers announced that he could no longer justify maintaining a nine-foot channel. That notice discouraged further talk about the Tennessee-Savannah link-up.[30]

A chimera is defined as an "unrealizable dream." Augustans experienced two chimeras during the '70s, a canal park maintained by the state, and a linkage to the Tennessee River. The notions titillated the citizenry for a while and then disappeared. The image of a power plant on the canal might be listed as another chimera except for the fact that it was about to reappear in the '80s.

CHAPTER FOURTEEN

A Brighter
Prospect,
1980–2000

━━━━━◦━━━━━

Among the interesting stories of the century's final decades, the most surprising is the burgeoning of public support for historic preservation in general and preservation of the canal in particular. "Augustans love their canal," reported *The Augusta Chronicle* after a "save our canal" rally in 1992.[1] That statement would not have been made at any earlier time in the canal's history, with the possible exception of the generation that built it in the first place.

Rediscovery of the river could be counted as a return to an age that depended on the river for commercial survival. The Riverwalk development of the '80s excited residents and tourists alike. The levee that had walled off the river was transformed into a grand park, with an esplanade along the top, adorned with all the flags that have flown over the region from the Spanish to the present Georgia flag. Plaques placed at overlooks explained the history of the river and the city, and below a wooded walk wound along the riverside. People turned to the river as never before for regattas, power boat races, pleasure boating and for concerts at the Jessye Norman Amphitheater. After a faulty start, the Port Royal condominiums attracted permanent residents. On its lower floors the National Science Center's Fort Discovery brought thousands of school children to its hands-on math and science exhibits, and incidentally to a fine view of the river. Visitors lodged at the new Radisson Hotel and felt privileged by their closeness to the river. Art fanciers strolled through the Morris Museum and its collection of southern paintings and admired the living riverscape outside.

The return to the river was only one aspect of the renewed interest in the past. A cursory listing of renovations and rehabilitations is impressive: the abandonment of the beautiful Sacred Heart Church in the '70s and its restoration by Peter Knox, Jr. in the '80s; Knox's rescue of a Victorian neighborhood and converting it into the Telfair Inn; the city's renovation of the Old Government House; Historic Augusta's drive to restore the Woodrow Wilson House and the adjacent Joseph R. Lamar House; William Moore's reconstruction of the Cotton Exchange and its function as a visitor's center; the new interest in Springfield Baptist Church as the oldest African-American congregation in the country. After the Augusta-Richmond County Museum moved into its spacious new quarters on Reynolds Street, its Board adopted the name "Augusta Museum of History" and installed a permanent exhibit on Augusta's history. The venerable Richmond County Historical Society published books on Augusta history, and Historic Augusta's membership increased dramatically in proportion to its success in promoting preservation. These and other examples of unprecedented public concern about the heritage of the community serve as a backdrop to the recent history of the canal. A series of threats to the canal climaxed in a movement to "save our canal."

The state's interest in the canal had generated some local interest during the '70s, but not until a series of intrusions upon the canal in the late '80s did its preservation become an organized movement. The first threat alone might not have caused much commotion because it had become so familiar. Like the nine-lived cat the hydroelectric plant reappeared on the city's agenda. If this narrative were a work of fiction, this author would not dare impose on the reader's credulity, as the historian is able to do because of the incredible nature of truth. Readers would not believe that a project so often killed would be as often resurrected, except that it happened. Mayor Millard Beckum had given up on the plans for a plant on the canal because the plant would consume so much water there would be too little left for the rapidly growing city. However, in 1981, the last year of Mayor Newman's administration, a new study claimed that there would be water enough after all; furthermore the plant would only cost $9.5 million and in 20 years it would make $60.1 million.[2] Edward McIntyre, the first African-American elected mayor in the city's history, entered office in 1982 with the new plant already on the drawing board. He embraced the plan, predicting that profits would soar to $63 million and even $120 million over a 20-year period. These were figures to tantalize property owners with the promise of a tax rollback. Historic preservation has seldom been able to compete with tax relief as a public priority. Mayor McIntyre asked the citizenry to vote for a bond issue of $18 million on October 13, 1982 and they responded by a three to one vote of approval.[3] A second study showed the cost estimate to be $18,469,000, or $5 million more than the cost the voters approved. Mayor

McIntyre sounded undaunted, "Regardless of the cost, it will be the best deal city taxpayers have ever received."[4]

McIntyre was instrumental in launching one of the great success stories in recent Augusta history. In partnership with a new group of public-minded citizens who formed "Augusta Tomorrow, Inc." in 1982, the city ordered a study by the American City Corporation to determine the best uses of the riverfront. The mayor envisioned a convention center, a marina, several restaurants and shops along the river.[5]

In 1982 the unique Waters Edge project neared completion. Developer L.D. Waters secured permission from the City of Augusta to construct residences on the river side of the levee between Hawk's Gully and 13th Street. The concept was bold, imaginative and attractive: houses perched on poles driven into the steep slope of the levee, affording residents a fine view of the river and the unspoiled South Carolina bank. Skeptics said that the houses would tilt, collapse, or sink into the levee; but after nearly twenty years they showed no signs of doing any of those things. Unfortunately, the proposed extension of the riverfront residential development led to Mayor McIntyre's downfall. He was convicted of violating the Hobbs Act for accepting a bribe in return for arranging the city's cooperation for the project, and sentenced to a term in prison. The City Council elected Councilman Charles DeVaney as acting mayor on May 4, 1984, and in October, the voters ratified the election. DeVaney dedicated his administration to carrying out the incipient riverfront plans. As the various features of the project unfolded Augustans and visitors alike marveled at the dramatic new use of the riverfront. The park called "Riverwalk," with its handsome esplanade along the summit of the levee, the historic flags and markers, the landscaped slope of the levee and the shady paths along the riverside, became the boast of the city.

For better or for worse Mayor DeVaney inherited that other holdover from previous administrations, the power plant on the canal. However, that project came under increasing criticism, not from the Georgia side of the river, the prospect of tax relief was still too strong for that, but from the Carolina side. Carolinians never liked the Augusta Canal very much from its inception. Now and again they filed lawsuits against the City of Augusta, none of which eased their fears of the entire river being emptied into Augusta. In 1983 a formidable figure in the person of Congressman Butler Derrick of Edgefield, South Carolina, filed a formal complaint against the proposed canal power plant, claiming that the plant would require so much water it would virtually dry up the stretch of river below the lock and dam at the headgates. The consequences for fish, wildlife and the environment would be disastrous. (Ten years later Augustans would use those same arguments against other threats to the canal.) On August 1, 1984 the State of South Carolina intervened to block the project. The Sierra Club filed its own objections.[6]

Councilman Herbert Elliott argued that plants and scenery would not be affected; City Engineer James Messerly observed that there would be two inches of water flowing over the dam at the locks and that should be enough for South Carolina.[7] When *The Chronicle* chided Congressman Derrick for his opposition to progress, he responded "I have been reading *The Augusta Chronicle* and the *Augusta Herald* for approximately thirty years or more and if their editorial writers have ever had the best interests of the people of South Carolina at heart it missed my attention."[8] Despite positive recommendations from South Carolina Senator Strom Thurmond and Georgia Senator Mack Mattingly, the Federal Energy Regulatory Commission decided to delay its approval pending environmental studies on the impact of the canal power plant by the City of Augusta.[9] Augusta officials dawdled, unwilling to do such a study and equally unwilling to abandon the project.

Meanwhile the seeds of interest planted by Joe Cumming, the state canal park idea, Sydney Carter's plan, and sporadic conferences by Augusta College's history department, slowly grew into fruition. Canal Authority member Bob Woodhurst tells of returning from San Antonio in 1985 full of excitement about the way that city had made attractive use of its waterway, and convinced that Augusta could do the same with its canal. He and downtown businessman George Harrison formed a canal committee that was incorporated into the Chamber of Commerce structure. Hugh Connolly, President of Augusta Tomorrow, Inc., conceived of the idea of a Canal Authority and in a letter of August 13, 1985, urged Mayor Charles DeVaney to "take steps that will work to the enhancement of this historic and otherwise valuable and unique local asset."[10] Again on May 10, 1988 Connolly urged the mayor to place the canal under the jurisdiction of its own authority.[11] Augusta Tomorrow commissioned Robert Norman, former Chairman of the Georgia Ports Authority, a long-time friend of Lester Moody and river development, and a member of Augusta Tomorrow, to draft legislation creating a Canal Authority based on the Ports Authority model, and the state legislature in its 1989 session adopted the measure. Hugh Connolly credited Jack Connell, Speaker pro-tempore of the Georgia House, with facilitation of the measure.

Mayor DeVaney accepted the "fait accompli" and appointed Bob Norman, Dick Fox, Tom Robertson, Jeanie Allen, and C. O. Hollis to the Authority. Fox, a self-styled "river rat," had helped sponsor Augusta's first rowing regatta as well as other river events. Robertson, a civil engineer and the primary designer of the successful Riverwalk project, had given lectures on the canal's history. Jeanie Allen, marketing representative for Georgia Public Broadcasting, had organized the first "Canal Canoe Cruise and Cookout" in 1988 when several dozen Augustans paddled down the canal, most of them for the first time, and enjoyed a barbecue at the historic George Walton's Meadow Garden. The success of the first cruise led Jeanie Allen to establish the outing as an annual event and in the process win friends for Georgia Public Radio and for the canal. Married to Richard Allen, she continued that family's interest in the canal dating back through two Mayors Richard Allen to Mayor J.V.H. Allen, an advocate of canal enlargement. C. O. Hollis, Senior Vice President of Pilgrim Life Insurance Company, informed Mayor DeVaney that the legislation creating the Authority required residency in Augusta and that he resided in Columbia County, otherwise he would have been delighted to serve.[12] The mayor accepted Hollis's resignation and appointed architect Bob Woodhurst in his place. When Bob Norman resigned in December 1990, Dennis Skelly replaced him. Skelly later moved to Columbia County and real estate executive Hugh Connolly succeeded him. Connolly's appointment was an appropriate recognition of his role in creating the Authority. His interest in the canal was shared by his wife, Nancy Cumming Connolly, a direct descendant of Henry H. Cumming and the daughter of Joe Cumming who had placed the canal on the National Historic Register. There were no other changes in the composition of the Authority until legislation expanded its membership in 1999.

The most important event of Bob Norman's chairmanship was a luncheon that featured Dr. Eugene Odum as speaker. Dr. Odum, a pioneer ecologist and the founder of the University of Georgia Laboratory at the Savannah River Site, proved an excellent choice for the fledgling Canal Authority.

Odum had the prestige to cause people to pay attention. He recommended that the Canal Authority draw up a master plan to develop a green belt through the city. He urged the Authority to include an "ecology laboratory" in its plans. "You've really got something here worth preserving," he told the luncheon audience.[13] His talk may be considered the turning point in the public recognition of the canal as an important nature center. The flood of 1990, curiously, played into the hands of canal preservationists. Heavy rains caused unusually heavy run-off from the creeks into the canal, creating a fault in the towpath above the Pumping Station. The City closed the towpath to motor vehicles to the immense satisfaction of the increasing number of hikers.

The electric plant has been mentioned as a continual threat to the canal. Although the project did not at first generate much local opposition, by the end of the '80s a canal clientele had formed, ready to protest intrusions. There was some muttering when the Department of Transportation began construction of the Murray Road extension, later known as the Riverwatch Parkway, connecting Interstate 20 with 15th Street at Hawk's Gully. The highway relieved traffic congestion on Washington Road, but at a cost to the wilderness area bounding the canal. Robert Pavey, later Outdoor Editor of *The Chronicle,* spoke for friends of the canal in his article of May 11, 1988: "In addition to removing shoreline foliage, the road project will destroy portions of the Bartram Trail used by hikers. It will also change forever the hidden inaccessible nature of the overgrown canal banks." Going west from downtown the parkway runs between the river and the canal, then above Lake Olmstead it crosses the canal and diverges as it approaches a junction with Interstate 20. The unspoiled triangular area bounded by the parkway, I-20 and the canal attracted the attention of San Jose developer Lee Brandenburg, who acquired 175 acres in 1987.

Another intrusion fomented open opposition. In the '80s the city lost interest in the headgate area. Fearing lawsuits from accidents, the city authorities posted "keep-out" signs and locked the access gates. However, the lure of the canal continued to attract hikers and bikers, some equipped with wire cutters. Augusta City Administrator Pete Brodie suggested to the Columbia County Commission that Augusta would not be averse to leasing the area. Columbia County needed a community center and the high bluff overlooking the headgates offered a picturesque setting. Mayor DeVaney met with the Columbia County Commission to work out the details. Columbia County agreed to respect environmental concerns, rehabilitate the decrepit pavilion, repair the lockkeeper's house, and reconstruct the barbecue pit. The county would contribute to the upkeep of the locks and headgates. To some it seemed a win-win situation for Augusta and for Columbia County.[14] However, the announcement of the arrangement was badly timed, coming only a month after Dr. Eugene Odum's plea to preserve the natural character of the canal, and it roused the opposition of environmentalists, nature lovers, and canal users.

The Riverwatch Parkway and the Columbia County Community Center annoyed so many citizens that when the hydroelectric scheme reappeared, it met with more local opposition than ever before. But whatever the friends of the canal might think, the City Council found the prospect of a power plant irresistible. On November 25, 1991, the City approved a proposal from the Fall Line Hydro Company of Duluth, Georgia to build and operate a plant on the canal and split the proceeds of the sale of electricity with the city. For an initial investment of $18 million, the city could expect a return of $370,000 annually.[15]

Almost simultaneous with the resurrection of the power

plant notion came a December announcement that Lee Brandenburg planned to build a golf course on the "island" between the canal and the river. He already owned 175 acres between the canal and Riverwatch Parkway and he proposed leasing 50 acres on the canal island from the city. Councilman Gerald Woods, Chairman of the city's waterworks committee, conferred with Brandenburg's representatives in January 1992 and told a reporter, "They want to build a mall, a full mall, like the Augusta Mall; if they build it, it's a big, big project." In addition there would be business offices, condominiums, parking lots, and, of course, the golf course across the canal. Woods cited the economic advantages, including an improved tax base, and the possibility of 2,800 new jobs. Two entrances off Riverwatch Parkway would be needed to handle the expected traffic. "We told them it's a project we take seriously, and have great interest in," said Woods, expressing the official city viewpoint.[16]

At almost any earlier time in Augusta's history Brandenburg would have built his mall and the citizenry would have cheered for progress. But by the '90s a gradual metamorphosis had set in. People began to define progress by counting quality of life intangibles such as opportunities for recreation and relaxation, respect for wildlife and plant life, an appreciation for the psychological value of a quiet place, and of the health benefits of clean, flowing water. The isolated mutterings became a movement with the organization of the Savannah Waterways Forum in December 1991.

The coincidental intrusions represented by the Columbia County Community Center, the hydroelectric plant and the Brandenburg development generated vocal opposition. When Margaret Brown and Dr. Tom Swift of the Savannah Waterways Forum invited Mayor DeVaney and Councilman Woods to a public meeting in the Parish Hall of Good Shepherd Episcopal

Church, the room was filled and the atmosphere electric. The mayor felt on the defensive as he listened to comments opposing the recent initiatives and as he fielded difficult questions.[17]

"Save the Augusta Canal" bumper stickers broke out like a rash across the city. The *Atlanta Journal-Constitution* picked up the story, quoting Augusta College biologist Dr. Judy Gordon who predicted a short-term economic gain but a long-term ecological disaster. Bob Butterworth of North Augusta told the reporter that if the power plant were built "You'll be able to walk across the Savannah River."[18] Canal Authority member Jeanie Allen provoked the mayor by publicly asking him to call a halt to the various projects while the Authority prepared a master plan. The mayor called the request unreasonable, and asserted that it caught him off guard. Allen commented that the mayor "wanted to save that golf course."[19]

The Waterways Forum counted the abandonment of the power plant as its first success. On February 9, 1992 Mayor DeVaney said that the continuation of the project depended on its profitability. On March 22, 1992 he wrote a guest editorial in *The Chronicle* to the effect that the power plant was not "economically feasible" and he agreed that the Authority needed time to prepare a master plan for the overall development of the canal. A "save our canal" rally at the Julian Smith Casino on March 25, 1992 maintained the momentum for canal preservation. Two days later, Canal Authority Chairman Tom Robertson drafted a bill that would designate the canal as a "National Heritage Area" and delivered the drafts to Congressman Doug Barnard and Senator Wyche Fowler.

In April the Georgia Department of Transportation allocated $130,000 to the Authority to fund a master plan. The Authority engaged two Boston consulting firms that had developed the master plan for Lowell's canal rehabilitation to do the study. Jonathan Lane and John R. Shields, representing the two companies, began work on the plan with a visit to Augusta in October 1992.²⁰ Tom Robertson of the Canal Authority described Jon Lane as "perhaps the preeminent planner of heritage areas in the United States."²¹ Lane and Shields proved to be masters at consensus building. Jim Wylie of the National Park Service provided in-kind technical assistance during the planning process and became an advocate for the canal in Atlanta. He buttonholed Governor Zell Miller in a grocery store and enlisted his help in getting congressional support for the designation of the canal as a National Heritage Area.

Throughout 1993 public interest remained high. The Columbia County Community Center survived because it had gotten underway before the opposition movement reached a critical stage, and also because there were good arguments for it. An attractively landscaped, well-policed, people-friendly lock and dam park was preferable to a neglected site with danger signs warning off the public. In fact the Canal Authority risked criticism in giving its approval to the Columbia County project in December 1991.²² The Brandenburg project went into limbo, with prospects dimming as time elapsed.

After the city decided against proceeding with the power plant and Councilman Woods declared it a "dead issue," the Federal Energy Regulatory Commission surprised everyone by its announcement that it was ready to hold hearings on the feasibility of the project. The city informed the commission that it did not intend to build a power plant or to cooperate with a private builder to construct one. However, the issue refused to die. In April 1996 the FERC informed the city that its license to divert water from the river for the purpose of building a power plant had expired and the city must reapply. In fact, the license applied for in 1929 when the city intended to cooperate with

Georgia Power had expired in 1979. The agency reminded the city that it had not done the environmental impact study necessary for re-application. All this might have been considered federal nonsense and therefore disregarded, except that if the city did not choose to reapply then any private company might do so. The Fall Line Hydro Company of Duluth, Georgia, the spurned partner of the city in its effort to build a plant, thereupon filed an application with the FERC to build a plant without the city's cooperation.[23] Here was a possibility almost surpassing belief. The 150-year-old waterway, constructed by the city with no outside help, and maintained with no outside help except for the WPA during the '30s, might now pass into the possession of a private agency because of a clause in an obscure Rivers and Harbors Act of 1898.

The Chronicle called the latest turn of events "a devastatingly bad development." The City and the Canal Authority sent protests to the FERC. In order to reestablish control over the canal the city had to file an application to construct a power plant that it had no intention of ever building. It filed a public notice of its intention on July 18, 1996. The cost of doing the necessary environmental impact study was estimated at $250,000. The proposed study fell hostage to the confusion of consolidation of city and county governments in 1996, and the consolidated government postponed consideration of the study until February 1999 when Max Hicks, Director of Utilities, announced that the cost of the study had escalated to $815,000. To keep the canal, the city had no choice but to go ahead with the study.[24] Though clearly annoyed at the bureaucratic interference, Mayor Bob Young promised to do whatever was necessary to preserve the canal.

The construction of a Petersburg boat in 1993 exemplified the new public interest in the canal and its possibilities.

Figure 57. Throngs cheered the launching of the Petersburg boat, the "Fort Augusta." *(Augusta Canal Authority Archive.)*

George Barrett, proprietor of a landscaping company, and a long-time friend of the canal, told a reporter that he had thought about building such a boat for at least ten years. In 1992 he assembled a group of volunteers who donated their time and he raised $38,530 from other interested persons to finance the actual construction. Barrett recruited Rusty Fleetwood, a boat-builder from Tybee Island, and they were joined by Mark Newell, an underwater archeologist. The team decided to use only techniques available in the 19th Century to construct the craft. The makeshift boatyard at Chafee Park attracted crowds of the curious as the boat took shape. Suspense mounted as the deadline for launching neared. Barrett invited the public to the launching on September 18, 1993, but did not know whether the boat would capsize, sink, or float. As 400 people anxiously looked on two mule teams pulled ropes connected to a block and tackle and laboriously moved the 45-foot-long, 6,500-pound vessel into the water. A cheer went up when the flower-bedecked craft, christened the "Fort Augusta" splashed into the canal, bobbed and settled onto an even keel. After several cruises on the canal, all of which drummed up support for canal preservation, Captain Barrett took the "Fort Augusta" all the way to Savannah. They carried a cargo representing what might have been carried by 19th Century riverboats: pine logs, granite from Elberton, and barrels of pitch. The "Fort Augusta" attracted attention of the throngs of Savannah tourists as it proudly cruised down that city's riverfront. Afterward the boat was retired to the Augusta Museum of History where it served as the centerpiece of the Augusta Story exhibit.[25]

After soliciting advice from the public and completing research, consultants Lane and Shields unveiled the Canal Master Plan on May 18, 1993. On May 12, 1994 a handsomely printed version was made available to the public. Well-written and attractive, the plan won approval from canal enthusiasts and the public generally. The *Augusta Focus* stressed the black community's desire to see the rewatering of the third level.[26] The plan set four major goals: the designation of the canal as a National Heritage Area by the United States Congress, the creation of a canal park of state-wide importance, the development of the educational potential of the canal including the establishment of an Augusta Ecology Center, and the facilitation of economic development in the downtown area.

Echoes of Sydney Carter and Eugene Odum reverberated from the pages of the report. The upper end of the canal should capitalize on its natural setting. The headgates and locks should be put in working order, and hiking trails and boat tours should be planned. The central area between Interstate 20 and

Lake Olmstead should house the Ecology Center. The Pumping Station should be opened for tours. The Bartram Trail should be plotted along the river. A kayak run could be planned along the Lake Olmstead spillway. The shores and lawns of Lake Olmstead should be landscaped. The "urban canal" from the Sibley Mill downward should emphasize the historic structures: the mills themselves, the Confederate Powder Works Chimney, the Harris House, the Butt Bridge, and Meadow Garden. Chafee Park should be designed as an entrance to the canal park. The plan envisioned a visitors center in the Granite Mill section of the then vacant Enterprise Mill. It suggested an extension of Saint Sebastian Way across the canal to connect the medical complex with the Enterprise Mill, Sacred Heart Cultural Center, upper Broad Street shops, Springfield Baptist Church and the Riverwalk. There could be an "embayment" at Hawk's Gully to serve as a marina. In the Laney-Walker area the third level should be rewatered and two lagoons created. The area would be ideal for a multi-cultural community center built near the historic Trinity Church, the Frank Yerby House, and Dyess Park. In short, the plan was so exhaustive, so specific, and so filled with interesting possibilities that it notched up public support to a new level.

More to the point, it served as a tool for the Canal Authority to get the attention of Congress. Democratic Congressmen Doug Barnard and his successor Don Johnson supported the Authority's application for National Heritage status. Unfortunately, the bill fell victim to partisan politics as all four Georgia Republican Congressmen voted against it. The bill, which would have recognized ten historic sites in all, was defeated by six votes.[27] Dr. Charles Norwood, elected in 1994 as a Republican, pledged to work for passage of a new bill. In 1995 Norwood collaborated with Republican Senator Paul

Coverdell on a bill to create the Augusta Canal National Heritage Area. The legislation would allow the Canal Authority to apply for federal funds and to enlist the cooperation of the National Park Service. Canal Authority Chairman Robertson and Norwood testified for the bill before the House Subcommittee on National Parks, Forests and Public Lands. Robertson invited the chairman of the subcommittee, Don Young of Alaska, to see the canal for himself. Norwood and the members of the Authority conducted the chairman on a tour of the canal on October 23, 1995. Robertson went back to Washington in December to help Senator Coverdell testify before the Senate Committee on Energy and Natural Resources. It seemed certain that a Republican sponsored bill would pass a Republican dominated Congress. Such was not the case; a majority of members in both houses did not want to create any more national parks or anything resembling national parks.[28]

Senator Coverdell refused to take no for an answer. He attached the Augusta proposal to a land management bill that had already passed both houses and was before a joint conference committee. The ploy worked. Both houses passed the land management bill and President Clinton signed it into law on November 12, 1996. The legislation created the Augusta Canal National Heritage Area as well as the South Carolina National Heritage Corridor that ran along the river opposite Augusta. John Stone, spokesman for Congressman Norwood, reflected on the tortuous route to enactment, "It's such a small bill. It doesn't involve a penny in spending, and yet it took two years to get it through."[29] Though no funding was contained in the bill, it was the golden key that could make the master plan come true. The legislation permitted the Canal Authority to apply for up to a million dollars a year until the year 2012 when such funding would be discontinued.

National recognition was as important as potential funding. Prominent individuals chose to associate themselves with the canal. On October 23, 1998 Senator Coverdell and Congressman Norwood cut a symbolic ribbon at Chafee Park indicating a start to the master plan renovation. "I've waited to see something like this happen since 1969," said Norwood.[30] A month later Secretary of the Interior Bruce Babbitt toured the canal and expressed genuine interest in the canal's history and future potential, "What I've seen today is a unique piece of American landscape and American history. It's a wonderful mixture of human history and the natural environment."[31] This was heady stuff. Augustans had long known that the canal was locally important, but to hear from a well-traveled national personage that it had national and even human implications caused them to look at the venerable waterway with a new respect. Even more surprising to many who had not appreciated the significance of the canal was an incipient international interest in the Augusta Canal. The Canal Authority in cooperation with The National Park Service hosted the Sixth Annual International Conference on Historic Canals on October 2nd through 6th 1995. Over sixty visiting canal enthusiasts toured the waterway and compared it favorably with those in New England and Great Britain.

During the period when the legislation made its way through Congress, other agencies recognized the importance of the canal. In July 1996 the prestigious National Trust for Historic Preservation promised to honor the canal if Congress did not. The Georgia Department of Community Affairs designated the canal as the first "Regionally Important Resource."[32] The designation lost some of its clout when Congress conferred national significance upon the canal.

By 1994 governmental agencies could no longer trifle

with the canal without the public noticing. When the Department of Transportation announced plans to build a new bridge over the canal and railroad tracks at 15th Street and to by-pass the Butt Bridge, it was greeted by a storm of opposition and protest. Augustans raised such a commotion that the *Atlanta Constitution* ran an article on it entitled "Augusta rallies to save bridge." Ross Snellings, leader of the opposition, invented the slogan that broke out all over the city: "SAVE OUR BUTT" and in lesser characters "Memorial Bridge." Snellings was quoted as saying, "I think the D.O.T. doesn't understand how people feel about the Butt Bridge. It tells people that if you conduct yourself honorably you'll be remembered."[33] The Department of Transportation backed down in face of the unexpected opposition. Mayor DeVaney festooned the bridge with lights, giving it and the canal the look of a Parisian riverscape to those with imagination.

Figure 58. Bumper sticker from the "Save Our Butt" campaign.
(Augusta Canal Authority Archives)

The positive effects of national recognition were soon evident. The Authority finally had enough money to hire an executive director. In April 1997 Glenn Coyne, Columbia County planning director, accepted the position. Dayton Sherrouse, Executive Vice President of Augusta Tomorrow, previously provided office space and staff support to the Canal Authority; when Coyne left the Authority on December 31, 1998 to become Director for the American Institute for Certified Planners in Washington, D.C., Sherrouse succeeded him as director. His resume listed long experience in city planning as Executive Director of the Augusta-Richmond County Planning Commission, Richmond County Administrator, Executive Vice President of Augusta Tomorrow, in addition to running his own consulting agency.

The year 1997 brought a welcome change to the blighted short second level of the canal. Architect Bob Woodhurst cleverly adapted an abandoned Georgia Ironworks building for the Davidson Fine Arts Magnet School, and drew the new buildings to complement the old structures. Earlier Woodhurst spruced up the Lake Olmstead area by designing an attractive baseball stadium for the local "Greenjackets" team.

Good things kept happening in 1997. Clayton Boardman, III bought the derelict Enterprise Mill, vacant since 1983. Boardman startled and gratified everyone by transforming the huge hulk into a handsome structure with modern amenities. Bricked-up windows were opened, a new roof installed, fresh coats of paint applied. Fifty-six loft apartments filled the top floor; business offices occupied the lower. After completion of the work, Clay Boardman told the *Metropolitan Spirit* that he had not initially realized the magnitude of the project. "I never really had a plan written out or thought out very well," he said. "It was pretty scary there for a long time." Costs ran as high as $50,000 a day and he had no outside financing at first. He had to sell some of his personal property to keep the work going. Later, he could have sold out to a Kentucky buyer, but by then he had "fallen in love" with the building. The final cost reached $17 million. Was it worth it? Though he felt that it would never be a moneymaker, for Clay Boardman it was worth it. He earned the gratitude of the entire community and made one of the recommendations of the master plan possible.[34]

Figure 59. The Augusta Canal Interpretive Center is housed in the renovated Enterprise Mill. *(Augusta Canal Authority Archives)*

The plan suggested that the Granite Mill be used as an industrial exhibit and visitors center. In 1999 the Canal Authority arranged to move its offices into the 10,000-square feet Enterprise "spooling room." There would be room for a visitors center, an industrial museum, a theater and staff offices. Boardman would activate the 1920 generators for the production of electricity. The Authority would be allowed to sell surplus electricity to Georgia Power. "We will finally be home – along the canal," Dayton Sherrouse told a reporter.[35] Meanwhile at its temporary offices on Cotton Row, the Authority gathered artifacts and compiled oral interviews of elderly mill workers. One of its treasured historic items was the personal hydrometer of William Phillips, the first Canal Engineer, donated by Mary Jo Reeves, the great-granddaughter of William Phillips. The instrument measured the flow of water in the canal.

The Canal Master Plan called for an ecology educational center and the Canal Authority found an ally in Dr. Gene Eidson who had long wanted to do just that. In 1997 Dr. Eidson founded the EcoSystems Institute to promote environmental education and research using Phinizy Swamp as a nature laboratory. [36] Eidson's interest in Phinizy Swamp began in 1989, and his opportunity to create a nature park occurred in 1993 when the Georgia Environmental Protection Division issued stricter guidelines for the discharge of wastewater into Butler Creek. The city could build a new treatment plant for $30,000,000 or the discharge could be purified by natural processes in the wetlands adjoining Butler Creek. Max Hicks observed that the latter option would require no operational or maintenance costs, and would provide wildlife habitat, "If constructed, Augusta would operate the Nation's largest wetland treatment system, placing our city in the forefront of environmental protection."[37]

In mitigation of the preemption of twenty-seven acres of wetlands the city provided seed money to permit the establishment of Eidson's EcoSystems. Eidson's original intention was simply to preserve the wetlands, but he was encouraged by unexpected public interest in the project to raise his objectives. He started the Southeastern Natural Sciences Academy that would act as an environmental educational institute with the Nature Park as a laboratory. Its ambitious "vision statement" called for twelve miles of trails and boardwalks, seven observation decks, a visitor center, an educational building, an outdoor pavilion, an herbarium, a butterfly house, and much more. In 2000 Eidson assumed the position of President. Director Jackie Maryak and staff set up offices in the Old Richmond Academy building on Telfair Street. After constructing the first boardwalks and observation platforms the Academy began to conduct tours of the Nature Park, as well as ecology tours of the Augusta Canal. Thus Gene Eidson helped meet Eugene Odum's challenge to establish an ecology laboratory well in advance of the Canal Authority's timetable. The enthusiastic public response to the project is evidence of the concern about quality of life at the dawning of the new millennium.[38]

The federal and state governments have also become ardent environmentalists in recent years. Georgia Power Company had to clean up its waste site adjacent to the canal and just east of the Butt Bridge in 1999. The Atlanta Gas Light Company faced a more serious challenge. It had to remove the contamination of over a century at the site of the gas works on the third level of the canal at 8th Street. Across the street from the gas works was the historic Trinity Church, founded by black Methodists from St. John Methodist on Greene Street, and considered by some authorities to be the mother church of the C.M.E. denomination. The courts ruled that Atlanta Gas Light had to compensate the Trinity congregation for the contamination of the church grounds.[39] There is the possibility that the building may be used as a museum when the clean-up is complete. In 2000 the Gas Company worked with Cranston, Robertson and Whitehurst of Augusta to create the rewatered third level canal envisioned by the master plan.[40] Mayor Young described exciting plans for a greenway development around the rewatered third level, with new housing, restaurants, and recreational facilities fronting the canal. And, of course, the environmental impact study demanded by the Federal Energy Regulatory Commission – whether the city wanted a hydroelectric plant or not – remained to be done as the first year of the new millennium came to a close.

What are the canal's prospects as the century turns? When asked that question Executive Director Dayton Sherrouse answered that he believed that an irreversible momentum has built up. The Congressional recognition of the canal's national significance has given the waterway credibility and prestige. He referred to the welter of on-going plans: for the headgate area, for the restoration of the locks, for Petersburg tour boats and docks, for the Enterprise Mill visitors center, for the extension

Figure 60. Visitors enjoying the Augusta Canal National Heritage Area.
(Augusta Canal Authority Archives.)

of Saint Sebastian Way, for the rewatering of the third level canal. None of these are pipe dreams, he emphasized; all have solid funding. He compared the interest in the canal in the year 2000 with the excitement generated by Riverwalk in the 1980's. Just as industrial progress motivated an earlier generation, Sherrouse believed that quality of life issues motivate this generation and will continue to do so.[41] The natural beauty of the canal will act as a lure to the new eco-tourists who value the curative qualities of a wilderness setting. The unique historical associations of the canal will appeal to heritage tourists. Thus the canal will continue to promote economic progress in the Twenty-First Century as it has in the two preceding centuries.

Notes

Chapter 2

1. James Axtell, *The Indians New South: Cultural Change in the Colonial Southeast* (Baton Rouge: Louisiana State University Press, 1997), 1.
2. Mike Toner, Access Atlanta, Presented in partnership with the *Atlanta Journal-Constitution*, 1999, Cox Interactive Media.
3. "Young Americans," *New Scientist*, 17 (October 1998); see website anthro.org/
4. Charles Hudson, *Knights of Spain: Warriors of the Sun: Hernando de Soto and the South's Ancient Chiefdoms* (Athens: University of Georgia Press, 1997), 418-19.
5. Carolyn Hanna Murphy, *Carolina Rocks! The Geology of South Carolina* (Columbia: Sandlapper Publishing Company, 1995), 172.
6. Kenneth E. Sassaman, "The Origins of Stallings Culture." *Legacy* vol. 1, no.2 (November 1996):6-7.
7. William H. Claflin, Jr., *The Stalling's Island Mound Columbia County, Georgia* (Cambridge: Peabody Museum of American Archeology and Ethnology, 1931).
8. Ibid., 21-22.
9. Kenneth E. Sassaman, "Life in a Stallings Community," *Legacy* vol. 2, no.1 (March 1997): 6-9.
10. David G. Anderson, *The Savannah River Chiefdoms: Political Change in the Late Prehistoric Southeast* (Tuscaloosa: University of Alabama Press, 1994), 108.
11. William Bartram, *Travels and Other Writings* (New York: The Library of America, 1996), 260.
12. Anderson, 159-60.
13. Ibid., 329.

14. Bartram, 260-61.

15. Edmond Randolf to Your Lordship, March 22, 1698/99, Records of the British Public Record Office Relating to South Carolina, pp. 78-81. Randolf reported to his superior, "Cutler talks of going to the Savanoe Town about 120 miles from hence with Loughton and Maybank to speak with Indian Traders, he premises (sic) great matters to those who inform him of mines."

16. Hudson, 461-62.

17. Ibid., 166-67. Hudson dates the crossing of the Savannah River April 17, 1540. He locates the crossing at Pace's Island; however, the descriptions of the chronicles fit the fall-line rapids as well. Furthermore, the natural trails led to the fall-line shoals.

18. Chapman J. Milling, *Red Carolinians* (Chapel Hill: University of North Carolina Press, 1940), 83. Archeologist Pat Garrow believes that there was some truth to the stories of Westos cannibalism. When conducting a dig at North Augusta, South Carolina's Hammond Hills, his team unearthed human remains, with a tooth embedded in a bone!

19. William Gascoyne, "Plat of the Province of Carolina in North America," London, 1685, British Library, London; Harold Maness, *The Forgotten Outpost: Fort Moore and Savannah Town 1685-1765* (Beech Island, S.C.: published by the author, 1986).

20. Letter of the Governor and Council of South Carolina to the Lords Proprietors, 1708, Records of the British Public Record Office Relating to South Carolina, cited in Dixon Hollingsworth, *Indians on the Savannah River* (Sylvania, Georgia: The Partridge Pond Press, 1976), 44.

21. Guillaume de Lisle, "Carte de la Louisiane it du Cours du

Mississipi," (1718), print copy in possession of the author.

22. Ibid., Milling, 170-72.

23. Thomas M.N. Lewis and Madeline Kneberg, *Tribes that Slumber: Indians of the Tennessee Region* (Knoxville: University of Tennessee Press, 1958), 139.

24. The similarity of Hogoheechee and Ogeechee suggests a connection between the Yuchis and the Ogeechee River, but I am not aware that anyone has established the connection.

25. Kristian Hvidt, ed., *Von Reck's Voyage: Drawings and Journal of Philip George Friedrich von Reck* (Savannah: The Beehive Press, 1980).

26. Bartram, 316-17.

27. Milling, 187.

28. Ibid., 189.

29. William Stephens Journal, December 9, 1737, in Allen D. Candler,ed., *The Colonial Records of the State of Georgia* (Atlanta: 1906) 4: 46-47.

30. Professor John Reps of Cornell University showed this writer a plat of New Savannah; however, the town was never actually surveyed and developed. The first grant of the land was to William (Billy) Gray, trader to the Chickasaws who accompanied them when Squirrel King volunteered to fight for Oglethorpe.

31. According to military historian Larry Ivers, "Squirrel King's Chickasaw Indians from near Augusta were the best warriors and even though they numbered only about thirty, their reputation placed their value equal to a hundred." Ivers, *British Drums Along the Southern Frontier: The Military Colonization of Georgia, 1733-1749* (Chapel Hill: University of North Carolina Press, 1974), 102.

32. Milling, 191.

33. Edward J. Cashin, *Lachlan McGillivray Indian Trader and*

the Shaping of the Southern Colonial Frontier (Athens: University of Georgia Press, 1992), 180.

34. Ibid., 194-97.

35. Arrell M. Gibson, *The Chickasaws* (Norman: University of Oklahoma Press, 1971), 64.

36. It was this writer's privilege to act as host to Chief James during his stay in Augusta.

Chapter 3

1. The lengthy South Carolina act of 1721 is cited in Harold Maness' *The Forgotten Outpost: Fort Moore and Savannah Town 1685-1765* (Beech Island, S.C.: published by the author, 1986), 101-102.

2. Samuel Eveleigh to Oglethorpe, November 20, 1734, *Colonial Records of Georgia* 20:105-108.

3. Oglethorpe's instructions to Roger Lacy dated June 14, 1736 are in Egmont Papers, 14202, Hargrett Collection, University of Georgia Libraries. William Stephens, who should have known better because he traveled up the Savannah River in 1736 and reported on the future site of Augusta, happened to put 1735 for Augusta's founding, and Augusta adopted that date. In fact, the city celebrated its 200th anniversary in 1935. By the 250th anniversary the city fathers had reluctantly accepted the proper date and observed the founding in 1986.

4. Robert G. McPherson, ed., *The Journal of the Earl of Egmont* (Athens: University of Georgia Press, 1962), 193-95.

5. Causton to Trustees, February 10, 1741, in Mills B. Lane, ed., *General Oglethorpe's Georgia* 2 vols. (Savannah: Beehive Press, 1975), 2:567.

6. For Rae's career, see George Fenwick Jones, "Portrait of

an Irish Entrepreneur in Colonial Augusta: John Rae, 1708-1772," *Georgia Historical Quarterly* 83 (Fall 1999): 427-47; for the formation of Brown, Rae and Company, see Kathryn H. Braund, *Deerskins and Duffels: Creek Indian Trade with Anglo-America, 1685-1815* (Lincoln: University of Nebraska Press, 1993), 45-47.

7. For McGillivray's career, see Edward J. Cashin, *Lachlan McGillivray, Indian Trader and the Shaping of the Southern Colonial Frontier* (Athens: University of Georgia Press, 1992).

8. Ibid., 24.

9. McGillivray acquired the tract from Thomas Smith in 1750, with houses and garden, see Georgia Colonial Conveyences, Book C-1, 54-55.

10. Edward R.R. Green, "Queensborough Township," *William and Mary Quarterly* 3rd ser., 17 (April 1960): 183-99.

11. For an account of the Battle of the White House, see Edward J. Cashin, *The King's Ranger: Thomas Brown and the American Revolution on the Southern Frontier* (Athens: University of Georgia Press, 1989), 114-120.

12. Martha F. Norwood, *A History of the White House Tract Richmond County Georgia, 1756-1975* (Atlanta: Georgia Department of Natural Resources, Historic Preservation Section, 1975).

13. Copy of a Contract Entered into Between G.B. Marshall of the One Part and Major M.M. Payne of the Other Part, *Richmond County History* 30 (Winter 1999): 22-25.

14. Kris Reynolds, "Major Skinner and the Skinner House," *Richmond County History* 10 (Winter 1978): 5-13. According to Michael White the dam, timbers, and clay quarry of the old Wells' mill remain intact in the creek today; nothing is left of the Skinner Mill.

15. Lt. Col. Archibald Campbell, "Journal of an Expedition against the Rebels of Georgia in North America under the orders of Archibald Campbell, Esquire, Lieut. Colol of His Majesty's 71st Regimt, 1778," ms. in State Library of Georgia, 14.

16. For the interesting but intricate account of the founding of Springfield and its relation to the two churches in Savannah that claim to be the oldest churches, see Edward J. Cashin, *Old Springfield: Race and Religion in Augusta, Georgia* (Augusta: Springfield Village Park Foundation, Inc., 1995).

17. Edward J. Cashin, *The Story of Augusta* (Augusta: Richmond County Board of Education, 1980), 44-53.

18. James Thomas Flexner, *Washington The Indispensable Man* (Boston: Little, Brown and Company, 1974), 199.

19. *The Augusta Chronicle*, June 8, 1799.

20. Ibid., February, 23, 1799.

21. The definitive history of Rae's Creek and everything about it is Michael C. White's, *Down Rae's Creek: A Famous Creek at Georgia's Fall Line Hills* (Aiken, S.C.: Howell Printing Company, 1996).

Chapter 4

1. Joseph Bryan Cumming, *A Sketch of the Descendants of David Cumming and Memoirs of the War Between the States* (Augusta, Ga.: privately printed, 1925), 10-11; henceforth, *Sketch*

2. W. Kirk Wood, "Henry Harford Cumming: Civic Virtue in the Old South," *Richmond County History* (Winter 1977): 5-9; Joseph B. Cumming, *Sketch*, 13-15.

3. Joseph B. Cumming, *Sketch*, 17-19; Carol Blesser's book of letters was published by University of Georgia Press, 1996.

4. H. H. Cumming to Board of Commissioners, July 20, 1852, Canal Commissioners Minutes, 1845-1853.

5. Charles C. Jones, Jr. and Salem Dutcher, *Memorial History of Augusta, Georgia* (Syracuse, N.Y.: D. Mason and Company, Publishers, 1890), 241. Henceforth, Jones and Dutcher.

6. Ronald E. Shaw, *Canals for a Nation: The Canal Era in the United States 1790-1860* (Lexington: University of Kentucky Press, 1990), 14.

7. Ibid., 13-14.

8. William H. Shank, *Towpaths to Tugboats. A History of Canal Engineering* (York, Pa.: The American Canal and Transportation Center, 1995), 15. As part of our September 1999 canal tour of New England, Canada, and New York, my wife and I stopped at York, Pennsylvania to visit the American Canal and Transportation Center. The Center turned out to be the home of William H. Shank, the historian of the Center. He received us graciously and provided us with useful information.

9. Jones and Dutcher, 441.

10. Ibid., 448.

11. The report of engineer W.W. Thomas, hired by the city to do a survey of the river between Augusta and Andersonville, South Carolina, is dated "November 1874" and included in the City Council Minutes, December 7, 1874.

12. Shaw, *Canals for a Nation*, 122.

13. Shanks, *Towpaths to Tugboats*, 34-35; Mark Finlay, "The Savannah and Ogeechee Canal," *American Canals* 103 (Autumn 1997), 8-11; the Savannah-Ogeechee Canal is featured on a website: http://www.georgianetweb.com/socanal/ . Bob Wilkinson treated my wife and me to a tour of the nature center and explained the long range plans for the

restoration of the waterway.

14. Shaw, *Canals for a Nation*, 123-24; The Loammi Baldwin Papers are at the William L. Clements Library at Ann Arbor, Michigan. According to the description of the collection on the Clements website, George R. Baldwin built the canal between the Altamaha and Turtle Rivers in Georgia. The discovery of fossils attracted the attention of the great pioneer geologist, Charles Lyell, see his *A Second Visit to the United States of North America* (New York 1849).

15. Patrick M. Malone, *Canals and Industry, Engineering in Lowell 1821-1860* (Lowell: Lowell Museum, 1983), 1-10; Arthur H. Frazier, "Early Hydraulic Science and Scientists at Lowell, Massachusetts," 1968, manuscript at Lowell History Center, University of Lowell, Massachusetts.

16. Benita Eisler, *The Lowell Offering: Writings by New England Mill Women 1840-1845* (New York: W.W. Norton and Company, 1977), 33.

17. Ibid., 28-29.

18. Frazier, "Early Hydraulic Science", 1-10; the canal tour was a highlight of our visit to Lowell in September 1999.

19. James A. Ward, *J. Edgar Thomson, Master of the Pennsylvania* (Westport, Conn.: Greenwood Press, 1980), 10-20.

20. Ibid., 25-33.

21. J. Edgar Thomson to Lemuel P. Grant, February 12, 1842, L.P. Grant Papers, Atlanta Historical Society.

22. Thomson to Grant, May 20, 1842, Grant Papers.

23. Thomson to Grant, October 4, 1845, Grant Papers.

24. Henry Clay to H.H. Cumming, March 31, 1844, in Cumming, Hammond, and Bryan Families: Papers 1737-1961, Reese Library, Augusta State University.

25. Thomson to Grant, November 2, 1844, Grant Papers.

26. H. H. Cumming to Julia Bryan Cumming, November 10, 1844, in Cumming, Hammond and Bryan Families Collection.

27. Minutes, March 28, 1848, Record of Reports and other Matters Appertaining to the Augusta Canal, Municipal Building, Augusta, Ga.

28. Minutes, January 7, 1846, Record of Reports and other Matters.

29. Ward, *J. Edgar Thomson*, 44.

30. *Augusta Chronicle*, November 11, 1842.

31. Ibid., January 2, 1845.

32. Ibid., February 3, 1845.

33. Ibid., November 1, 1850.

Chapter 5

1. Minutes, March 15, 1850, Ledger entitled "Augusta Canal May 1ˢᵗ 1645 to Feb. 10, 1847"; and on the inside title page, "Record of Reports and other Matters Appertaining to the Augusta Canal William Phillips, Secy and Bookeeper," Vaults, Municipal Building, Augusta, Georgia. Henceforth Minute Book 1845-47. The titles of the many ledgers depended on the clerks fancy.

2. *The Augusta Chronicle and Sentinel*, November 1, 1850. Henceforth, *Chronicle*.

3. Ibid.

4. Minutes, March 15, 1850.

5. Ibid.

6. *Chronicle*, March 15, 1845.

7. Charles J. Jones, Jr. and Salem Dutcher, *Memorial History of Augusta, Georgia* (Syracuse, N.Y.: D. Mason and Company, Publishers, 1890), 401-404.

8. March 18, 1845, Minutes "Canal Board of Commissioners, March 18, 1845 to November 5, 1853," Henceforth Minute Book One.

9. Report of Engineer Sanford, April 30, 1845, Minute Book One.

10. September 24, 1845, Minute Book 1845-47.

11. May 17, 1845, Minute Book One; *Chronicle*, May 30, 1845.

12. Ibid., June 19, 1845.

13. July 2, 1845, Minute Book One.

14. *Chronicle*, July 17, 1845.

15. Jones and Dutcher, 405-10.

16. *Chronicle*, December 11,12,13, 1845; January 3, 1846.

17. July 15, 1845, Minute Book One.

18. November 26, 1845, Minute Book One.

19. March 6, 1846, Minute Book One.

20. March 29, 1848, Minute Book One.

21. *Chronicle*, April 24, 1848.

22. April 30, 1845, Minute Book One.

23. October 30, 1846, Minute Book One.

24. December 18, 26, 1845, Minute Book One.

25. Baldwin's report, April 16, 1846, Minute Book 1845-47.

26. William Phillips, Special Report, August 18 56, p.7, Reese Library Special Collections, Augusta State University.

27. April 16, 1846, Minute Book 1845-47.

28. April 19, 1847, Minute Book 1845-47.

29. *Chronicle*, November 23, 1846.

30. Ibid., December 31, 1846.

Chapter 6

1. Cumming to L.D. Ford, April 19, 1847, Records Augusta

Canal May 1, 1845 - February 1847, Augusta Municipal Building Vaults. On title page, Record of Reports and Other Matters Appertaining to the Augusta Canal, William Phillips, Secretary and Bookkeeper. Henceforth, Phillips Records.

2. *Chronicle*, January 19, February 11, March 3, 1847.

3. Ibid., May 3, 12, October 28, 1847.

4. Ibid., June 20, May 21, July 17, 1847, March 24, 1848, February 1, 1849.

5. Minutes, May 5, 1847, January 12, 1849, Minutes Canal Board of Commissioners, March 18, 1845 to November 5, 1853, Augusta Municipal Building Vaults. Henceforth, Canal Minutes.

6. Minutes, March 23, April 8, 1847, Canal Minutes.

7. Minutes, March 28, 1849, Canal Minutes;   Henry H. Cumming report, July 29, 1846, November 28, 1849, Phillips Records. The reference to "unseemly lagoons" might remind readers of Augustus Baldwin Longstreet's description of Springfield as a swampy place in his famous *Georgia Scenes*.

8. Cumming report, January 26, 1850, Canal Minutes; Phillips reports, February 27, June 26, 1850, Phillips Records,

9. Phillips report, August 28,1850,   Phillips Records.

10. Phillips 1877 report

11. C. O. Sanford to H.H. Cumming, December 11, 1847, E. D Sanford to H.H. Cumming, December 29, 1847, March 29, 1848, J. E. Thomson to H.H. Cumming, February 17, 1848, Phillips Records.

12. Minutes, April 23, 1849, Canal Minutes.

13. Jones and Dutcher, 410.

14. Cumming to City Council, September 1, 1848, Phillips Records.

15. Cumming to City Council, September 13, November 1, 1849, Phillips Records.
16. Jones and Dutcher, 410.
17. Minutes, August 28, 1850, Canal Minutes;   Phillips reports, August 28, September 25, 1850, Phillips Records.
18. Phillips report, October 30, November 27, 1850, Phillips Records.
19. Phillips report, December 25, 1850. The hard-working Phillips wrote his report on Christmas Day.
20. Phillips reports, February 26, April 30, May 28, 1851, Phillips Records; Canal Minutes, May 30, 1851, Canal Minutes.
21. Phillips reports, June 25, September 26, 1851, January 28, March 31, 1852, Phillips Records.
22. Phillips reports, June 30, July 28, July 29, 1852, Phillips Records.
23. Phillips to Canal Commissioners, September 29, 1852, Minutes Council, September 27, 1852 to November 3, 1859. On inside title page of ledger "A Record of Reports and other matters in connection with the Augusta Canal, William Phillips, Secretary." Henceforth, Council Minutes.
24. Phillips to Canal Commissioners, March 30, August 25, 1853, Council Minutes.
25. Phillips to Board of Managers, January 7, 1854, Council Minutes.
26. Minutes, September 1, November 3, 1853, Canal Minutes.
27. Phillips report, December 24, 1854, Council Minutes.
28. Phillips reports, July 2, September 5, 1855, Council Minutes.

Chapter 7

1. Council Minutes, October 4, 1861, in Minutes of Council,

April 5th 1861 to December 28, 1865, City Council ·
Vaults, Augusta, Georgia. Henceforth for citations during
the above dates, "Council Minutes."

2. Col. (General) Geo. W. Rains, *History of the Confederate
Powder Works* (Augusta, Georgia: Chronicle and
Constitutionalist Print., 1882), 4. Henceforth, Rains,
History.

3. *Augusta Chronicle*, January 24, 25, 1861.

4. Ibid., January 5, 1861.

5. Ibid., April 20, 1860.

6. Augusta Unit, Federal Writers' Project in Georgia, Works
Progress Administration, *Augusta* (Augusta: City Council
of Augusta, 1938), 201. Henceforth, Federal Writers,
Augusta.

7. *Augusta Chronicle*, February 2, 1861.

8. Federal Writers, *Augusta*, 202.

9. Phillips' Report, July 31, 1861, Council Minutes.

10. Minutes, October 4, 1861, Council Minutes.

11. *Augusta Chronicle*, May 23, 1862.

12. Edward J. Cashin, *The Story of Augusta* (Augusta:
Richmond County Board of Education, 1980), 121.

13. Shaler Smith became nationally prominent after the war
for his designs of large bridges. The Smithsonian has an
exhibit of his work.

14. Florence Fleming Corley, *Confederate City* (Columbia:
University of South Carolina Press, 1960), 53.

15. Deed of 200 acres purchased from Judge Starnes, August
2, 1862, Microfilm Records for Freedman's Bureau of
Georgia (M798) Reel #36, National Archives. Henceforth
Freedman's Bureau Records.

16. Warren's Deed, August 9, 1852, Freedman's Bureau
Records. A plat accompanying the deed shows Starnes 200

acres, the old Arsenal Tract, Warren's property, and the location of the Rae's Creek wasteway.

17. Machine Works Property (Deed to), August 19, 1862, Freedman's Bureau Records. The plat accompanying the deed shows the location of the buildings on the tract.
18. Most of the details of the process are from Rains, *History*.
19. Ibid., 21.
20. Corley, *Confederate City*, 59.
21. Rains, *History*, 27.
22. Corley, *Confederate City*, 47, 48.
23. *The Augusta Chronicle*, January 15, 1865.
24. Ibid., 47.
25. Phillips' Report, July 2, 1862, Council Minutes.
26. Ibid., June 3, December 2, 1863, Council Minutes.
27. Minutes, October 1, 1863, Council Minutes.
28. Minutes, August 3, 1863, Council Minutes.
29. Minutes, October 1, 2, 1863, Council Minutes.
30. Minutes, October 2, 1863, Council Minutes.
31. Virginia Ingraham Burr, ed. *The Secret Eye: The Journal of Ella Gertrude Clanton Thomas 1848-1889* (Chapel Hill: University of North Carolina Press, 1990), 229.
32. Phillips' Report, February 3, 1864, Council Minutes.
33. Mayor's annual message, October 7, 1864, Council Minutes.
34. Minutes, May 9, 1865, Council Minutes.
35. Corley, *Confederate City*, 98.
36. Ibid.

Chapter 8

1. *The Augusta Chronicle*, November 3, 1865.
2. Virginia Ingraham Burr, ed. *The Secret Eye: The Journal of Ella Gertrude Clanton Thomas 1848-1889*, (Chapel

Hill: University of North Carolina Press, 1990), 277.

3. *Chronicle*, August 17, 1865.

4. Ibid., May 4, 1856

5. Joseph B. Cumming, *A Sketch of the Descendants of David Cumming* (Augusta: privately printed, n.d.), 20.

6. *Chronicle,* April 15, 1866.

7. In fact this author first called the years 1870 to 1890 the "Janus" years as the title of Chapter Nine in *The Story of Augusta* (Augusta: Richmond County Board of Education, 1980).

8. *Chronicle,* August 1, 1866.

9. Minutes, February 1, 1867, Council Minutes July 1866 to September 1870.

10. Phillips Report, February 5, 1868, in Council Minutes, February 7, 1868.

11. Council Minutes, August 8, 1868.

12. *Chronicle,* January 31, 1869.

13. Ibid., November 30, 1868, December 3, 1868.

14. Council Minutes, January 1, 1869.

15. Information about the drowning of Phillips' wife was given to Dayton Sherrouse, Director of the Augusta Canal Authority by Mary Jo Reeves, Phillips' great-granddaughter.

16. *Chronicle,* February 21, 1869.

17. Council Minutes, April 2, 1869.

18. Ibid., May 7, 1869.

19. Ibid., November 5, 1869.

20. Ibid., November 26, 1869.

21. *Chronicle,* April 28, 1970.

22. Council Minutes, April 1, 1870.

23. Ibid., June 28, 1870.

24. Ibid., August 5, September 12, 1870.

25. Jones and Dutcher, *Memorial History,* Part II, 1.
26. Council Minutes, December 8, 1870, in City Council Minutes, November 4, 1870 to April 7, 1879.
27. Ibid., August 7, 1871, Thomas X. Grasso, President of the Canal Society of New York State, in a communication with Jeanie Allen, confirmed that Olmstead worked on the Erie Canal both before he came to Augusta and after he completed the enlargement.
28. *Chronicle,* June 27, 1871.
29. Council Minutes, August 7, 1871.
30. Ibid., August 21, November 6, 1871.
31. *Chronicle,* May 29, 1872.
32. Ibid., August 17, 1872.
33. Council Minutes, November 4, 1872.
34. Ibid., December 5, 1872.
35. Ibid., June 2, 1873; Robert C. Jorgensen, "Russell and Simmons Factory," Historic American Engineering Record, 1977.
36. *Chronicle,* May 7, 1873, in "Augusta Newspaper Digest," 117-18. The typescript volumes of the Works Progress Administration writers' project is in the reference room of the Reese Library, Augusta State University.
37. Cashin, *Story of Augusta,* 150.
38. Council Minutes, January 5, 19, 1874.
39. *Chronicle,* March 26, 1874.
40. Robert L. Spude, "Augusta Canal," Historic American Engineering Record, 1877, p. 11.
41. Thomas' report is dated November 1874, and is contained in Council Minutes, December 7, 1874; Cashin, *Story of Augusta,* 170.
42. *Chronicle,* October 24, 1874.
43. Ibid., November 12, 1874.

44. Council Minutes, November 1, 1875.

45. Ibid., December 7, 1876. Though the council minutes are silent on the matter, *The Augusta Chronicle* reported in its December 15, 1876 issue that the canal had been formally turned over to the City Council by virtue of the failure of the Augusta Canal Company to repay bonds in the amount of $40,000.

46. Council Minutes, January 1, 1877.

47. Ibid., January 4, 1877.

48. Ibid., April 2, 1877.

49. William Phillips*, Report upon the Topography and Hydrography in the Vicinity of Augusta, Ga.* (Augusta: publisher not given, 1892), 24.

50. Council Minutes, September 7, 1874, March 1, April 5, September 4, 1875. Phillips actually did three maps, one showing fire districts, one wards, and the other lots.

51. Council Minutes, February 5, 1877.

Chapter 9

1. Robert L. Spude, "Augusta Canal," Historic American Engineering Record, 1977, 15. Henceforth HAER.

2. Spude, "Enterprise Manufacturing Company." HAER, 3.

3. Ibid., 4.

4. Jones and Dutcher, 420.

5. *Chronicle*, May 14, 16, 1885.

6. Spude, "Enterprise," 6.

7. Robert C. Jorgensen, "Pendleton and Boardman," HAER, 2-3.

8. Jorgensen, "The Augusta Machine Works (Augusta Lumber Company)," HAER, 2-4.

9. Jorgensen, "Russell and Simmons Factory," HAER, 2-5.

10. Jones and Dutcher, 420. Robert Spude, writing for the

Historic American Engineering Record, identifies the Paragon Mill with Alfred Baker's 1859 flourmill. William Phillips report of February 1, 1865 refers to "Stovall's Excelsior Mill," Minutes of Council, April 5, 1861 to December 28, 1865.

11. Spude, "Paragon Mill," HAER, 2-4.

12. Robert C. Jorgensen, "Dartmouth Spinning Company (Sutherland Mill)," HAER, 2,6.

13. *Chronicle*, December 3, 1877.

14. Ibid., November 1, 1879.

15. Ibid., February 15, May 27, 1880.

16. Jorgensen, "Sibley Manufacturing Company," HAER, 2-4; *Chronicle,* October 28, 1881.

17. *Chronicle,* August 1, 1882.

18. Jorgensen, "Sibley Manufacturing Company," HAER, 6.

19. Jones and Dutcher, 421.

20. Ibid., "Biographical Sketches," 30-42; Judge King lived another five years, dying at his residence on March 19, 1887.

21. *Chronicle*, July 11, 1882.

22. Mayor's message, Council Minutes, July 27, 1882.

23. *Chronicle*, May 13, January 28, 1885.

24. Lee Ann Whites, "Paternalism and Protest in Augusta's Cotton Mills: What's Gender Got to Do With It?", in Edward J. Cashin and Glenn Eskew, eds. "Paternalism in a Southern City: Race, Religion and Gender in Augusta, Georgia," (manuscript in process of publication at the University of Georgia Press), 133. Henceforth, Cashin and Eskew.

25. Edward J. Cashin, *The Quest: A History of Public Education in Richmond County* (Augusta: County Board of Education of Richmond County, 1985), 26-28.

26. Ibid., 28.

27. *Chronicle*, January 16, 1887.

28. Ibid., October 25, 1882, August 3, 1881.

29. Julia Walsh, "Rolling Religion Down the Hill: Mill Workers and Churches in Augusta," in Cashin and Eskew, eds, 359-60.

30. *Chronicle*, June 15, 1886.

31. Ibid., August 31, September 1, 2, 1886.

32. Council Minutes, September 6, 9, 1886.

33. Ibid., September 9, 1886.

34. *Chronicle,* September 14, 15, 19, 1886.

35. Ibid., November 5, 1886.

36. Ibid., January 29, 1887.

37. Council Minutes, August 5, 1878.

38. Ibid., January 9, 1879.

39. Ibid., February 7, March 7, June 1, July 12, July 27, 1881.

40. Engineer's Report, Council Minutes, April 5,1886. The illness John Cartledge contracted because of his work in the sewer caused his death on September 14, 1886.

41. *Chronicle*, November 5, 1881, May 10, 1882.

42. Council Minutes, August 2, 1886.

43. Council Minutes, August 1, 1887.

44. Ibid., November 7, 1887, March 5, 7, 1888, *Chronicle* put out a special "Exposition Issue" dated May 1888.

45. *Chronicle*, September 11, 12, 13, 1888.

46. Council Minutes, September 13, October 1, 1888.

47. *Chronicle*, December 7, 8, 12, 17, 1888.

Chapter 10

1. Richard Henry Lee German, "The Queen City of the Savannah: Augusta, Georgia, During the Urban Progressive Era, 1890-1917," (Ph.D. dissertation, Florida State University, 1973), 84. Henceforth, German;

Chronicle, August 31, 1887.

2. German, 86

3. Ibid., 88-89.

4. Council Minutes, April 6, 1897, in Minute Book January 2, 1893 to December 27, 1897.

5. Council Minutes, August 2, 1897

6. *Chronicle*, September 27, 1896.

7. Ibid., May 13, 1897.

8. Ibid., July 1, 14, 1897.

9. Dorothy Haynie Murray, "William John Henning: The Man: The Publisher," *Richmond County History* Vol. 2, no.1 (Winter 1970), 7-12.

10. *Chronicle*, November 2, 1892; November 7, 1894.

11. Ibid., July 3, 1897.

12. Council Minutes, November 23, 1998.

13. *Chronicle*, November 22, 23, 1898.

14. Ibid., December 3, 1998.

15. German, 116. 184.

16. *Chronicle*, October 15, 1909.

17. Mr. Joseph B. Cumming told this writer that Dyer's full name was "Daniel Boone Dyer." Dyer invariably signed his name "D. B. Dyer."

18. Council Minutes, February 12, June 27, 1890; *Chronicle*, October 6, 1890.

19. Council Minutes, February 12, 1890, *Chronicle*, October 6, 1890.

20. *Chronicle*, May 30, August 17, October 6, 1890.

21. Ibid., October 6, 1890; *Chronicle Exposition Edition*, 1891; Chateau Levert became the convent for the Sisters of St. Joseph around 1916. This writer recalls noticing how the floor of the old house sloped more than Colonel Dyer's addition.

22. Council Minutes, August 1, 1892. It will be recalled that the city had a temporary illumination of Broad Street in 1882.
23. Ibid., July 29, November 4, 1895.
24. Cashin, *Old Springfield*, 81-82.
25. *Chronicle,* June 9, 1900, May 12, 1901.
26. Council Minutes, February 22, 1889, February 1, 1892, January 6, 1896.
27. Ibid., June 3, 1895.
28. Ibid., September 2, 1895, October 9, November 12, December 2, 1897.
29. Council Minutes, December 14, 29, 1897; Council Minute Book from January 3, 1898 to December 31, 1901, Minutes, January 3, 18, February 7, April 4, September 5, 1898.
30. Ibid., September 26, November 3, 1898.
31. *Chronicle*, December 22, 1898.
32. Ibid., March 20, 22, 1899.
33. Council Minutes, June 5, August 7, September 4, 1899; for a history of the Augusta Water Works, see Thomas H. Robertson, "Development of the Augusta Water Works," *The Georgia Operator* (Spring 1977), 8-16, 38
34. German, 165.
35. Alan J. Steiner, "Georgia Iron Works," HAER, 6.

Chapter 11

1. *Chronicle*, March 11, 1891.
2. Ibid., July 30, August 1, 1902.
3. Cashin, *The Story of Augusta*, 190-91.
4. *Chronicle*, March 25, April 7, May 31, 1906, November 6, 1907.
5. Ibid., January 3, 1909.

6. Ibid., January 22, 1909, November 12, 1911, December 23, 1912.

7. Ibid., September 25, 27, 28, 1912.

8. Ibid., October 10, 1912.

9. Ibid., February 15, 17, 1914.

10. Thomas S. Arnold, "A Man Called Archie," *Richmond County History* (Summer 1991), 4-17.

11. *Year Book of the City Council of the City of Augusta, Georgia,* 1905, 30; Henceforth *Year Book.*

12. Alan J. Steiner, "Augusta Water Works," (HAER), 14.

13. *Year Book*, 1905, 64.

14. *Year Book*, 1905, 76; 1906,12.

15. Edward J. Cashin, *The Story of Sacred Heart* (Augusta: Sacred Heart Cultural Center, 1987), 17.

16. Report of Nisbet Wingfield, January 8, 1919, in Minutes of the Flood Commission, January 30, 1919. Henceforth Flood Commission. I am grateful to Herbert Elliott for lending me his personal copy of the Minutes of the Flood Commission. The originals are in the vault of the Municipal Building on Greene Street. Wingfield's report was also published in the *Chronicle*, February 2, 1919.

17. Ibid., also Minutes of Flood Commission, March 10, 1909.

18. Wingfield Report, January 8, 1919, Flood Commission, January 30, 1919.

19. Flood Commission, January 31. 1910.

20. *Year Book*, 1912, 25-30.

21. Wingfield Report, January 8, 1919, Flood Commission, January 30, 1919.

22. Flood Commission, September 24, 1912.

23. Ibid., January 8, August 15, 1913.

24. Ibid., June 2, 1914, March 2, 1915.

25. Ibid., January 27, February 25, 1913. Wingfield actually

managed to wheedle $218,000 out of the Corps of Engineers for work on the river bank.

26. Ibid., June 21, 1915, February 8, 1917.
27. *Chronicle*, January 9, 1917.
28. Flood Commission, October 10,1916, April 12, 1918.
29. *Year Book*, 1919, 16.
30. Ibid.
31. Flood Commission, January 30, April 29, 1919.
32. *Year Book*, 1915, 29.
33. *Year Book,* 1917, 7.
34. Calvin J. Billman, "The 1916 Augusta Fire: An Unnecessary Tragedy?" *Richmond County History* (Summer 1975), 77-99.
35. Ibid.
36. *Year Book*. 1917, 14.
37. Ibid., 23.
38. Ibid., 21-29.
39. *Chronicle*, January 17, 1919.
40. Ibid., October 3, 6, 7, 8, November 27, 1919.

Chapter 12

1. *Yearbook* of the City Council of Augusta, Georgia, 1932, 5, 9. Henceforth *Yearbook*.
2. *Yearbook*, 1907, 59.
3. *Yearbook*, 1911, 47.
4. *Yearbook*, 1919, 10.
5. *Chronicle*, November 22, 1921.
6. *Yearbook*, 1921, 8.
7. *Yearbook*, 1922, 7.
8. *Chronicle*, August 20, 1924; *Yearbook*, 5-6.
9. *Yearbook*, 1924, 60.
10. *Chronicle*, September 30, October 2, December 23, 1924.

11. Robert Spude, "The Enterprise Manufacturing Company."
    HAER, 1977;   Robert C. Jorgensen, "Dartmouth Spinning
    Company (Sutherland Mill)" HAER, 1977.
12. *Yearbook*, 1927, 59.
13. *Yearbooks*, 1927, 62; 1928, _
14. *Chronicle*, July 14, November 5, 1926.
15. Ibid., June 27, 1929.
16. Ibid., November 17, 1931, February 19, 1932.
17. *Yearbook*, 1934, 10.
18. *Chronicle*, August 17, 25, November 22, December 4,
    1935.
19. Wade H. Wright, *History of the Georgia Power Company,
    1855-1956* (Atlanta: Georgia Power Company, 1957), 282.
20. Cashin, *The Story of Augusta*, 268.
21. Ibid., 270.
22. *Chronicle*, August 17, 1928, September 28, 1929.
23. Ibid., September 28, 30, October 1, 2, 3, 1929.
24. Wise's unusually lengthy report is in *Yearbook*, 1929, 51-
    61; the report of M.B. Cooper is in the same book, 70-71.
25. *Yearbooks*, 1932, 40, 1933, 59, 1934, 66.
26. *Yearbook*, 1936, 6-11, 70-76.
27. *Yearbooks*, 1936, 70-76, 1937, 7, 71.
28. *Chronicle*, July 17, 1933.
29. Ibid., September 6, 1934.
30. Ibid., September 10, 1934.
31. Ibid., September 18, 23.
32. *Yearbook*, 1941, 62.

Chapter 13

1. Although there is some uncertainty about exactly when the
   Augusta Factory ceased operations, it must have been in or
   after 1937. The Year Book of the City Council for 1937

lists the Factory among the mills in operation for that year.

2. *Year Books*, 1941, 62; 1942, 60; 1943, 3.
3. *Year Book*, 1943, 64.
4. *Year Book*, 1947, 68.
5. *Year Book*, 1948, 5, 42.
6. *Year Book*, 1950, 44-45, 51, 46.
7. *Year Book*, 1952, 42.
8. *Chronicle*, April 28, May 29, June 26, 28, October 26, 1951.
9. *Year Books*, 1955, 42, 1956, 43.
10. *Year Book*, 1960, 42-44.
11. *Chronicle*, December 9, 1962.
12. *Year Books*, 1968, 4; 1966, 8.
13. Norman Kaylor, "The Augusta Canal," *Publication of the Augusta Chamber of Commerce* (Fall 1966), 27-29, 40, 42.
14. *Chronicle*, March 13, December 23, 1969, January 25, 1971.
15. Ibid., March 23, 1969, September 20, 1970; *Year Book*, 1971. 8.
16. *Chronicle*, July 26, 1971.
17. *Year Books*, 1973, 7, 1974, 6.
18. *Year Book*, 1974, 6.
19. Martha Norwood, "The White House Tract," (Atlanta: Department of Natural Resources, 1975).
20. Cashin, *The Story of Augusta*, 275-76.
21. Sydney Carter, "The Augusta Canal and Environs Study," Augusta-Richmond County Planning Commission, 1975.
22. On August 22, a judge ruled against local farmers' complaint that the sludge had damaged their farmlands, and denied them compensation, *Chronicle*, September 15, 2000.
23. Robert L. Spude, "The Augusta Canal," Historic American Engineering Record, (1977), 14.

24. *Year Book*, 1978, 8.

25. *Year Book*, 1980, 1.

26. *Year Book*, 1980, 40-41.

27. *Chronicle*, March 6, 1975.

28. Ibid., June 22, 1969.

29. Ibid., May 17, 1971.

30. Ibid., July 7, 1978.

Chapter 14

1. *Chronicle*, March 13, 1992.

2. Ibid., March 5, 1981.

3. Ibid., October 14, 1982.

4. Ibid., July 14, 1982.

5. Ibid., June 20, 1982.

6. Ibid., June 30, 1984.

7. Ibid., July 21, August 5, 1984.

8. Ibid., June 30, 1964.

9. Ibid., November 8, 1983.

10. Hugh Connolly to Mayor DeVaney, August 13, 1985, Augusta Tomorrow Files.

11. Same to same, May 10, 1988, copy in possession of Hugh Connolly.

12. C.O. Hollis to Mayor DeVaney, November 14, 1989, Canal Authority Files.

13. *Chronicle*, November 2, 1990.

14. Ibid., December 13, 1990.

15. Ibid., November 26, 1991.

16. Ibid., February 27, 1992. Gerry Woods has told this writer that he himself had mixed feelings about the benefits of the project.

17. Ibid., January 3, 1992.

18. *The Atlanta Journal-Constitution*, date missing, Canal

Authority files.

19. *Chronicle*, February 18, 1992.
20. Ibid., February 9, March 18, 22, 27, October 4, 1992.
21. Communication to the author, September 6, 2000.
22. Ibid., December 13, 1991.
23. Ibid., February 9, 1993, April 26, 1996.
24. Ibid., April 26, May 1, 1996, February 34, 1999.
25. Ibid., June 30, November 14, 1994.
26. *Augusta Focus*, February 11-17, 1993.
27. *Chronicle*, September 28, 1994.
28. Ibid., September 8, October 14, 1995.
29. Ibid., October 5, 1996.
30. Ibid., October 24, 1996.
31. Ibid., November 21, 1996.
32. Ibid., July 25, 1996.
33. *Atlanta Constitution*, March 4, 1995.
34. *Metropolitan Spirit*, January 20-26, 2000.
35. *Chronicle*, February 13, 2000.
36. *Metropolitan Spirit*, February 26, 1998.
37. City Council Yearbook 1993, 59.
38. I am indebted to Jackie Maryak and Bebe Johnson for the information they provided on the Southeastern Natural Sciences Academy.
39. It was this writer's privilege to testify to the historical importance of Trinity Church during the arbitration proceedings.
40. *Headgate*, Vol 1, No.1 (May 1999). *Headgate* is the official newsletter of the Canal Authority.
41. Interview with Dayton Sherrouse, August 28, 2000.

Index

M

McCellan, Charles, 93-94

McCord, Z., 158

McGillivary, Lachlan, 25, 30-34

McIntyre, Edward, 258-59

Mackay House, 32-33, 222, 250-51

Mahone, Charles, 133-37, 143

Maness, Harold, 19

Mann, Luke, 71

Mason's Plantation, 16

Mattingly, Senator Mack, 260

May, Robert, 104, 118, 121-23, 158, 162, 169, 172-73, 191

Messerly, James R., 252-53, 260

Metcalf, Thomas, 85, 96, 125

Meyer, John U., 131, 145-46, 162

Middlesex Canal, 44-45, 50

Mill Branch, 11

Mill villages, 178

Miller, Andrew J., 67, 71-72, 96

Miller, Thomas W., 63

Miller, Zell, 267

Mississippian culture, 15

Molineux, General Edward L., 123

Moody, Lester, 228-29, 239, 254-55, 261

Mooney, James, 17

N

Nelson, Matthew, 72

Newell, Mark, 269

Newman, Mayor Lewis, 238, 251-53, 258

New Savannah, 23, 124, 226

Nichols, Johanna, 9

Nixon, Scott, 255

Norman, Robert, 261-62

Norwood, Representative Charlie, 271-73